Reading Goethe

Studies in German Literature, Linguistics, and Culture

Reading Goethe

A Critical Introduction to the Literary Work

Martin Swales and Erika Swales

CAMDEN HOUSE
Rochester, New York

First published 2002 by Camden House
Revised and reprinted in paperback 2007
Transferred to digital printing 2012

Camden House is an imprint of Boydell & Brewer Inc.
668 Mt. Hope Avenue, Rochester, NY 14620, USA
www.camden-house.com
and of Boydell & Brewer Limited
www.boydellandbrewer.com
PO Box 9, Woodbridge, Suffolk IP12 3DF, UK

Paperback ISBN-13: 978-1-57113-358-8
Paperback ISBN-10: 1-57113-358-5
Hardback ISBN-13: 978-1-57113-095-2
Hardback ISBN-10: 1-57113-095-0

Library of Congress Cataloging-in-Publication Data

Swales, Martin.
    Reading Goethe: a critical introduction to the literary work / Martin and
Erika Swales.
        p. cm. — (Studies in German literature, linguistics, and culture)
    Includes bibliographical references and index.
    ISBN 1–57113–095–0 (alk. paper)
    1. Goethe, Johann Wolfgang von, 1749–1832 — Criticism and
interpretation. I. Swales, Erika, 1937–   II. Title. III. Studies in
German literature, linguistics, and culture (Unnumbered)

PT2177.S94 2001
831'.6—dc21

                                                                    2001037384

A catalogue record for this title is available from the British Library

This publication is printed on acid-free paper
Printed in the United States of America

Contents

Preface

THIS BOOK IS MODEST IN SCOPE, size, and intention. Its aim is to offer English-speaking readers a short, critical, and by that token lively introduction to Goethe's literary achievement. We firmly believe that, for all the interest of his autobiographical, scientific, and journalistic writing, of his letters and indeed of his life, it is through the literary work that Goethe most richly and urgently speaks to us today. This is not to say that every item of his oeuvre is worthy of reverent attention. On the contrary: Many of his literary productions are flawed. But equally we are convinced that his finest works truly repay detailed study. And it is a measure of his creativity that they occur in all three major literary genres — poetry, drama, and prose narrative.

It may be helpful to highlight three interrelated aspects of that literary output at the outset: they are factors that explain why Goethe's works "travel" well, so to speak. One aspect has to do with his mastery of the German language. As we know, for English speakers, the German language poses particular difficulties. It is an inflected language, and it makes weighty demands in terms of structure and word order. But it is precisely these structures which, as we shall see, Goethe exploits to unforgettable expressive effect. This capacity is one all-important part of the revelation that he can offer us: what, on occasion, can seem an irritating linguistic property of German becomes experientially immediate in his hands. This is generally true, of course, of all the great writers of the German literary tradition. But it is particularly true of Goethe: On the one hand, he constantly draws on the ability of the German language to sustain a flexible and sophisticated discourse of philosophical abstraction and speculation; on the other hand, he capitalizes on colloquial registers, and stays close, even in written from, to the language in its everyday condition. This aspect points back to the legacy left by Luther's great Bible translation. Goethe can make the vernacular sing in a way that few other German or indeed European poets can. He puts us immediately in touch with the expressive force and range of the German language.

The second strand derives from the first, and it concerns his feel for the specifically lyrical potential of the German language. Goethe is one of Europe's greatest poets, yet sometimes it seems difficult to identify precisely what makes his poetry so miraculous. Compared with other masters of the European lyric, he seems less idiosyncratic, less identifiable in terms of stylistic and thematic characteristics. Yet if there is a definition of Goethe's lyric genius, it is perhaps the following: time and again, he is able to express a moment that is weighty both experientially and cognitively, to capture a mood where feeling and reflection come into quickened and quickening interplay. Goethe's finest poetry touches a nerve that is both visceral and mental. This ability may well explain why his works have so frequently attracted the attention of great composers. Goethe's own sense of — and taste in — music may, admittedly, have been mediocre. Of course, it does not follow that great creative writers will, by virtue of their talents, be able to appreciate other forms of supreme creativity. But even so, it is difficult not to be surprised and disappointed that Goethe was impervious to Schubert's genius — even to the point of failing to acknowledge settings of his poems which the composer sent him. Yet, although blinkered in the matter of music, Goethe produced poetry that spoke with incomparable force to a whole range of German composers: Beethoven, Schubert, Schumann, Liszt, Mendelssohn, Wolf, Brahms, Mahler, Richard Strauss, Pfitzner, Alban Berg, and many others. And this has meant that his poetry travels like no other: it is familiar worldwide to music lovers who have no knowledge of German literature, but to whom Goethe texts seem somehow to be the natural vehicle for the human voice at its most thoughtful and passionate.

The third facet concerns his ability to make both the specific universal and the universal specific. This, too, may apply to all great writers; but in the case of Goethe it is again particularly evident. As we have already noted, his creativity was wonderfully at home in his own language. He was also richly and complexly engaged by his own time and his own culture. He was fully aware of the critical energies liberated by the Enlightenment; he was touched by the emotional release generated by the culture of *Empfindsamkeit* or sentimentalism, and by the turmoil of Romantic art and thinking. He was a secular spirit who could also respond to the appeal of fervent inwardness as expressed in the religious ardor of Pietism. He was the product of two German towns — of Frankfurt am Main, with the lively civic and bourgeois culture of the Free Cities of the Holy Roman Empire, and of Weimar, where he played a very full part in court life. Yet, for all the "Germanness" of these, and other, formative experiences, Goethe was remarkably open to energies and impulses from the wider world. It is no coincidence that he coined the term "Weltliteratur": he had a lively sense of both European and Eastern cultures. He esteemed specificity but he abhorred narrowness. And that understanding allowed, and allows, him to travel. It is because he was so thoughtfully, fluidly, in touch with his own world — both historically and linguistically, geographically and culturally — that he did and does speak to other ages and cultures.

This study is dedicated to the task of understanding and explicating that particular transferable specificity. It is also dedicated to the generations of students who have studied Goethe with us at our two universities. On many occasions, their comments, questions and insights have helped us to see more clearly what we were, or ought to have been, trying to say. Additionally, our debt to fellow Goethe scholars is great, particularly to colleagues within Anglo-Saxon German Studies who have contributed to our thinking by both the written and the spoken word: Jeremy Adler, Nick Boyle, Barker Fairley, Robin Harrison, Bill Larrett, Barry Nisbet, Jim Reed, Roger Stephenson, and John Williams. Moreover, we are especially grateful to the editors of and contributors to the *Goethe Handbuch*. Secondary literature on Goethe has become well-nigh overwhelming. The *Handbuch* performs the inestimable service of helping one to find one's bearings within the current climate of critical discussion. It is a fine tribute to Germany's greatest writer.

Wherever possible, sources for quotations from Goethe's works have been given in the most readily accessible form. That is to say: poetry and verse dramas are cited by means of line numbers. Letters are identified by the recipient and date, conversations with Eckermann by the date, *Maximen und Reflexionen* by *MUR*, followed by the Hecker number. Prose works are identified by page numbers, which refer to the Hamburger Ausgabe (HA), but also to the Frankfurter Ausgabe (FA), the Münchner Ausgabe (MA), and the Weimarer Ausgabe (WA).

Three previously published papers have fed into the argument of this study: Erika Swales, "Johann Wolfgang von Goethe, 'Urworte. Orphisch,'" in *Landmarks in German Poetry,* ed. Peter Hutchinson (Oxford and Bern: Lang, 2000), 57–71; Martin Swales, "'Das Bild, o König, soll uns nicht entzweien': Image and Image-making in Goethe," *PEGS,* 66 (1996): 42–52; "Goethe's Prose Fiction," in *The Cambridge Companion to Goethe,* ed. Lesley Sharpe (Cambridge: Cambridge UP, 2001), 129–46. In each case we are grateful to the editors for allowing the borrowing to occur.

E. S.

M. S.

August 2001

Abbreviations

Note: The translations provided for quotations from Goethe are in every case our own. They make no claim to literary quality, but we hope that they will help readers to find their way through the German.

1: Introduction

B EFORE WE COME TO detailed consideration of Goethe's literary works, we wish to explore three aspects which combine to constitute what one might call the "Goethe phenomenon." They are: his life, his thought, and, for want of a better word, his image. All great writers tend to generate in the minds of their readers a sense both of the historical person who wrote the literary works and of the mentality, the creative persona from which these works emanated. Moreover, the thinking of great writers tends to play a role in the cultural (and even, on occasion, socio-political) traditions of their native land. As we shall see, all three propositions apply with particular force to Goethe. As regards the third aspect, his role as an icon within Germany's culture and politics has been both complex and, on occasion, problematic.

To convey a sense of the issues involved, let us begin with a quotation from Friedrich Gundolf's magisterial study of 1916, which is entitled simply *Goethe*. In the introduction he reflects on and justifies that one-word title in the following terms:

> Das nachfolgende Buch ist betitelt "Goethe" ohne weiteren Zusatz. Es ist schon daraus zu entnehmen, worauf es wesentlich ankommt: auf die Darstellung von Goethes gesamter Gestalt, der größten Einheit, worin deutscher Geist sich verkörpert hat.[1]

> [This book is entitled "Goethe" pure and simple. From this fact one can gather what essentially it aims to do: to explore the whole entity that is Goethe, the greatest unity in which the German spirit has expressed itself.]

And, a few paragraphs later, we read the following:

> Goethe ist das größte verewigte Beispiel der modernen Welt, daß die bildnerische Kraft eines Menschen, mag sie als Instinkt oder als bewußter Wille wirken, den gesamten Umfang seiner Existenz durchdrungen hat.[2]

> [Goethe is the greatest and most lasting exemplification in the modern world that the forming energies of a person, whether they express themselves as instinct or as a deliberate act of will, can permeate the full extent of his being.]

Here, Gundolf claims that a particular wholeness and centeredness informs every facet of Goethe's life, experience, thinking, writing. His key terms are "wesentlich," "gesamte Gestalt," "größte Einheit," "deutscher Geist," "das größte verewigte Beispiel," "bildnerische Kraft," "den gesamten Umfang seiner Existenz." We shall return later to the particular issue of uses (and abuses) of Goethe within German culture. At this stage let us simply register the ways in which, and the extent to which, he has been held by generations of commentators to enshrine a wholeness that is greater than the sum of the many parts which made up his life and work. In one form or another this contention has informed many responses to Goethe, and this applies by no means only to German voices. Hence, this study begins by offering some contextualizing glimpses of that complex package, that "Goethe phenomenon," which embraces his life, his philosophy, and the many responses to him during his life time and thereafter.

The basic outlines of his life can be rapidly summarized. Goethe was born on 28 August 1749 in Frankfurt am Main. His father, Johann Kaspar Goethe, was a retired lawyer, his mother, Katharine Elisabeth Textor, was the daughter of a senior city official. Goethe spent his childhood in Frankfurt, where he was privately educated. In October 1765 he went to Leipzig to study law. At that time Leipzig was a fashionable and elegant city known as "Little Paris" because of the esteem in which French manners and culture were held. His stay there was curtailed by a grave illness involving some kind of total nervous collapse, and he returned home in the summer of 1768. At this point, he was briefly influenced by Susanna von Klettenberg, who belonged to a Pietist sect, and he began to take an interest in mystical philosophers and writers. By 1770 the crisis had passed, and he was able to resume his legal studies, this time in Strasbourg. Here he was overwhelmed by the discovery of Gothic architecture as embodied in the great cathedral. He put Leipzig and the so-called cosmopolitanism of French neo-classicism behind him and hailed Gothic as the true "German" style. This crucial shift of artistic sensibility was underpinned by his contact with Johann Gottfried Herder (1744–1803), who advocated the importance and beauty of primitive poetry. Herder also encouraged him in his enthusiasm for Shakespeare, who, for Goethe and his contemporaries, came to embody the energy of nature and of genius, in answer to, and in repudiation of, all neo-classical rules. The all-important attachment to nature acquired personal and erotic force in Goethe's brief love affair from 1770 to 1771 with Friederike Brion, a clergyman's daughter living in the nearby village of Sesenheim. She inspired some of his finest early poetry whose linguistic and emotional immediacy can still be felt today. The exultant sense of connecting with a kind of linguistic and experiential bedrock also produced in 1771, with a second version in 1773, Germany's first great historical drama, *Götz von Berlichingen* (1773). The play is a key docu-

ment of Sturm und Drang, a culture of energetic revolt which characterized the young generation in the 1770s.

Goethe completed his legal studies in August 1771, and returned
briefly to Frankfurt. The turmoil of the Strasbourg years erupted again
during his time spent working as a lawyer in Wetzlar, which was a key legal and administrative center of the Holy Roman Empire. His involvement with a young woman, Charlotte Buff, who was engaged to, and
subsequently married, Johann Georg Christian Kestner, produced the
novel *Die Leiden des jungen Werther* (1774). It was an explosive success,
the first great European best-seller to come out of Germany. *Götz* and
Werther, the major literary achievements of the years 1771–75, caught the
attention of Duke Carl August of Weimar. In some ways, it seems a
somewhat odd meeting of minds: the works of the 1770s had given
Goethe the reputation of a tearaway and rebel, certainly not the kind of
figure who would find favor at a small court. But Carl August clearly was
taken with Goethe, and invited him to Weimar in 1775. If the invitation
was astonishing, the fact that it was accepted was even more so. Goethe
had grown up in a Free City. Yet he seems to have welcomed the chance
to be associated with a court culture. With one spectacular interruption,
Weimar was to remain his home for the rest of his life.

The first ten years spent there are remarkable for his involvement in
practical administrative work. It has to be remembered that many of the
courts of the Holy Roman Empire were, to put it mildly, very small-scale,
and Weimar was one of these. Goethe became involved in running the
mines, the forests, and the army; he also helped to organize the exchequer.
Court life for him was, in other words, like being on a town or county
council nowadays and was much less grand than we tend to assume.
However valuable the early Weimar years were, they conspired to frustrate
much of his work on his literary projects. He wrote some poetry, but pro-
gress on larger works such as *Faust, Egmont, Torquato Tasso,* and the *Wilhelm
Meister* novel was slow. Any notion, then, that Goethe was the leisured
and pampered writer-in-residence at a glittering court, paid a retainer in
return for the cultural eminence he purveyed, is wide of the mark. He was
a conscientious administrator; and a great deal of his effort was very much
"hands-on," as we might put it nowadays. He manned, for example, the
chain of buckets to put out a fire.

If frustration characterized his creative life in Weimar, it was also a
feature of his emotional life. He developed a passionate attachment to an
influential lady at court, Charlotte von Stein, the wife of the duke's Master
of the Horse. It seems that, in terms of intellectual and cultural interests,
they were very much equals. Certainly, Goethe's letters to Charlotte talk
with real ease of philosophical, aesthetic and other matters; one does not
feel that he has to make any allowances. But in emotional terms, there

was manifestly a sense of distance, which derived not only from Charlotte's position as a married lady occupying a very visible position at court, but also from her own emotional make-up. Admittedly, during this first Weimar phase Goethe began some of his scientific work on, for example, anatomy, botany, geology. But even so, one has the impression that he was in a condition of suspended animation, of being less than fully alive, certainly by comparison with the years up to 1775.

No doubt in response to some growing sense of personal crisis, Goethe in September 1786 took an extraordinary step. He was away from the court on leave, at Carlsbad, and he departed in dramatic secrecy and with extraordinary, almost desperate, haste to Italy. He was away for nearly two years. The time in Italy seems to have been one of extraordinary personal happiness. Clearly he rejoiced in being free of court duties; and his accounts of the Italian experience bear witness on every page to his delight in inhabiting a physically outgoing culture. The discovery of classical art and architecture was, it seems, part and parcel of the experience of coming emotionally, sexually alive. When he returned from Italy, he scandalized Weimar society by taking Christian Vulpius, a woman of humble origins, as his mistress and later, in 1806, as his wife.

On his return to Weimar, Goethe had a reduced administrative load. This was welcome to him; but it also seems symptomatic of growing human and spiritual isolation. In this context the friendship with Schiller was crucial. Their theoretical discussions, sustained both through letters as early as 1794, and increasingly, after 1799 when Schiller moved from Jena to Weimar, through direct personal contact, were of inestimable value. Their thoughts about art, morality, and politics stimulated both of them to striking productivity in all literary forms: the richness of their achievements has come to be known as "Weimar Classicism." Part of that classicism, it should be stressed, was an urgent debate with and response to the emergent forces of modern culture. The most acute expression of that modernity was, of course, the French Revolution. Goethe had personally glimpsed the ramifications of that momentous event: in 1792 he accompanied the Duke and the German armies on an invasion of France, driven by the aim to restore the monarchy. His relationship to the events that occurred on French soil was deeply ambivalent: on the one hand he was appalled by the violence and destruction; on the other he manifestly had a sense of the world-historical significance of such turmoil.

The years from 1786 to 1810 witnessed intense creative output: in addition to the poetry, there are the plays *Egmont* (1787), *Iphigenie auf Tauris* (1787), *Torquato Tasso* (1790), the Bildungsroman *Wilhelm Meisters Lehrjahre* (1796), the first part of *Faust* (1808), and the novel *Die Wahlverwandtschaften* (1809). Moreover, the scientific work, in particular on (anti-Newtonian) optics and color theory, continued apace. Yet the death of

Schiller in 1805 was a bitter blow and remained for years with Goethe. This is all the more striking as he could, on occasion, be very adept at shedding people who, for whatever reason, moved out of his experiential sphere. The works of his late phase consist of poetry (including the "Persian" collection the *West-östlicher Divan* of 1819), novels (*Wilhelm Meisters Wanderjahre* of 1821 and 1829), drama (*Faust II*, 1832), and of a great deal of autobiographical writing (most notably the *Italienische Reise* of 1816–17). In addition, there are the conversations with Johann Peter Eckermann, which appeared after Goethe's death (22 March 1832).

In many ways it is not easy to know how to interpret Goethe's biography. True, it was a long life, but it could be argued that, apart from the Italian journey, it was not entirely filled with vital and varied incident. Some commentators have, for example, regretted the years spent in Weimar officialdom. Yet, if Goethe could play safe at times, there also were moments where he seems to have been capable of a kind of spectacular rebirth. Strasbourg was one, Italy another — as was the Rhine journey and the attachment to Marianne von Willemer in 1814–15 that generated the *Divan,* and, at the age of seventy-four, the embarrassingly desperate infatuation with the seventeen year old Ulrike von Levetzow, which produced three poems entitled the "Trilogie der Leidenschaft." On the one hand, then, the life seems to be intensely self-protective; yet on the other there are moments of tumultuous self-discovery.

In order to give an idea of the issues raised by Goethe biographies we want to refer briefly to three test cases. All of them are studies by English scholars. This may seem very parochial in focus. But, as we have already indicated with reference to Gundolf and his legacy, there can be a particular socio-cultural loading to German biographies of Goethe. Hence, in terms of exploring the issues raised by the life itself, it is illuminating to consider works by non-German scholars, simply because they are free from any particular corporate ideological freight.

Three English commentators, over the past half century, have each taken a different phase of Goethe's life and have found in it the key to Goethe's creative biography. For Barker Fairley, in his *Study of Goethe,* that center is the ten years in Weimar prior to the flight to Italy. Paradoxically (or so it seems at first sight) Fairley insists that the whole Charlotte experience was both foreign to, but also necessary to, Goethe's personal development. Goethe needed that "unnaturalness" as a corrective to his early years, which were a phase in which "rapture so intimately mingles with melancholy, confidence with despair, idyll with tragedy" that the upshot was "a state of being so contradictory and so unresolved that only youth in its hey-day could sustain it, and then only for a time."[3] In short, the repressions of that first Weimar decade, the frustrations felt at so many levels of his being and consciousness, were a necessary respite from his own volatility. In a key passage Fairley twice invokes the notion of crisis: "The ten years of Charlotte, rightly understood, give us the measure of his crisis; they tell us more forcibly than anything else in his biography how real the crisis was and how inveterate in himself the condition that had produced it."[4] In Fairley's view, Goethe's life evolved through crises. At every crucial juncture in his life he somehow managed to find the balancing corrective that would allow the disturbance to be lived through and, ultimately, to become enriching. If Charlotte, then, was the corrective to the early years, Italy was the corrective to Charlotte:

> only the long subservience to Charlotte with its queer dichotomies
> and its forcing on him of a kind of sensibility, a philosophy that he was
> bound to throw off sooner or later, could account for the extremity of
> his feelings about Italy and the persistence with which he held to
> them.[5]

Ultimately, for Fairley, Goethe's life, evolving as it did, not smoothly but through lurches, was successful. That life was long, rich and coherent, and it produced an oeuvre that affirmed the value and purpose and dignity of human existence on earth. In the closing pages of his study Fairley ruefully wonders whether Goethe was not (as it were) so successful, so totally housed in, and at ease with, the world as inhabited and interpreted by him that he thereby forfeited the ability to speak to the modern (i.e. post-Romantic world), with its delight in *poètes maudits*.

Nicholas Boyle, in his monumental life of Goethe, of which to date two volumes have appeared,[6] offers us the portrait of a splendidly heterodox life, as heterodox as the Holy Roman Empire from which that life came. Boyle stresses that Goethe's was a resolutely secular temperament, one which derived its governing sense of value from its own framework of signification (Goethe is, for example, acutely aware not just of his birthday but also of the various anniversaries that define his life). He derives pattern and meaning from those subjectively perceived and configured recurrences. But, Boyle argues, three experiences helped him to know that subjectivity writ large came perilously close to solipsism. One of the experiences had intimately to do with his own psyche, whereas the other two were more in the nature of public revolutions. As regards the psychological issue, we need to take note of Boyle's claim about the role and place of the Italian journey in the psychic economy of Goethe's creativity. For many commentators, that journey represents the experiential moment when Goethe comes to life again, makes contact with the deepest sources of his energy as both man and poet. Boyle is unpersuaded:

> Goethe certainly learned something new in Rome, something useful
> for the rest of his life; he had, in the end, nearly two years of sus-

tained and partially systematic study of a subject, the history and practice of art, under the tutorship, sometimes formal, of professionals and scholars. It was the nearest he came to a true university education and it was the foundation of his mature knowledge of culture. But it was no rebirth for his poetry. On the contrary, nothing demonstrates so clearly the continuity of Goethe's Italian journey with the sterile years immediately preceding it as its failure to stimulate him to any lyrical poems of note, or indeed to any substantial literary work at all. The ten years after Goethe's Roman "rebirth" brought him practically no *new* literary flowering; there was one remarkable cycle of poems, and there was, in its own way, the equally remarkable completion of some long-standing projects, but otherwise there was only some of his most obviously mediocre writing, and a resounding silence. These were years of a great illusion, of the belief that the alternative to the poetry of desire was a poetry of possession. Only at their end did Goethe realize that the true alternative, the only alternative that could inspire *him*, was a poetry of renunciation.[7]

We have quoted Boyle at considerable length because the passage reflects the central argument of his study: it suggests that Goethe was able most richly to know and express the modes of fulfillment available to a posttheological culture precisely by coming to understand the necessity of renunciation. For Boyle, Goethe is, then, either the poet of anticipation or the poet of renunciation; but he is not, as many commentators have claimed, the spokesman of fulfilled living in the immediate experiential world. And that decisive personal-psychological recognition interlocks with the two other — public — experiences which express the, as one might put it, world-historical appropriateness of renunciation. One was the French Revolution. Goethe disliked the violence, the fracturing of tradition, the conviction that Reason should be allowed to devalue custom and convention. He perceived the coming into being of that field of force of modern politics made up of ideology, mass urban movements, and the will to bureaucratic rationality. Of all these energies Goethe was deeply suspicious; yet he also had no doubt that the French Revolution was the primary example of emergent modernity, that the clock could not be turned back. The French Revolution made him see that the modern world was not set to evolve in accordance with his hopes and wishes, that, in consequence, renunciation was the appropriate response that fully acknowledged the otherness of the world's processes. Similarly, the Kantian revolution in philosophy, according to Boyle, taught Goethe to attend more to the processes by which human structures of belief came about than to the beliefs themselves. Once again, this time as a response to Kant's critical enterprise, renunciation comes to the fore as the definition of that enforced modesty of expectation that alone would allow sensible and purposive living in the modern world. Because, for Boyle, Goethe accepted these constraints, he was able to live aright in the modern world; to find a worldliness that was reverent rather than reductive, that was modest rather than euphoric, that was joyous without being hedonistic.

Boyle's argument has been both implicitly and explicitly challenged by T. J. Reed. For him, the center of gravity of Goethe's life and work is to be found neither in the Charlotte years (Fairley) nor in the French and Kantian Revolutions (Boyle) but in the Italian journey — most particularly in the diary of that journey which Goethe kept at the time (rather than in the later, more polished and stylized account in the *Italienische Reise*). Reed stresses the coexistence in the diary of Goethe's pleasure in the physical world, his exultant sense of solidity and materiality on the one hand, and his delight in thinking, reflecting, speculating in order to make connections on the other. In Italy, then, Goethe displays both empirical and theoretical vivacity. He is eager to touch and to inquire, to know in both modern and biblical senses of the word. The Goethe of that journey is both eager tourist, delighting in the Mediterranean warmth that seems to reach every corner of his body, and also an artist, anthropologist, botanist, meteorologist, geologist, cultural critic, and lover. Reed argues that the "Römische Elegien," the great upshot of the Italian experience, are not poetry of loss, deprivation and longing. Rather, they capture love's fulfillment in the bodily and mental Here and Now. At the end of his introduction to the *Tagebuch,* Reed writes "we feel we too are seeing the world aright through Goethe's eyes."[8] This affirmation is reminiscent of Fairley's sense of Goethe's intense belief in the rightness of the world and of human indwelling within it. For Fairley Goethe needed, as it were, to renounce in order to be able to affirm; for Boyle, Goethean renunciation is the only form of right indwelling in modern secular culture; for Reed, the greatest truth of Goethe's life and work is his radiant, complex worldliness, his celebratory ability to see the world aright.

We have summarized three different views taken of Goethe's life not in order to score points, but rather in order to suggest two shared aspects which unite these biographical approaches, despite their deeply felt differences in emphasis. Fairley and Boyle and Reed have an urgent sense that Goethe's life matters profoundly, and that it does so because it expresses something that is not readily expressed by modern, that is, post-Romantic literature: the sense that human life in the world can be fulfilling, meaningful and therefore worthwhile. The other concern that unites Fairley, Boyle, and Reed is the view that Goethe's life is present in, and is a kind of guarantor of, his creative work. Not that any of them seek crudely to "test" the literature against the life. But all three of them believe that there is an important human affirmation in what Goethe's literary work has to say; and that affirmation has everything to do with a recognizable human self that is manifestly concerned to express and explore manifold forms of worldly experience. Admittedly, that view is far removed from current critical orthodoxy, which asserts the death of the author and holds that the birth of the reader-text dialogue is the only true locus of literary signification. As regards this study, we shall not engage in any thorough-going way with Goethe's life as a necessary framework of reference. Moreover, we very strongly believe that Goethe's oeuvre has nothing to lose in the present climate of theory: we shall stress frequent moments of thematic self-consciousness and textual self-reflexivity in the literary work. But even so, the resonance of the biography will not allow itself to be banished; Goethe's literary work, however much it responds to post-modern notions of textuality, has a voice which, at every turn, is in dia-logue with us. It urges us to acknowledge, rather than to suppress, the plural significations of Goethe's selfhood, of our selfhood, and of the cul-tural texts within which we dwell. Goethe's oeuvre, in its multiple interac-tions with us, resists reductions and simplifications. It does so not in the name of elusive pan-textuality, but rather in the name of a complex living subject. That human entity is one that is inseparable from the forms and modes of its lived experience; this is why we have commented at some length on the issue of Goethe biography. Moreover, it is also inseparable from a whole set of thoughts about the place, philosophically speaking, of the human subject in the material world. For many commentators Goethe is a source not of philosophical adventurousness nor of spiritual profun-dity, but rather of applied intelligence, of helpful insight into the living process. To this issue of Goethe's worldly wisdom, as one might call it, we now wish to turn, bearing in mind what it has to offer us now and also what has been made of it over the years.

When one comes to consider Goethe's thought — and many com-mentators have been concerned to explicate and evaluate it — one thing is particularly striking: Goethe did not produce any single definitive com-pilation of his central beliefs. Rather, he contented himself with essays, notes, miscellaneous maxims and aperçus. In a sense, the most extensive state-ment of many of his cherished beliefs is to be found in the scientific work. We shall return to the matter of Goethean science at the end of this study. Suffice it to say at this stage that the science is animated by many of his most firmly held convictions. This is not to deny that the science is im-pelled by genuinely scientific questions; it is that, but it is also the medi-ated form of a philosophy of man's place in the material world. Goethe's science, then, is never value-free; rather, it is one particular expression of an ethos of applied worldliness. And perhaps that notion of worldliness gives us our best access to the recurring preoccupations of his thought. In a letter to his friend Johann Caspar Lavater of 28 October 1779, Goethe refers to himself as a "sehr irdischer Mensch" (very earthly person), This sense of attachment to the earth and all that it stood for (and all that stood on it) never left him throughout his life. Typically, to Eckermann on 25 December 1825, he speaks of having "eine Phantasie für die Wahrheit des Realen" (an imagination for the truth of the real). It is noteworthy that even in that early crisis when he returns from Leipzig as a young man in utter disarray and feels himself powerfully drawn to Pietistic beliefs, he holds fast to a sense that he is on this earth to be a writer and that this calling implies sustained and sustaining worldliness:

> mein feuriger Kopf, mein Witz, meine Bemühung und ziemlich gegründete Hoffnung, mit der Zeit ein guter Autor zu werden, sind jetzt, daß ich aufrichtig rede, die wichtigsten Hindernisse an meiner gänzlichen Sinnesänderung und des eigentlichen Ernsts die Winke der Gnade begierig anzunehmen.[9]

> [My fiery head, my wit, my energy, and my pretty much justified hope of becoming in time a good writer — these are all, to be perfectly frank, the most weighty obstacles to any profound change of heart on my part and to my eagerly acknowledging the signs of grace.]

In fact Goethe was consistently skeptical in matters of religious belief. He once described himself as a "dezidierter Anti-Christ"[10] (decided anti-Christian), and he was particularly disapproving of the strain of anti-worldliness and anti-bodiliness that was, for example, strongly in evidence in Christianity's central symbol of the crucified Son of God. In a letter to Karl Friedrich Zelter, he refers at one point to "das leidige Marterholz, das Widerwärtigste unter der Sonne"[11] (the dreadful cross of torture, the most repulsive thing under the sun).

Goethe was, however, able to esteem religion where it offered an affirmation of life and being in the world (hence his fondness for the figure of the Virgin Mary and for certain forms of Eastern belief). The force of his views on religious matters is vigorously expressed in the *Tagebuch der italienischen Reise*. There he registers the presence of pagan, pre-Christian culture with its complex, often tragic acknowledgement of bodiliness, and he regrets the subsequent transformation of that culture when it is overlaid by the tenets and mindset of Christian belief.

The Goethe of the Italian journey is, one feels, utterly in love with materiality. He writes to Frau von Stein from Rome:

> Wer mit Ernst sich hier umsieht und Augen hat zu sehen muß solid werden, er muß einen Begriff von Solidität fassen, der ihm nie so lebendig ward. Mir wenigstens ist es so als wenn ich alle Dinge dieser Welt nie so richtig geschätzt hatte als hier.[12]

> [Whoever looks seriously around himself here, and has eyes to see, must achieve solidity; he must come up with an idea of solidity more

lively than ever he saw before. At any rate I feel as though I had never appreciated the things of this world as rightly as here.]

It is a lovely remark, beginning as it does with a generality (wer) and with a concept (solid werden), and ending with the disarming particularity of one person's sense (mir wenigstens) that things are coming alive with a new kind of intensity and urgency. Yet that delight is not wild hedonism or gushing effusion. One thinks of his precise perception of a simple crab in a rock pool:

> Was ist doch ein Lebendiges für ein köstlich Ding! Wie abgemessen zu seinem Zustande, wie wahr, wie seiend.[13]

> [What a lovely thing is a living creature! How attuned to its condition, how true, how full of being.]

Without the least hint of affectation or pretentiousness the perception of the small creature in its world becomes transmuted into a reverent ontology. At one point, Goethe speaks of his awareness of the dangers of effusiveness, of wallowing in well-being:

> Ich lebe sehr diät und halte mich ruhig damit die Gegenstände keine erhöhte Seele finden, sondern die Seele erhöhen.[14]

> [I am living very frugally and keep calm so that things do not find an exalted soul, but rather exalt the soul.]

What is ultimately so moving about these statements of the Italian experience is that they figure as the tangible, sensuous basis of sustaining beliefs. In a late essay Goethe speaks of his sense that the human self only truly knows itself in interaction with physical objects:

> [...] daß mein Denken gegenständlich tätig ist [...] daß mein Anschauen selbst ein Denken, mein Denken ein Anschauen sei. Hierbei bekenn' ich, daß mir von jeher die große und so bedeutend klingende Aufgabe: erkenne dich selbst! immer verdächtig vorkam [...]. Der Mensch kennt nur sich selbst, insofern er die Welt kennt, die er nur in sich und sich nur in ihr gewahr wird. Jeder neue Gegenstand, wohl beschaut, schließt ein neues Organ in uns auf.[15]

> [... that my thinking is object-directed ... and that my observation is itself an act of thinking, that my thinking is observation. At this point I confess that the injunction "know yourself," which has for so long been revered as great and important, has always struck me as suspect.... Human beings only know themselves insofar as they know the world, which they are only aware of insofar as it is in them and they are in it. Every new object, carefully observed, opens up a new organ within us.]

Precisely that kind of thinking becomes also an artistic principle and reminds us of that earlier remark that his destiny as a *writer* blocks any firm commitment to religious belief. At one point in his autobiographical work *Dichtung und Wahrheit,* he likens "wahre Poesie" (true poetry) to "ein weltliches Evangelium"[16] (a worldly gospel).

These articles of worldly faith are, then, at the very heart of Goethe's creative personality. And it is important to stress that they come together in an intimation not of achieved totality, not of definitively acquired wholeness, but of ceaseless process and interactive movement. Of course, Goethe was fascinated by his own selfhood; but that self was not a solipsistically secure possession, it was constantly in flux, constantly in debate with its surroundings. Hence, his concern with self was also a concern with the world. His belief in nature was an affirmation of energy rather than a totalizing possession. He writes in an early note:

> Was den Menschen umgibt wirkt nicht allein auf ihn, er wirkt auch wieder zurück auf selbiges, und indem er sich modifizieren läßt, modifiziert er wieder rings um sich her. Die Natur bildet den Menschen, er bildet sich um, und diese Umbildung ist doch wieder natürlich.[17]

> [What surrounds human beings does not simply influence them, they in their turn influence it. And, since they allow themselves to be changed, they change things around them. Nature forms human beings; they change their forms, and this re-forming is once again natural.]

The parallelism of the clauses here mirrors Goethe's profound sense of reciprocity in action; and the colloquialism of "doch wieder" deliciously confirms the sense that what is being formulated conceptually is a truth that is enacted every day. A similarly colloquial verve can be heard in the famous remark (from a letter of 23 November 1818): "Zustand ist ein albernes Wort; weil nichts steht und alles beweglich ist" (State is a foolish word because nothing is in stasis and everything is in flux). Goethe's belief in process rather than stasis gives an omnipresent sense of complementary energies to which he often applied the term *Polarität.* What he had in mind was the necessary interplay, in human affairs, of interactive energies — light and dark, heat and cold, breathing in and breathing out, expansion and contraction (as in the alternating diastole and systole of the heart's rhythmic beating). Moreover, for Goethe, that whole process had a dynamic built in to it; it was not, in other words, an inexorable sameness, a sterile, repetitive interplay of colliding energies, because *Polarität* generated *Steigerung,* generated a qualitative transformation of energy. Goethe saw this deeply cherished model of the living process as a mental construct that was intimately responsive to the very rhythms of natural life.

Goethe's thought is, then, both down to earth and sophisticated. Hence, it cannot be too strongly stressed that, for all his belief in the right and necessary links between the human self and the natural world, he was no enemy of speculative thought. Nicholas Boyle has, for example, suggested that Goethe was much more aware of developments in philosophical and theoretical thinking (Kant, the Romantics) than has hitherto been allowed. Time and again we sense his elated engagement with the life of the mind; yet he was also concerned to break a lance for empiricism, properly understood. One might, for example, think of two maxims that spell out the conceptual yield engendered by the interplay of analysis and synthesis, of particularizing and generalizing, of distinguishing and likening:

> Jedes Existierende ist ein Analagon alles Existierenden; daher erscheint uns das Dasein immer zu gleicher Zeit gesondert und geknüpft. Folgt man der Analogie zu sehr, so fällt alles identisch zusammen; meidet man sie, so zerstreut sich alles in's Unendliche. In beiden Fällen stagniert die Betrachtung, einmal als überlebendig, das andere Mal als getötet. (*MUR*, 554)

> [Everything that exists is an analogy for the whole of existence; for this reason being strikes us at one and the same time separate and interconnected. If one goes too far in pursuing the analogy, then everything coalesces and becomes identical. But if one avoids the analogy, then everything degenerates into infinite particulars. In both cases, contemplation falters — on the one hand there is an excess of vitality, on the other a deadness.]

This is Goethe in discursive philosophical mode. He expresses the same insight with the charm of a double riddle when he writes:

> Was ist das Allgemeine? Der einzelne Fall. Was ist das Besondere? Millionen Fälle. (*MUR*, 558)

> [What is the general? One specific case. What is the particular? Millions of cases.]

Fundamentally, Goethe insists on the necessary and quickening relationship between theory and practice, between idea and concretion. He registered, for example, that, within the human sphere, that which matters is never simple, unmediated matter; it is, rather, matter rendered significant by theory — as he once put it: "Das Höchste wäre zu begreifen, daß alles Faktische schon Theorie ist"[18] (The greatest thing would be to understand that all factual arguments are already theorized). Or again, one could recall a marvelous passage which spells out the various stages in that process which takes us from looking at something, via noticing that something, to musing, then connecting, before reaching the final phase of theorizing:

Denn das bloße Anblicken einer Sache kann uns nicht fördern. Jedes
Ansehen geht über in ein Betrachten, jedes Betrachten in ein Sinnen,
jedes Sinnen in ein Verknüpfen, und so kann man sagen, daß wir
schon bei jedem aufmerksamen Blick in die Welt theoretisieren.[19]

[For simply to look at a thing cannot get us any further. Rather, every
act of looking becomes observation, every act of observing becomes
contemplation, every contemplation is an act of connecting; hence,
one can say that, with every attentive glance at the world, we are already
theorizing.]

The passage is dominated by verbal nouns — "Anblicken," "Ansehen,"
"Betrachten," "Sinne," "Verknüpfen" — and all of them, by virtue of
their very grammatical form, conspire to suggest the ceaselessly energetic
processes of human existence in the world. Elsewhere, and in similar vein,
Goethe speaks of theory as a tribute that the mind pays to the concrete
world, a tribute couched in what he calls "tender empiricism":

zarte Empirie, die sich mit dem Gegenstand innigst identisch macht
und dennoch zur eigentlichen Theorie wird. (*MUR*, 509)

[tender empiricism, which makes itself utterly identical with the object and yet develops into a genuine theory.]

It is noteworthy that the meeting which brought Goethe and Schiller together had everything to do with a central philosophical issue. They met
in Jena after a lecture which both of them disliked because it took a very
piecemeal approach to the understanding of nature. Goethe walked home
with Schiller and eagerly explained his notion of the "Urpflanze" (or
"symbolische Pflanze" as he then called it). Schiller was fascinated, but offered the important corrective "das ist keine Erfahrung, das ist eine Idee"
(that is not an experience, that is an idea). To which Goethe countered.
"Das kann mir sehr lieb sein, daß ich Ideen habe ohne es zu wissen, und
sie sogar mit Augen sehe"[20] (That can be congenial to me — that I have
ideas without knowing it and even see them with my own eyes). It is a
wonderfully expressive anecdote. Schiller is, of course, right that any such
notion of a primal plant is a construct, a product of the human mind rather
than of the material world. Yet it is utterly characteristic of Goethe's mindset that he should insist that ideas and concepts which unify and explain the
natural world must also be grounded in the natural world. It was his way of
emphasizing that his sense of the living process was rooted in the interplay
of sentient human selfhood on the one hand and the material universe on
the other.

That interplay gives him his sense of being dependent on occasions in
his life, on the operation of a world outside himself and other than that

self. At the same time he knew that some occasions were more conducive for him than others. As he writes in *Dichtung und Wahrheit:*

> Es kam nur auf die Gelegenheit an, die einen Charakter hatte, so war ich bereit und fertig. Wie ich nun über diese Naturgabe nachdachte und fand, daß sie mir ganz eigen angehöre und durch nichts Fremdes weder begünstigt noch gehindert werden könne, so mochte ich gern hierauf mein ganzes Dasein gründen.[21]

> [Everything depended on the opportunity that had the right configuration, and I was ready and willing. As I then reflected on this gift of nature and found that it was given particularly to me and could be neither furthered nor damaged by any extraneous elements, I was content to base my whole existence upon it.]

The notion of "Gelegenheit" implies a restriction of the self, implies its dependence on the configuration of external circumstances. It is this which, as we have noted, sets Goethe's urgent sense of self poles apart from solipsism.

We have summarized a number of features that are part and parcel of Goethe's worldview not only because of their inherent interest, representing as they do a generous, unideological, heterodox view of life, but also because particular versions of that Goethean worldview have played a culturally and politically important role in the German image of Goethe and Germany. In itself this is neither surprising nor evil; as we have already remarked, great writers can at various times play key roles in the self-understanding of the nations to which they belong. But there is something monolithic about the role Goethe has played in Germany. All too often, he has been linked with the problematic political issue of German unity. In other words: he has been stylized into some spokesman and ambassador for human wholeness who, in the years before 1871, symbolized the aspirations for unity within the German-speaking lands, and after 1871 provided that invention of tradition that confirmed the foundation of the Wilhelmine Empire as the only right and necessary way forward for Germany in her world-historical role. We all know that great writers can be pressed into the service of patriotic ends. By no means all the German images of Goethe have been pernicious; but some of them have been just that. The studies by Wolfgang Leppmann, Karl Robert Mandelkow, and Hans Schwerte can help us to get the measure of the use and abuse of a great writer.[22] There is, in our judgment, no need to labor the point, least of all when we come to the Fascist image of Goethe. But even where the cultural loading was not overtly heinous, the image-making often contrived to do Goethe an immense disservice, specifically in respect of the reception of his literary work. If we put him in the company of the other obvious European "Greats" (Cervantes, Dante, Molière, Shakespeare) we immediately note that he is, in many different ways, especially close to our contemporary tastes. He is, for example, much more varied than the other great writers: his oeuvre embraces all three literary genres and takes in philosophy and science. Moreover, his life is more urgently present, more fully documented and explored than is the case with, say, Shakespeare or Cervantes. Finally, and most obviously, Goethe is closer to us in time and linguistic forms. Yet paradoxically he has, within his own culture at any rate, frequently been seen as a pre-modern, rather than as a modern classic. Because of the range, scope, and resonance of his life and creativity, he has often been held to be the last whole man in an age of increasing specialization and fragmentation. He is, as it were, the universal spirit who provides the antidote to modernity. To make this claim for Goethe is, however, to do him a disservice. Ultimately, this perspective runs the risk of subscribing to notions of wholeness and wholesomeness which coalesce with images of Goethe the Olympian and the Sage of Weimar. In short, this is to marginalize him and his oeuvre within modern culture which, in the eyes of many, is held to be most urgently articulated by the fraught and torn spirits, such as Hölderlin, Heine, and Baudelaire.

It is worth remembering that Goethe's name is used officially to represent German culture abroad. That representation is entrusted to organizations that are known as "Goethe Institutes"; on occasion, this poses practical problems for foreigners because the name "Goethe" is difficult to pronounce. By contrast, English culture is represented abroad by the British Council and not by the Shakespeare Institute, and French culture by "L'Institut Français" and not by "L'Institut Molière." Moreover, generations of Germans have been encouraged to move *Mit Goethe durch das Jahr,* a yearly almanac, which contains a Goethe text, a wise saying, a maxim, intended to provide daily guidance through the vicissitudes of the year. Some of that quasi-sacramental resonance can be felt at the end of Friedrich Meinecke's historical essay *Die deutsche Katastrophe* (1947), an anguished analysis of Germany's slide into barbarism. He asks himself what might be the way forward out of the physical and spiritual rubble. He suggests the formation of "Goethe Gemeinden" (Goethe congregations), in which the best and finest of German culture might help to restore the shattered heart, mind, and soul, and, in the process, the nation.

Some of this adulation and, arguably, ideological overloading extends even to the scholarly realms of academe. It is, for example, a fascinating and instructive exercise to consult Hans Pyritz's *Goethe Bibliographie,* which started to appear in 1961, its most recent volume being published in 1968. Three fearsome volumes bear witness to the scholarly interest which Goethe generates and, of course, to the compilatory zeal of the editorial team. One would assume that a bibliography is a relatively value-free enterprise; its aim, after all, is to offer as full and detailed a compilation as possible. And yet, even within this seemingly disinterested scholarly enterprise, ideological undercurrents can be detected. The various sub-headings speak volumes. They are as follows:

Goethe Forschung
Goethe Editionen
Goethes Ganzheit
Goethes Entwicklungsgeschichte
Goethes Lebensbeziehungen
Goethes Persönlichkeit
Goethes Bildungsreich und geistige Kultur
Goethes Weltbild
Goethe als Naturforscher
Goethe in seiner staatlichen und organisatorischen Tätigkeit
Goethe als Bühnenpraktiker, als bildender Künstler, als Publizist
Goethe als Dichter
Goethes Werke in der wissenschaftlichen Spezialliteratur
Goethes Wirkungsgeschichte[23]

[Goethe scholarship
Goethe editions
Goethe's wholeness
Goethe's development
Goethe's relationships
Goethe's personality
Goethe's intellectual awareness and spiritual culture
Goethe's view of life
Goethe as natural scientist
Goethe in his civic and organizational activities
Goethe as man of the theater, as visual artist, as publicist
Goethe as creative writer
Goethe's works in specialized scholarship
Goethe's influence]

What strikes us as very strange indeed is that "Goethe als Dichter" comes so low down the list, clearly relegated to a secondary position compared to his "Ganzheit," "Persönlichkeit," "Weltbild," and so on. There are deeply felt reasons for such emphasis, and they become clear at particular moments when Pyritz allows the mask of disinterested scholarship to slip, and one hears the urgent voice of cultural diagnosis. At one point (he is writing in 1955) he refers to the "Kulturverfall unseres Zeitalters"[24] (cultural decline of our age); it seems that he resents above all else the atomization of Goethe scholarship, the proliferation of specific studies, of aspectival monographs and articles, because they serve to erode the all-important wholeness of Goethe. There is, in other words, a cultural and moral agenda behind Pyritz's aspiration to biographical completeness; the great bibliography will validate the wholeness that is everywhere under threat:

> Das Auge des heutigen Forschers, an Goethes eigener Morphologie geschult, erblickt die sich entwickelnde Gestalteinheit, in der sich alles mit allem verbindet. Und das Goethe-Schrifttum, wie ein riesiges Netz über das Ganze der Goetheschen Existenz gebreitet, faksimiliert ihr Gestaltgesetz und ihren Entfaltungsgang, indem sich innerhalb dieses Schrifttums bei jeglichem Thema (mag es der jeweilige Verfasser noch so gesondert verhandeln) sich alles mit allem berührt.[25]

> [The eye of the scholar today, if it is trained in Goethe's own morphology, discerns the unfolding unity of form in which everything is connected to everything else. And Goethe scholarship, spread like an enormous net over the whole of Goethe's existence, replicates his formal laws and their unfolding, so that within this body of writing every individual theme (even if it is dealt with separately by the author) connects with every other.]

Twice, in two sentences, and with almost talismanic force, the notion is expressed that Goethe is and represents a unity in which everything is connected with everything else. If the critics have lost sight of this, then the bibliographer can make good the deficit, can re-assert wholeness. In the prefatory section to the chapter on "Goethes Entwicklungsgeschichte," there is one particular point in the bibliography where the full fervor of Pyritz's agenda erupts. He laments that there is no serious study of the early, crisis-riven years in Frankfurt (1768–70), because they embody

> jenen in der Weltgeschichte wohl einzigartigen Prozeß, der nicht nur einen jungen, scheinbar am Ende stehenden Menschen und Dichter vom Grund aus erneuert und umformt, vom physischen Heilwunder an bis hinunter in die geheimsten Bezirke des geistigen Lebens, der vielmehr innerhalb weniger Monate den ausgebrannten Heimkehrer, den Gescheiterten einsenkt in den Wurzelboden seiner ganzen künftigen Wesensentfaltung, ihn reift und durchorganisiert und mit Überkräften rüstet zur Empfängnis des dionysischen Feuersturms der Straßburger Ära, den Leipziger Rokoko-Epigonen bereit macht für seinen Weg zur geistigen Weltherrschaft, für seine den Weg des Menschen in der Welt vollendende Lebensleistung.[26]

> [that process, which is doubtless unique in world history, whereby a young man and poet, seemingly at his wits end, is renewed and transformed from the very basis of his being by a cure that extends from the miraculous physical healing of the body to the most secret

areas of spiritual life. That process in the space of a few months plunges the broken man, the burnt out homecomer, into the roots and soil of his future development, matures him, re-organizes him and endows him with superhuman powers ready to meet the Dionysian firestorm of the Strasbourg era and makes the Leipzig poet, that mere copier of the rococo style, ready to take his path to spiritual world domination, to a living substance that completes the being of the human self in the world.]

This is, to put it mildly, a remarkable piece of rhetoric. In the reference to the "ausgebrannten Heimkehrer" one hears an acknowledgement of the generation damaged by the war. The intensity of the claim made for Goethe links with an impassioned perception of that wholeness and healing which contemporary culture desperately needs but is unable to provide. At times Pyritz's voice is hectoring, strident, embattled. But he is not merely idiosyncratic: in essence, he challenges the fragmentation and dislocation of the modern world in the name of a much older tradition, one which has, as we have seen, revered Goethe as the bringer of wholeness.

In the 1950s, Pyritz was not alone in his wish to privilege the integrative energies of Goethe's life, work, and personality. Something similar can be heard in the commentary sections of what is still a hugely influential edition of Goethe's works — the Hamburger Ausgabe (HA). Here is Erich Trunz on "Mailied":

Goethes lyrische Sprache war mit ihm jung und wurde mit ihm alt. Die Deutschen wissen erst durch ihn, daß Jugend eine eigene Sprache hat [. . .]. Das Fest der Natur und der Seele wird Klang, jubelnd, leicht, tanzend und zugleich feierlich [. . .]. Für den Satzbau charakteristisch: Ausrufe, die das Gedicht von Anfang bis Ende beherrschen; Ausruf drückt Jubel am unmittelbarsten aus. Völliges Einssein von Natur und Mensch in der Sprache. [. . .] Das liebende Mädchen, das liebende Ich sind Natur und sind darum eins mit dieser festlichen Landschaft. [. . .] Goethes Sprache ist Einheit.[27]

[Goethe's lyrical language was young with him, and it grew to old age with him. It was through him that the Germans discovered that youth has a language of its own. . . . The celebration of nature and the soul becomes song, rejoicing, light, dancing and yet solemn. . . . The sentence structures are characterized by exclamations that dominate the poem from beginning to end, exclamations are the most direct articulation of rejoicing. Complete oneness of nature and human being in language. . . . The loving girl, the loving self are nature and are at one with this celebratory landscape. . . . Goethe's language is unity.]

It is a wonderfully engaged and passionate commentary about a passionate poem. And it rightly highlights the interplay of human and natural spheres (both animal and vegetable) that animates the poem. The point at which we would dissent from Trunz's commentary is when he speaks of "völliges Einssein von Natur und Mensch in der Sprache" (complete oneness of nature and human being in language). The poem, we would suggest, is not so much concerned with identity and sameness as it is with modes and processes of reciprocity. That, surely, is enshrined in the particle "wie" (which can mean both "how" and "like"). This small word, then, can have exclamatory force (wie herrlich leuchtet / Mir die Natur; How gloriously nature glows in my eyes), and it can also speak as simile, as likeness and kinship: "Wie Morgenwolken" (like morning clouds); "So liebt die Lerche / Gesang und Luft [. . .] wie ich dich liebe [. . .]" (Just as the lark loves song and air, so do I love you). It is a measure of Goethe's acute feel for linguistic possibilities that this poem of love centers on the connection between liking and likening, on the link between intensity of experience and kinship of experience.

We have no wish to problematize this splendidly immediate poem. Rather, we wish to highlight its immediacy which can be heard, for example, in the Frankfurt vernacular rhyme of "Zweig" and "Gesträuch"; but that immediacy coexists with notions of mediacy, of mediation as the expression of human self-consciousness. The glory of which the poem speaks is both literally given and metaphorically made.

The reference to Trunz's commentary on "Mailied" is not meant to score points off a scholar whose edition still is a superlative achievement; but it serves to sketch in a particular view of Goethe which may come between contemporary readers and the work of one of the very greatest of European writers. By contrast, it should be noted that the two most recent editions of Goethe — the Münchner Ausgabe (MA) and the Frankfurter Ausgabe (FA) — aim to offer a precise historical contextualization of Goethe's creativity and to acknowledge the many ways in which his art fruitfully engages with modern textual approaches. But neither of these editions bears the stamp of one editor (as is the case with Trunz's presence in the Hamburger Ausgabe); nor do they have that sense, which Trunz's edition so powerfully expresses, of the coherent unfolding of Goethe's creative personality.

The clock, then, has moved on, taking us beyond that particular form of Goethe reception that is characteristic of (especially German) reactions to Goethe in the hundred and twenty-five years or so after his death. In the immediate aftermath of the Second World War, Pyritz, Trunz and Emil Staiger cling to the belief in Goethean wholeness. But the politicized 1970s rejected that legacy as so much high-bourgeois ideological ballast and advanced a sternly skeptical view of "The Great Man and His Works."

Of late, in the climate of deconstruction and theory, that trend has given place to more sophisticated textual debates with Goethe. But his overall position in contemporary German culture is still strangely unclear. The Goethe Year of 1999 produced both a boom in Goethe memorabilia on the one hand and on the other laments that nobody reads Goethe any more. Theatre producers were often demonstrably unsure as to how to approach his "classic" works.

This study seeks to capitalize on the fluidity of the contemporary critical climate and, by that token, to suggest that Goethe's literary work powerfully and cogently explores the thematics and stylistics of our (as it were) post-modern condition. But we shall also be mindful of that older legacy of Goethean wholeness. It cannot merely be dismissed as some strange chimera to which German literary scholarship succumbed because of the need for a riposte to, and redemption from, the problematic course of German history (der deutsche Sonderweg). Matters are nowhere near so simple as that, not least because the presence of a dynamic and multiple richness to Goethe's creative achievement is indisputable. Yet it is crucially important, to see this richness as symptomatic of a generous and open approach to experience, a non-reductive acknowledgement of both mind and matter and their dialectical interplay. As we have stressed, it is this aspect which may speak most strongly to the modern reader.

After all, and this is a point to which we attach great importance, Goethe was creatively and thoughtfully aware of modernity. Two of the great projects — the *Faust* drama and the *Wilhelm Meister* novels — that occupied him throughout his creative life have everything to do with a debate with modern culture. He was acutely perceptive about the energies released by modern culture, and about the dangers that that culture would bring in its train even though he says very little about socio-economic specifics. His key concept of "Entsagung," of renouncing certain modes and forms of experience, links with his sense of the unavoidable specialization and narrowing of the personality that the modern world imposes. Moreover, his scientific work is animated by the need to debate with the scientific temper of modern culture. Ironically, it was none other than Schiller, his key collaborator, who, with his great essay on modern culture, *Über naive und sentimentalische Dichtung,* did Goethe a great disservice, because that essay has contributed to a pigeonholing of Goethe as some unreflective and by that token premodern voice. This was certainly not Schiller's intention and nothing could be further from the truth, as we hope this study will demonstrate.

But now, after all this preliminary consideration of the life, the thought, the image, it is time to turn to the literary work.

2: Poetry

IN ORDER TO HAVE SOME MEASURE of structure, this chapter will address Goethe's poetry under various thematic headings: nature, divinity, love, reflectivity. However, we must stress at the outset that these thematic categories are anything but watertight divisions: more often than not, the nature poetry, for example, is inseparable from the love poetry and the love poetry is implicated in the philosophical poetry. This interrelation lies at the very heart of Goethe's poetic oeuvre and makes him perhaps the greatest lyric poet of modern Europe. For him, feeling and mood modulate into thought and concept, and vice versa. For this reason his poetry, taken as a whole, gives us powerful access to his experiential and imaginative world.

As far as his worldview is concerned, even the early poetry prefigures what was to become his mature philosophical stance. The Sesenheim and Frankfurt poems largely bespeak a sense of being at home in the world, being at one with nature. There are somber moments, but more often than not, affirmation gains the upper hand. Thus a poem's conclusion may typically turn its back on troubling reflectivity and assert a conciliatory "und doch" — "and yet." In "Willkommen und Abschied" (1771, revised 1789), sorrow yields in the last two lines

> Und doch, welch Glück, geliebt zu werden,
> Und lieben, Götter, welch ein Glück!

> [And yet what bliss to be loved,
> And to love, you Gods, what bliss it is!]

A similar example is "Warum gabst du uns die tiefen Blicke" (1776), a love poem to Charlotte von Stein. The text abounds in motifs of suffering, yet it ends on a note of reconciliation:

> Glücklich, daß das Schicksal, das uns quälet,
> Uns doch nicht verändern mag.

> [Happy that destiny that torments us
> Cannot in fact change us.]

Such structures of affirmation are often accompanied by themes and images of oneness. In "Mahomets Gesang" (1772–73), we find the ever-recurrent image of water, the river merging with countless other rivers, seeking fulfillment in the sea. "Ganymed" (1774) is another famous example: Ganymed, beloved of the god Zeus, seeks union with divine nature. Like Werther, he is cradled by "Blumen" and "Gras," but his spirit, driven by yearning, strives upwards: "hinauf, hinauf strebt's." And the spirit of the divine father responds:

> Abwärts, die Wolken
> Neigen sich der sehnenden Liebe,
> Mir, mir!
> In eurem Schoße
> Aufwärts,
> Umfangend umfangen!
>
> [Downwards, the clouds
> Bend down to the longing of love.
> To me, to me!
> In your womb
> Upwards
> Embracing and embraced!]

The juxtaposition of "hinauf" and "abwärts" generates a sense of total fusion which is crystallized in the image of "Schoß" and in the phrase "Umfangend umfangen!" We shall return to this poem later. Suffice it to say at this stage that in "Ganymed," as in so many poems, feeling is transformed into purest form, grammatical and syntactical structure.

In the early 1770s, this worldview is essentially anchored in feeling, in mood; with the move to Weimar, it deepens into a firmly held view, a profound attitude. This development is inseparable from the scientific studies which Goethe soon takes up. His pursuits in mineralogy, botany, anatomy, and other fields of enquiry are driven by the quest for a unifying principle, the desire to discover how nature brings forth her infinite variety. These scientific studies are grounded in a holistic vision which has no room for any fundamental dualism, unbridgeable division. Thus his later philosophical poetry may challenge us to reason, to differentiate; but tracing difference is ultimately in the service of synthesis, of perceiving coherence. Take, for example, the following phrase from his trilogy of 1820, dedicated to the English natural scientist Howard:

> Dich im Unendlichen zu finden,
> Mußt unterscheiden und dann verbinden.
>
> [To find yourself in the infinite
> You must distinguish and then connect.]

It is this holistic stance which makes him reject Newtonian science as mechanistic, divisive, deadening. For Goethe, there is but one world, one force, extending from the lowest forms of inorganic nature to the highest realms, the human sphere, its creative activities. In this sense he views his own work, its wide spectrum of different forms, as ultimately rooted in that one and same force of formation, in "Bildungstrieb." All forms, even the most unusual ones, are ultimately related to their primordial entities — Goethe's term is "Urphänomene." These entities have their own encoded law of being and development, the blue-print of their evolution. This view is at the heart of the poem on the evolution of plants, "Die Metamorphose der Pflanzen" (1798).

> Alle Glieder bilden sich aus nach ew'gen Gesetzen,
> Und die seltenste Form bewahrt im geheimen das Urbild.

> [All the segments evolve by eternal laws,
> And even the rarest form preserves in secrecy its primal shape.]

A similar notion applies to the human being: each one represents indivisible and unique individuality, with its own innate law, its inborn destiny, entelechy.

In philosophical terms, the central concepts and tenets which sustain Goethe's literary and scientific work are indebted to both Benedictus de Spinoza (1632–77) and Gottfried Wilhelm von Leibniz (1664–1716). For Spinoza, there is only one divine substance, and matter and mind are but its aspects. In essence, his philosophy amounts to pure pantheism in that God is Nature, and Nature is God. Goethe first encountered Spinoza's thought in 1773, and he repeatedly acknowledges how much he owes to this philosopher. Certainly, one could trace numerous Spinozan elements, particularly in his poetry. But for Goethe overall, and for eighteenth-century German thinking, Leibniz is the decisive figure. He perceives of the universe as a perfect dynamic order, secured by a divine pre-established harmony. God created it as the best of all possible worlds. It is made up of myriads of so-called monads, centers of energy: each one is windowless, and yet endowed with the capacity to reflect within itself the universal divine order. Leibniz's conception is much more dynamic than that of Spinoza, and in this sense it is at the heart of Goethe's thinking, which is utterly informed by the idea of unceasing energy and change within ultimate order.

Goethe's terms for this dynamic force are manifold: "Werden," "Regen," "Bilden," and the most famous is, of course, "Streben." The danger that this energy might run riot is philosophically kept at bay by the idea of an overriding design, a harmony, which, as in Leibniz's scheme, keeps energy in check. This is crystallized for example in such poems as "Dauer im

Wechsel" (1803) or "Eins und Alles" (1821). The very titles speak volumes, and they also alert us to a central aspect of Goethe's thinking, the notion of *Polarität,* polarity. Put in a nutshell, the potentially excessive flow of energy is held in check by the interaction of polar opposites. For Goethe, the basic rhythms of the living organism are deeply symbolic: breathing in and out, "Ein-" and "Ausatmen," and the expanding and contracting heart muscle ("Diastole" and "Systole") symbolize the force of polarity which regulates energy. This notion of polarity as a creative interplay of opposites pervades Goethe's work in countless variations.

The most fundamental polarity is that of freedom and order — nature epitomizes the harmonious interplay of these two opposites. The following extract from the poem "Metamorphose der Tiere" (1800) illustrates this perfectly. Here, we are told to delight in nature's incessant interchange of energy and containment, of freedom and limitation, and to take it as a guide for our own life:

> Dieser schöne Begriff von Macht und Schranken, von Willkür
> Und Gesetz, von Freiheit und Maß, von beweglicher Ordnung,
> Vorzug und Mangel erfreue dich hoch! [. . .]

> [This lovely concept of power and constraints, of contingency
> And law, of freedom and moderation, of moving order,
> Of advantage and lack, — let it delight you.]

All this sounds very abstract indeed, but Goethe's poetry invariably finds the objective correlative for these concepts and ideas. As John Williams so memorably suggests, in Goethe's lyric oeuvre, landscape and inscape interact ceaselessly.[1] Precisely this interlocking of outward and inward worlds, of lived experience on the one hand and of the interpreting, transforming mind of the poet on the other, gives Goethe's lyric work its unmistakable urgency. In an early observation (1781), he thanks the gods for the gift of poetic articulation, for "die Gabe [. . .] in nachklingende Lieder das eng zu fassen, was in meiner Seele immer vorgeht" (HA 2, 429; the gift [. . .] of capturing precisely in reverberant song the things that are going on in my soul). One should note the stress on poetry not as stenography of experience but as its concentration and distillation (eng zu fassen). Poetry by this process modulates the particular into the universal. In 1820, looking back at a poem he had written in 1777, "Die Harzreise im Winter," Goethe said:

> Was von meinen Arbeiten durchaus und so auch von den kleineren
> Gedichten gilt, ist, daß sie alle, durch mehr oder minder bedeutende
> Gelegenheit aufgeregt, im unmittelbaren Anschauen irgendeines
> Gegenstandes verfaßt worden, deshalb sie sich nicht gleichen, darin
> jedoch übereinkommen, daß bei besondern äußern, oft gewöhn-

lichen Umständen ein Allgemeines, Inneres, Höheres dem Dichter vorschwebte. (HA 1, 393).

[What applies to all my works, and hence even to the smaller poems, is the fact that they all, triggered by occasions of greater or lesser importance, were composed in the act of immediate contemplation of one object or another; for this reason they are all different, yet they have in common that, in the context of these particular, external, and often ordinary circumstances, something general, inward, higher hovered before the mind's eye of the poet.]

At the heart of his poetry, then, is the ability to find in the experienced world instances of revelation. In this context, we should recall Goethe's gloss on the symbol as a "lebendendig-augenblickliche Offenbarung des Unerforschlichen" (*MUR*, 314). In the fluidity of that creative process, as manifested in the poetry, it is therefore less than helpful to distinguish between "Erlebnislyrik" and "Gedankenlyrik," because his poetry explores the quickening interaction of immediate physical experience on the one hand and the workings of reflectivity on the other.

In the introduction to this study, we have touched on "Mailied" as it is indeed an excellent starting point in any consideration of Goethe's poetry. "Mailied" (first version 1771, revised 1789) is one of the early "Sesenheim" lyrics, and it illustrates perfectly the energizing interrelation of landscape and inscape. The poem exemplifies perhaps the very essence of what Goethe's nature poetry has to offer. It is rapturous in mood and utterance, and its song-like mode celebrates the sense of oneness that is at the heart of human loving:

> O Mädchen, Mädchen
> Wie lieb ich dich!
> Wie blickt dein Auge,
> Wie liebst du mich!

> [O maiden, maiden
> How do I love you!
> How your eyes shine,
> How you love me!]

The reciprocity between the lovers is confirmed and magnified by the all-pervasive sense of kinship between the human world and all the other orders of nature. The indefinite verb "es dringen" (there thrusts), which opens stanza two, has for its compound subject the blossoms of vegetable nature, the sounds of animal nature (Und tausend Stimmen / Aus dem Gesträuch), and finally (by implicit extension) all natural entities including the human (Und Freud und Wonne / Aus jeder Brust). If the sequence of the statement in stanzas two and three moves, then, along a chain of related being (a notion very dear to the eighteenth century), that same journey is undertaken in reverse order in stanzas six and seven:

> Wie blickt dein Auge,
> Wie liebst du mich!
>
> So liebt die Lerche
> Gesang und Luft,
> Und Morgenblumen
> Den Himmelsduft [. . .].
>
> [How your eye shines,
> How you love me!
>
> This way the lark loves
> Song and air,
> And morning flowers
> The fragrance of heaven.]

Yet no sooner has the utterance reached the animal kingdom than we move instantly back into reconnection with the human sphere (Wie ich dich liebe / Mit warmem Blut [As I love you with warm blood]). The poem is remarkable, then, for the delight and energy with which it brings together separate experiential spheres. This much is suggested in the little word *wie* which dominates the poem. It functions both as an exclamation of intensity ("Wie herrlich leuchtet" [How gloriously does shine]) and as simile, the expression of likeness ("Wie Morgenwolken" [like morning clouds]). These two functions are, of course, related in the poem: it is the sheer urgency of experience that generates the relatedness of experience. That relatedness is expressed in the first stanza with the metaphor of the meadow's laughter, "Wie lacht die Flur!" (How the meadow laughs!). Not a remarkable instance of figurative speech, perhaps; but in the context of the poem as a whole it acquires almost ontological force. The poem closes with the promise that this present experience of rapturous relatedness will become some kind of lasting benchmark for any and every future happiness: "Sei ewig glücklich / Wie du mich liebst" (Be eternally happy / As you love me!). The poem, then, is about human feeling, about human reflectivity, about the need to make metaphors of experience. Tellingly, it closes on a moment of self-consciousness.[2] The poem (in this, its second, version) is called "Mailied": the final stanza speaks of the girl as inspiring the poet "Zu neuen Liedern." Our poem, then, is a song about song, perhaps even a song of songs. It is the Song of May, and the genitive in that formulation is, one senses, both objective and subjective. It is the song that May sings; and it is the song that the human self sings about

May, about spring and early summer as the temporal and emotional context of and metaphor for human joy.

A similar interplay of literal and metaphorical statement informs "Über allen Gipfeln" (Over All Mountain Tops, 1780;) the second of the two "Wandrers Nachtlieder." When Goethe chose to publish them as a pair of poems, he indicated their pairing by giving the second poem the simple title "Ein Gleiches" — one more of the same. The poem evokes the calm of evening, and registers peace as indwelling in the mountain tops, the tree tops, in the birds, and it closes with the promise that soon that peace will reach the human subject:

> Warte nur, balde
> Ruhest du auch.
>
> [Wait a little, soon
> You too will rest.]

As E. M. Wilkinson suggests,[3] the details invoked in the poem are by no means randomly associative, but form a sequence: they trace the historical process of the creation of the world: from inorganic matter (rock) via organic matter (trees) and animate life (the animal kingdom) to the sentient being of the human self. The sequence also moves from distant realms to the immediate surroundings of the human subject, from distant heights to the human habitat on earth. In short, our poem both derives from, and conveys, the sense of a chain of being, of which the human subject is necessarily, but complexly, part.

The poem is a miracle of sound enshrining sense, and the echoes and rhymes establish a measure of consonance between the human self and the natural world. The "ist Ruh" of line two is echoed and transformed by the "Ruhest du" of the final line. The human subject becomes the grammatical subject of the verb "to rest" in the closing cadence of the poem. But here, a central question arises: Why is the human self, although umbilically connected to nature, unquiet, and why does it have to wait for the peace that fills the landscape to fill his or her heart too? The answer, as the poem suggests, has to do with human self-consciousness: Close reading reveals that within the lyrical formation there is also a drama of self-reflexivity. This may seem a large claim, for, on the overt level of the poem, there is no "Ich," but only a "du": "Spürest du" in line four, the second person singular imperative form "Warte nur" in the penultimate line, and finally an explicit reference again in the concluding phrase "ruhest du auch." Who are the parties to this conversation? The title of the poem, with its singular genitive form "Wandrers," makes it clear that this is the night song of one and only one person. And that person both is, and is aware of being, in communion with himself or herself.

Physically, there is only one self in the poem; but in terms of the consciousness displayed, there are two selves: an "ich" that talks to itself in the "du" form. Grammatically and cognitively, the human subject is self-conscious, and is, by virtue of that condition, more unquiet than the mountain tops, the tree tops, and the birds, more complexly constituted.

The final line expresses the promised goal of waiting — peace. It is, and this is true of the verbs throughout the poem, couched in the present tense. "Ruhest du" echoes the strands of "Ist Ruh" and "Spürest du," but with a difference: The final clause is introduced by "balde." In short, this is a grammatical and cognitive present that has not yet come about — the sense of the present tense is in fact future. The temporal dimension is decisive. The final two lines of the poem suggest that the human subject is not completely absorbed in, not integrally coterminous with, the present. By virtue of its self-consciousness, it knows of more than the present moment, the present context. Hence its restiveness. The poem closes with the word "auch," with an implied connection of comparison and similarity: nature rests, so too will you. The combination of futurity with similarity invests "Ruh" and "ruhen" with future and metaphorical meaning — and thereby with the association of death. This is not, it must be stressed, to convert the poem into a meditation on death. It is not that. It is a meditation on rest and peace, which metaphorically extends its meaning to encompass death. This issue of the metaphorical extrapolation can be heard in one tiny detail of the poem's linguistic mode. T. J. Reed has drawn our attention to the poem's fondness for suppressing and adding an "e" at frequent points.[4] On two occasions the "e" that one would expect in standard written German is not in evidence — "Wandrers" in the title, and "Ruh" in line two. Such elisions give the poem an intimate, colloquial feel. But on five occasions an "e" is added: "Spürest," "Vögelein," "Walde," "balde," "ruhest." On the whole, the added "e" lifts the register of the language, gives it a more melodic, poetic, perhaps even a more solemn, feel. The fluidity of Goethe's diction, then, moves the poem between colloquial statement of associative mood and feeling on the one hand and a grander register of weighty reflectiveness on the other. And in the context of the potential metaphorical presence of death, the issue of the extra "e" is particularly important. In the iconography of death, on memorials and tombstones, there is a familiar phrase which expresses the hope that the dead person is "resting in peace." The metaphorical substitution of rest for death is consoling. In German that phrase is often inscribed in the optative subjunctive form — "er / sie ruhe in Frieden" (let him/her rest in peace) — and that subjunctive form is signaled by the presence of the added "e." Perhaps, then, even this tiny detail of Goethe's language, this delicate shift invites us to hear, amongst other things, the consciousness of the human subject as one poised between literal and metaphorical forms of awareness, between, literally, rest and, metaphorically, death.

Let us now turn to another poem that explores the relationship between the human self and the natural world: "Herbstgefühl" (Autumn Feeling, 1775, revised 1789).

Fetter grüne, du Laub,
am Nebengeländer
hier mein Fenster herauf!
Gedrängter quellet,
Zwillingsbeeren, und reifet
schneller und glänzend voller!
Euch brütet der Mutter Sonne
Scheideblick; euch umsäuselt
des holden Himmels
fruchtende Fülle;
euch kühlet des Mondes
freundlicher Zauberhauch,
und euch betauen, ach!
aus diesen Augen
der ewig belebenden Liebe
vollschwellende Tränen.

[Grow more lushly green, you foliage,
On the vine trellis,
Here up to my window.
Swell more tightly,
Twin berries, and ripen
More quickly and more lustrously full.
You are bred from the farewell
Glance of the maternal sun, you are
Fanned by the fruitful fullness
Of the lovely sky.
You are cooled by the moon's
Friendly magic breath,
And you are bedewed, alas,
By the fully swelling tears
Of eternally enlivening love
From these eyes.]

The poem opens, remarkably, with a human voice commanding nature outside the window to move the season forward more swiftly: "grüne," "quellet," "reifet" (green, flow, ripen) are all imperative forms. Yet in the course of the poem the grammatical mode and the mood of the poem change. The impatience, the urge to accelerate natural processes has gone, seemingly banished by the all-important noun "Scheideblick" (parting glance) which invokes separation and parting as the inevitable consequences of time passing. The remainder of the poem addresses the grapes by the window through the frequently repeated form of the plural accusative "euch." The human self, then, addresses natural entities; and the phrasing suggests that there is a form of kinship that links human and natural spheres: the swelling tears of love replicate the shape of the grapes — the "glänzend voller" (with fuller radiance) prefigures the "vollschwellende Tränen" (fully swelling tears) — and the tears that fall from human eyes are metaphorically akin to nature's dew, "betauen." Yet kinship is not identity. The grapes are different from the humans who delight in them; the interplay of relatedness and separation is suggested by the subtle modulation of sound patterns in the lines:

> Euch kühlet des Mondes
> Freundlicher Zauberhauch,
> Und euch betauen, ach! [. . .]

> [You are cooled by the moon's
> Friendly magic breath,
> And you are bedewed, alas! . . .]

Assonance takes us from the "euch" of the grapes via "Hauch" to "betauen" and then to "ach." The register of human lament derives from a drama of relatedness and difference, expressed by the shifting sound patterns. The human self begins and ends the poem in a condition that separates it from nature. In the opening lines the voice speaking is peremptory. It knows, in advance of their occurrence, the shapes and forms that nature assumes in the course of the year. Hence, it makes comparisons between what is and what can be and will be, just as, at the end of "Über allen Gipfeln," the present tense "ruhest du" expresses future meaning. The mental act of comparing present with future generates the comparative form of adjectives, adverbs, participles: "fetter," "gedrängter," "schneller," "voller." If that form of separation is one that, as it were, knows better than nature, by the end of the poem the self grieves over the separation in the "ach." Comparison can bring entities together, but it can also separate them.

Yet we have to ask ourselves to be more precise about the cause of the grief. What is it that afflicts the human subject in this poem? One answer is implied by the title — "Herbstgefühl" — by the autumnal feelings that can overcome the human mind, a sense of transience and loss. Feelings about autumn are also feelings of the autumnal self as it reflects on the passing of time. Once again the issue of self-consciousness comes to the fore. It figures in the address to nature which informs every line of our poem. It is also present in the way in which, at the beginning and end of the poem, Goethe creates a demonstrative linguistic gesture in respect of the speaking self. One thinks, for example, of the "Hier mein Fenster herauf!" (here, up to my window) in line three, and "Aus diesen Augen" (from these eyes) in the third line from the end of the poem. The "hier," "mein," "diesen" all indicate a self that ultimately is, and knows itself to be, an onlooker at its own experience. The self-thematizing of the human self in the poem is an unmistakable rhetorical gesture, and it is also part of the poem's theme, which interrogates the overlap and distinction between the human self and the natural world.

In his nature poetry, Goethe speaks of the comfort and shelter afforded by the omnipresence of natural processes; but he never simplifies the relationship between two very different orders of being. It is noteworthy that on certain occasions he even speaks of the incommensurability between human and natural spheres. In this context the ballads come to mind: they often conjoin a seeming sturdiness and simplicity of literary mode with a disturbing perception of what can happen to human entities within the natural world. One key example is a poem that has become especially famous because of its amazing musical setting by Schubert: "Erlkönig" (Erl King, 1782).

> Wer reitet so spät durch Nacht und Wind?
> Es ist der Vater mit seinem Kind;
> Er hat den Knaben wohl in dem Arm,
> Er faßt ihn sicher, er hält ihn warm.
>
> Mein Sohn, was birgst du so bang dein Gesicht? —
> Siehst Vater, du den Erlkönig nicht?
> Den Erlenkönig mit Kron und Schweif? —
> Mein Sohn, es ist ein Nebelstreif. —
>
> "Du liebes Kind, komm, geh mit mir!
> Gar schöne Spiele spiel ich mit dir;
> Manch bunte Blumen sind an dem Strand,
> Meine Mutter hat manch gülden Gewand."
>
> Mein Vater, mein Vater, und hörest du nicht,
> Was Erlenkönig mir leise verspricht? —
> Sei ruhig, bleibe ruhig, mein Kind;
> In dürren Blättern säuselt der Wind. —
>
> "Willst, feiner Knabe, du mit mir gehn?
> Meine Töchter sollen dich warten schön;
> Meine Töchter führen den nächtlichen Reihn
> Und wiegen und tanzen und singen dich ein."

Mein Vater, mein Vater, und siehst du nicht dort
Erlkönigs Töchter am düstern Ort? —
Mein Sohn, mein Sohn, ich seh es genau:
Es scheinen die alten Weiden so grau. —

"Ich liebe dich, mich reizt deine schöne Gestalt;
Und bist du nicht willig, so brauch ich Gewalt."
Mein Vater, mein Vater, jetzt faßt er mich an!
Erlkönig hat mir ein Leids getan! —

Dem Vater grauset's, er reitet geschwind,
Er hält in den Armen das ächzende Kind,
Erreicht den Hof mit Mühe und Not;
In seinen Armen das Kind war tot.

[Who rides so late through night and wind?
It is the father with his child;
He has the boy secure in his arms,
He holds him tightly, he keeps him warm.

"My son, why do you hide your face so fearfully?"
"Do you, father, not see the Erl King?
The Erl King with crown and robe?"
"My son it is a wisp of mist."

"Come now, you sweet child, go with me!
I will play very lovely games with you;
There are many fine flowers on the shore,
My mother has many golden garments."

"My father, my father, and do you not hear
What Erl King softly promises me?"
"Be calm, stay calm, my child;
The wind is rustling in the dry leaves."

"You lovely boy, will you come with me?
My daughters will attend to your every need;
My daughters lead the nightly round dance,
And they will rock and dance and sing you to sleep."

"My father, my father, and do you not see there
In the gloomy place Erl King's daughters?"
"My son, my son, I see it all clearly;
It is the grey sheen of the old willow trees."

"I love you, I am excited by your beautiful form;
And if you are not willing I shall use force."

"My father, my father, now he has caught hold of me!
Erl King has done me great hurt."

The father shudders, he rides fast,
He holds in his arms the groaning child,
Reaches the courtyard with effort and pain;
In his arms the child was dead.]

Like so many ballads, this poem has an energetic narrative thrust: a father rides through the night with his child; in his terror the child sees a ghostly figure who beckons to him and finally attacks him; when the father arrives at his journey's end, the child is dead in his arms. Much of the poem — and this again is a recurring feature of the ballad form — is sustained by dialogue. In this case there are three speakers, in addition to the narrative voice which introduces and ends the poem in the first and final stanzas: the father, the son, and the Erl King. Goethe draws very fully on the expressive potential of the traditional form; and he does so in order to create a world invaded by terror, a terror not assuaged by the narrative framing which insists on the protective role of the father, holding the child in his arms. Death has the last word. And the terror of death stalks the stanzas in which the three figures speak. Much of the power of Goethe's great poem derives from the interpretative uncertainty it creates. At the concrete, that is non-supernatural, level we can hear two possibilities. One is that the child is frail, perhaps ill; at any rate, he is so terrified by the shapes and sounds that surround him on his journey through the dark landscape that he dies. Within this framework of understanding there are powerful interpretative possibilities at work: most parents, we suspect, will hear in the poem the nightmare of a child slipping away into death. At a more general, philosophical level we note that the father is the voice of rationality and common sense. He claims to see accurately (ich seh es genau), and to perceive only natural — not supernatural — phenomena ("es ist ein Nebelstreif; in dürren Blättern säuselt der Wind" [it is a wisp of fog; the wind is rustling in the dry leaves]). Yet no amount of robust reasoning can exorcise the child's vulnerability and terror. Moreover that terror, captured unforgettably in the hammering octaves of the pianist's right hand in Schubert's setting, echoes powerfully within our own memories of being ill as children, of the raised heartbeat of fever, of nameless fear, with the comforting voice of the well-meaning parent utterly distant. We note the terrified doubling of the boy's appeal to the father — from "Vater" in stanza two to "mein Vater, mein Vater" of subsequent stanzas. The father is, it seems, invaded by the urgency of his child's terror as he moves from "mein Sohn" to "mein Kind" and then, finally, to "mein Sohn, mein Sohn."

There is, then, a primary level of non-metaphysical terror to the poem's statement. But even that primary level has further implications that need to be spelled out. One all-important issue involves gender. We have the son and the father, but no reference to the boy's mother. No female figures appear in their own right, although the Erl King's attempts at seduction constantly invoke the charms of women figures — the mother with her golden garments and the daughters with their alluring dances. Perhaps we begin to hear in the poem some kind of drama of male desire as it unfolds in the little boy's mind. The father figure speaks as a promulgator of reason and law, endeavoring to hold the child's desires in check. But the other male authority figure, the Erl King, is complicit in the forces of desire; he spells out the possibilities of seduction, both heterosexual and homosexual. The sense of mounting sexual tension is superbly captured in the following line, which is repeated in the Schubert setting:

Und wiegen und tanzen und singen dich ein.

[They rock and dance and sing you to sleep.]

One notes the repeated "und," the wickedly ambiguous force of "wiegen," and the compound form of the verbs with "ein" which suggests enveloping, cocooning to the point of self-abandonment (perhaps to orgasm, sleep, or death). Yet the voice that promises bliss is also alive with threat; and the Erl King's final couplet speaks of mounting desire (mich reizt deine schöne Gestalt), and culminates in something very close to an act of rape.

Even within a non-supernatural reading, then, the poem is deeply unsettling. Yet it also asks to be heard as an acknowledgement of entities, forces, powers quite beyond the parameters of the familiar world. When the Erl King enters the poem, he establishes an irresistible presence by virtue of the fact that his voice dominates stanzas three and four completely. No other voice is allowed to countermand his insidious authority. Moreover, the little boy initially refers to him with the definite article, as a creature from folklore — "den Erlenkönig." But subsequently the definite article disappears as the antagonist become overwhelmingly real to the boy:

Erlkönig hat mir ein Leids getan!

[Erl King has done me harm!]

Perhaps, then, there are supernatural agents in the world. We would do well to note that the title of the poem is not "der Erlkönig" but, starkly, "Erlkönig." And while we, as modern readers, may of course choose to doubt the existence of spooks and ghosts, we have to acknowledge that the final line registers a death in the real world. Throughout the poem all the verbs are in the present tense. The one exception is the final line:

> In seinen Armen das Kind war tot.

> [In his arms the child was dead.]

No constraints of rhythm, meter, rhyme would have prevented Goethe from writing "ist." But he chose to write "war," perhaps because that past tense is, by tradition, the tense of narratives of events that really happen (news reports, documentaries, histories, and so on). The change of tense at the end of the poem means that we feel ourselves to be in the presence of an event in the real world, our world. So what causes the death in this poem? We cannot be sure. And our anxiety is compounded by that little world "Hof" in the penultimate line. Of course, it means "yard" or "farm." But could it not also mean "court," the court of the Erl King whose voice, once heard, can never be banished?

"Heidenröslein" (Little Heath Rose, 1771) is similarly indebted to the ballad tradition. We have a simple event-sequence: a boy notices a wild rose and decides to pick it; the rose retaliates by digging its thorns into the boy's flesh but cannot thereby prevent the act of destruction. Once again we have dialogue, in this case between the boy and the rose. Moreover, and this is a balladesque feature that is not in evidence in "Erlkönig," we have a refrain which occurs in line two and lines six and seven of each stanza. The story is simply told; but it is not without complexity. We note the speed with which the boy's delight in the flower —

> Lief er schnell, es nah zu sehen,
> Sah's mit vielen Freuden —

> [He ran quickly to see it from close by,
> Saw it with many joys.]

modulates into the desire to possess the flower and, by that act of possession, to destroy it. In itself, the act of picking a flower (depending on the cultural context) is not necessarily a heinous one. But in our poem the issue of transgression is highlighted by virtue of the dialogue which allows the rose to defend herself. Both agents in this battle of wills are young; the boy is "der wilde Knabe" (the wild boy), and in the final stanza the rose "so jung und morgenschön" (so young and beautiful as the morning). In this sense, the scene has a certain spontaneity, even perhaps innocence. Yet behind that casualness there vibrates a sense of wantonness and brutality. The poem has an elaborate rhyme scheme which is both disarming and hauntingly expressive, almost hallucinatory. The refrain generates the identical end-rhyme in lines two and seven of each stanza; the additional rhyming component occurs in line five with "Freuden," "leiden," and "leiden," and charts the modulation of joy into suffering. The one line that does not rhyme within the seven-line stanza ends on the word "rot," which expresses the colorful glory of the rose, and, by implication, the red of the blood that results from the thorns penetrating the boy's hand. It is difficult not to hear behind "rot" the word "tot"; for the poem ends with the extinction of the flower. The poem (and Schubert's setting respects this entirely) stays wonderfully within the foregrounded simplicity of the folksong mode: one thinks, for example, of the insistent presence of the diminutive ending "lein," of the suppressed articles and pronouns in "War so jung" (was so young); "Knabe sprach" (boy spoke); "Röslein sprach" (Little Rose spoke); and "Röslein wehrte sich" (Little Rose resisted). Yet behind such disarming naiveté one senses darker implications, of the human agent that thoughtlessly despoils the natural world, of the youthful self that casually destroys the beauty that crosses its path, of the male self that deflowers what it desires.

Precisely the issue of innocence that may be callousness feeds into a number of poems in which Goethe explores the responsibilities that go with the human endowment of self-consciousness. A key poem in this regard is "Das Göttliche" (The Divine, 1783) which will allow us to make the transition from Goethe's nature poetry to his poetry concerned with the place of the divine in human affairs. In "Das Göttliche" Goethe reflects on the human capacity to make choices. The poem opens by enjoining the human subject to aspire to the morally good life; because, and this is the heart of our poem, it is that ability to choose, to make distinctions, that distinguishes human beings from other orders of being:

> Denn das allein
> Unterscheidet ihn
> Von allen Wesen,
> Die wir kennen. (3–6)

> [For that alone
> Distinguishes him
> From all beings
> That we know.]

Stanzas two, three, and four speak of the extent to which nature is a realm of moral indifference. By contrast, human beings know of the moral freedom, and the moral obligation, to make choices. In an explicit echo of the opening stanza we are told (and the pronoun "er" refers to "der Mensch"):

> Er unterscheidet,
> Wählet und richtet. (39–40)

> [He distinguishes
> Chooses and judges.]

Stanzas six, seven, and eight reflect intensely on the forms of human obliga-
ion. Human beings are at the mercy of nature's whims; there are, inevita-
ly, innumerable material constraints which press in upon the human self:

> Nach ewigen, ehrnen,
> Großen Gesetzen
> Müssen wir alle
> Unseres Daseins
> Kreise vollenden. (32–36)

> [According to eternal, iron
> Great laws
> We all must complete
> The circles of
> Our lives.]

Goethe is resolutely aware of the constraints acting upon human life — as
we shall see when we come to discuss "Urworte. Orphisch" and the drama
Iphigenie auf Tauris. Here, in "Das Göttliche" the modal verb "müssen"
speaks volumes, yet the very next stanza modulates the argument:

> Nur allein der Mensch
> Vermag das Unmögliche. (37–38)

> [Humankind alone
> Can do the impossible.]

The human subject, it seems, uniquely among the creatures of the known
world, can perform the impossible, can countermand the inroads of de-
termining agencies by making choices. Two key modal verbs — "können"
and "dürfen" — embody the dimension of moral autonomy:

> Er kann dem Augenblick
> Dauer verleihen.

> Er allein darf
> Den Guten lohnen,
> Den Bösen strafen [. . .]. (41–45)

> [He can give duration
> To the moment.

> He alone may
> Reward the good man
> And punish the evil man.]

Thus far we have concentrated on the moral implications of our poem.
But we would do well to recall its title — "Das Göttliche." In the second

stanza we learn that the good human being is a model and prefiguration of the higher beings whom the human race reveres. Goethe returns to the issue of divinity at the end of his poem, and suggests that divinity is the conceptual focus for all that is most truly and most finely human: The immortals emerge primarily as human constructs, images of the best that humanity is capable of, expressions of the full conjectural possibilities of being human. They are metaphors of what human beings aspire to be. Precisely this note of the metaphorical and the conjectural is central to Goethe's poem. "Das Göttliche" begins with an injunction, couched in the third person optative form which employs the subjunctive mode:

> Edel sei der Mensch,
> Hilfreich und gut!

> [Let humankind be noble,
> Helpful and good!]

The poem ends with a stanza in which every single verb is in that subjunctive mode:

> Der edle Mensch
> Sei hilfreich und gut!
> Unermüdet schaff er
> Das Nützliche, Rechte,
> Sei uns ein Vorbild
> Jener geahneten Wesen! (55–60)

> [Let noble humankind
> Be helpful and good!
> May they tirelessly bring about
> That which is useful and right,
> Let it be to us a model
> Of those intuited beings.]

Here, in the very linguistic mode of the poem's closing cadence, we touch upon the mystery of humanity at its finest: the human subject does not simply dwell in facts, in the immediate and material present, but also in the conjectural and metaphorical dimension of what could or might be. Human beings have need for the subjunctive because it expresses a transcendence of the given, the literal, the factual; because they can exist in the subjunctive realm they can conceive of a more than physical realm, a metaphysical dimension where humanity resembles (and, by resembling, creates) divinity. We shall have occasion to recall this remarkable poem later in this study when we come to look at the verse drama *Iphigenie auf Tauris*.

"Das Göttliche" brings us to consider a number of poems which reflect on the nature of divinity and the role played by metaphysical belief in human affairs. The obvious starting point is two early poems which Goethe published as a pair of complementary (and contrasting) statements: "Ganymed" (1774) and "Prometheus" (1774). Both, it should be noted, are poems which speak through the persona of a figure from Greek mythology; on the one hand Ganymed, the beautiful boy who is lifted up to Olympus to be Zeus's cup-bearer, and on the other, Prometheus, who defies the god in the name of the value and dignity of human experience. The presence of mythological components should not deceive us. The sentiments are characteristic of the early Goethe, of the Sturm und Drang mood of the 1770s. The expansive ecstasy that fills "Ganymed" recalls "Mailied." Once again, the experience of nature's beauty is total and embraces every gender of being: the masculine of "Frühling, Geliebter!" (Spring, Beloved), the neuter of "heilig Gefühl" (holy feeling), and the feminine of "Unendliche Schöne" (infinite beauty). The language speaks of intense reciprocity and blissful surrender. The human self feels almost penetrated by the intense presence of nature:

> Mit tausendfacher Liebeswonne
> Sich an mein Herz drängt
> Deiner ewigen Wärme
> Heilig Gefühl.

> [With thousand-fold loving bliss
> The holy feeling
> Of your eternal warmth
> Presses upon my heart.]

Or again:

> Und deine Blumen, dein Gras
> Drängen sich an mein Herz.

> [And your flowers and your grass
> Press upon my heart.]

The verb "sich drängen" embodies extraordinary physical intensity. And that ecstasy acquires an upward direction in the final stanza, one in which perfect reciprocity is sustained: the urgently repeated "hinauf" (beyond) and "aufwärts" (upwards) are answered by the descending clouds which move "abwärts" (downwards), which "neigen sich" (bend down) to meet the force of human yearning. And in a superbly simple and expressive line — "Umfangend umfangen" (embracing embraced) — active and passive principles merge in a conjoining of two grammatical forms of one and the same verb which are only (just) separated by the one consonant "d." The godhead that is celebrated in "Ganymed" is, then, one that is utterly immanent in human experience.

By contrast, the deity against whom Prometheus rages is one that is utterly hostile to, and divorced from, human experience. Goethe planned, but abandoned, a drama on Prometheus. The poem borrows the sentiments and some of the phrasing from the two-act fragment that is extant, and it has a powerful declamatory feel. According to Prometheus's angry catalogue of their failings, the gods are dependent upon human weakness for tribute, are envious of those beings (such as himself) who are, in every sense of the word, self-sufficient. The poem is shot through with the violent clashing of pronouns: Prometheus's proudly assertive "ich," "mich," "mir," "mein" collide with the second person forms (du, dich, dein). In line 6, the god is even denied his pronoun (Mußt mir meine Erde / Doch lassen stehn [you will have to leave my earth standing]). The battle culminates in the near-blasphemous note of the final stanza:

> Hier sitz ich, forme Menschen
> Nach meinem Bilde,
> Ein Geschlecht, das mir gleich sei,
> Zu leiden, zu weinen,
> Zu genießen und zu freuen sich,
> Und dein nicht zu achten
> Wie ich! (52–58)

> [Here I sit, forming humans
> In my image,
> A race that should be like me,
> To suffer, to weep,
> To exult and rejoice,
> And not to notice you
> Like me!]

The human self claims to create a race of men in its own image, a race that will scorn the gods.

Any discussion of Goethe poetry that addresses the issue of divinity must attend to the late poem "Urworte. Orphisch" (Primal Words. Orphic, 1817) in which concepts from a religious scheme are used in order to define the character of human experience. It is a statement that encapsulates much of Goethe's thinking. The mode of expression is highly expository and discursive, yet at the same time thought is constantly transmuted into poetic shape. "Urworte. Orphisch" takes from the Orphic religion of Ancient Greece the notion that the poet's song is indestructible and may become the conduit for mysterious, even oracular speech. This legacy can be heard in the diction of the poem. At one level it is clear to the point of being schematic; but it also leaves much to challenge the interpretative mind. The poem looks intimidating: the Greek headings were too much even for Goethe's contemporaries, hence he added the German translations and provided brief commentaries on each of the stanzas. The five stanzas develop Goethe's conception of the human condition, particularly in the polarity between subjective freedom and the constraints of the outer world. The overall conceptual sequence is clear: the opening stanza posits inalienable selfhood; stanzas two, three, and four reflect on the forces which impinge on (and interact with) our individuality; and the fifth stanza asserts our capacity for freedom, in spite of all constraints.[5]

The first stanza invokes the term "Daimon"; it stands for the central Goethean notion of entelechy which perceives each instance of individuality as inscribed with its unique law of being and destiny. The individual self is seen as part of the cosmic order; the law of unfolding being betokens not fixity but constancy of developmental energy. Yet the individual self is not, of course, a law unto itself. As stanza two acknowledges, it is constantly acted upon from outside. Chance — "das Zufällige" — is quite literally what befalls us, in our interaction with the outside world. These processes are seen to be made up of good and bad fortune (bald hin-, bald widerfällig, 13); but the tone here is conciliatory, easy-going even. "Zufall" is seen, then, as essentially benign or amiable — "gefällig." One central input into the experiences that impinge upon the self from outside and mould it irrevocably is Eros. The third stanza speaks of the sheer flux of erotic energy, of its capacity to sow confusion:

Da wird ein Wohl im Weh, so süß und bang. (22)

[There comes about a well-being in pain, so sweet and troubled.]

However the conclusion is edifying; it envisages containment, purposiveness, certainty:

Gar manches Herz verschwebt im Allgemeinen,
Doch widmet sich das edelste dem Einen. (23–24)

[Many a heart floats away into generality,
Yet the noblest spirit dedicates itself to one task]

Yet the next stanza changes tone and rails against notions of limitation. The stanza speaks, with no little bitterness, of the processes of (self-) censorship:

Das Liebste wird vom Herzen weggescholten — (29)

[Dearest things are censored out of the heart]

as the heart not only relinquishes its deepest desires but represses the inadmissible at every turn. Even willing, it seems, is willing what we are
programmed to will:

> aller Wille
> Ist nur ein Wollen, weil wir eben sollten. (26–27)

> [all will
> Is only a willing because we simply must.]

The tone here, sharpened by its unmistakable colloquial sting, is fiercely
resentful. But that resentment is the precondition of the release which the
final stanza celebrates. All categories of fixity and constraint (Grenze,
Mauer, Pforte) are set aside as the soaring energies, the sheer lift-off of
hope, of creative energy endow the self with wings. For Goethe, in the
last analysis, the energy invested in the human personality has an inher-
ently liberating force. And one can hear that energy throughout the poem,
above all in those colloquial moments which undercut the austerely systematic, even schematic, structure of the poem. One thinks, for example,
of such lines as:

> Und handelst wohl so, wie ein anderer handelt. (12)

> [And you presumably behave just as others do.]

and:

> Die bleibt nicht aus. (17)

> [It is not missing.]

and:

> Da ists denn wieder. (25)

> [There it is again.]

We have noted an occasion when the colloquial register speaks of the entrapment of the psyche in processes of self-censorship. But far more frequently that register speaks of the vitality of the self that will not allow
itself to be constrained. That decisive tonality culminates in the final line
which dispenses with a main verb altogether and celebrates the human
ability, with one pulse of self-assertion, to (as we might put it now) "get
away from it all":

> Ein Flügelschlag — und hinter uns Äonen! (40)

> [One beat of the wings — and aeons are put behind us.]

Goethe's poem respects and works with the categories and systematic entities of Orphic thinking; but the centrally affirmed philosophical truth is less a system than the transformative energies of the self.

That capacity for self-renewal is nowhere more richly in evidence than in Goethe's love poetry. Let us begin with the early "Willkommen und Abschied" (Welcome and Parting, 1771/1789), more precisely with the second version of the poem. The title itself, together with the experiences embodied, speaks urgently of contrasts, of (to use a favorite Goethean term) a polarity between arrival and departure, between expectation and retrospection. The poem is noteworthy for its intimation of energy and pace. It depicts a journey on horseback as the poet rides through the night to meet his beloved — only then to leave at daybreak. Twice in the first stanza the little temporal particle "schon" conveys a sense of no-sooner-one-thing-than-another. The thought instantly begets the deed; and the deed merges into the journey which is the governing theme of the remainder of the poem. Nature partakes vividly of the dynamic of that journey; elements of the landscape assume human shape and capacities — the oak tree, the moon, the winds. As such, the animism could be synonymous with eeriness; yet one exultant line puts paid to any such notion:

> Die Nacht schuf tausend Ungeheuer,
> Doch frisch und fröhlich war mein Mut [. . .]. (13–14)

> [The night bred a thousand monsters
> Yet fresh and joyous was my spirit.]

The energy in the natural world seems to invigorate — rather than to over-awe — the human self. The third stanza pictures the goal of the journey:

> Dich sah ich, und die milde Freude
> Floß von dem süßen Blick auf mich [. . .]. (17–18)

> [You I saw and abundantly gentle joy
> Flowed from your sweet glance to me.]

The lovers' meeting has an idyllic feel — as in the "rosenfarbnes Frühlingswetter" (rose-tinted spring weather) that departs radically from the mood of the nocturnal forest — and on that account feels more like a vision than an actuality. Indeed, moments of seeing and picturing are central to the poem, as Wellbery reminds us.[6] In the first two stanzas, nature sees the poet, in stanza three, the poet sees the girl, in the final stanza, the girl sees the poet leaving. Hence, we find ourselves asking if there is any moment of meeting between the processes of "Willkommen" and "Abschied," if (as it were) the poem ever comes to rest. In any event, the meeting is one of eyes and glances rather than of people. Stanza four reinstates the journey, signaled once again by the "schon" of temporal acceleration. The poet leaves; and our last image of the beloved is of someone transfixed by grief. Yet grief does not have the last word: the poem distils from the flux of its narratively mediated story of arrival and departure a sense of abiding worth, and that worth has everything to do with passion and energy and very little to do with stability and possession. Hence — and this is characteristically Goethean — the contradictory force of the poem's polarity is ultimately affirmed as a source of experiential drive (one notes the "doch" of line one and line seven in the final stanza). Affirmation insists on the value of experience in the present. The exclamatory mode of

> In meinen Adern welches Feuer!
> In meinem Herzen welche Glut! (15–16)
>
> [In my veins what fire!
> In my heart what ardor!]

and of

> Und doch, welch Glück, geliebt zu werden!
> Und lieben, Götter, welch ein Glück! (31–32)
>
> [And yet, what bliss to be loved!
> And to love, you gods, what bliss it is!]

locates these statements and sentiments in an implied present tense. The closing cadence of the poem asserts the abiding value deriving from the flux and movement of human experience.

As we have seen, in "Willkommen und Abschied" the beloved exists chiefly as a component within the experiential energy of the male subject. However, in some of his other, and very finest, love poems, Goethe does confront the challenging tensions and contradictory responses which the very experience of love may generate. This is particularly evident in the poems which center on Goethe's relationship with Lili Schönemann. "An Belinden" (1775), like "Willkommen und Abschied" and so many other love poems, tells a story. It begins and ends in the present, with the poet regretting the girl's irresistible sway which transports him into a world of blissful splendor (Pracht). Yet that very state is anything but welcome, hence the questioning mode of the poem's opening — "Warum ziehst du mich?" (Why do you pull me?) — and the "Ach" at the beginning of the second line, which carries negative undertones and yet links by assonance with "Pracht." The poet looks back into the past, to a time of untried innocence, of fantasies about loving, undisturbed by any attempt at the complexities of the real thing. The present situation is unsettling (conjoining "Ach" and "Pracht"); but the previous condition, its unreal bliss, offers no consolation:

> War ich guter Junge nicht so selig
> In der öden Nacht?

> [Was I not, sweet little lad, so blissful
> In the empty night?]

The return to the present, to the enslavement to the girl, compounds the unease. The poet, now in a world of bright lights and gaming tables, scarcely recognizes himself. In the magnificent final stanza, that incredulity modulates into a complex sense of the bewilderingly different, yet valid forms that love, as natural emotion, can take:

> Reizender ist mir des Frühlings Blüte
> Nun nicht auf der Flur;
> Wo du, Engel, bist ist Lieb und Güte,
> Wo du bist, Natur.

> [No longer is the blossom of spring
> In the meadow more charming to me,
> Where you, angel, are is love and goodness,
> And where you are is nature.]

The reference to "Blüte," together with the rhyme pair that conjoins "Flur" and "Natur" evokes a powerful intertext: "Mailied." Just as, within the psychological theme of the poem, the self articulates the change that has come on him — "Bin ichs noch?" — so, too, Goethe reflects on the process of change in his poetic utterance. "Mailied" celebrates a natural world and natural loving, whereas the closing cadence of "An Belinden" recognizes that the place of present loving is not nature, not meadows, but rather, and in sharp contrast, social space, rooms. The present form of loving would seem to be shadowed by notes of repudiation in the phrase "Reizender ist mir des Frühlings Blüte"; yet this is forcefully cancelled out by the emphatic "Nun nicht" in the next line. In short, the last two lines of the poem celebrate the love which Belinde inspires: despite her evident worldliness and sophistication, that love also constitutes a natural force. Within the complex realm of human eros, then, natural desire is seen to work through a whole number of often uncomfortable, indeed seemingly "unnatural" configurations.

Take the famous love poem "Warum gabst du uns die tiefen Blicke" (Why Did You Give Us the Deep Glances) of 1776. Goethe sent it to Charlotte von Stein as part of a letter, and it retained its utterly private character until it was first published in 1848. The poem quite simply embodies the agony of unfulfilled desire, and the poetic, musical structure is so intense that literally every note counts. The poem starts and ends on the note of the vowel "a": The opening line asks Fate: "Warum gabst du uns die tiefen Blicke," and the last two lines assert: "Glücklich, daß das Schicksal, das uns quälet, / Uns doch nicht verändern mag" (happy that the destiny that torments us / cannot in fact change us). In German, "a" is a complex sound, and its many meanings are captured in the particle "ach" which the poem repeatedly employs: *ach* speaks of pain, of longing, but also of joy, of marvel and wonder. Throughout the poem, this "a" sound countermands the sound of "u" which in the first stanza informs the opening syllables of five out of eight lines. For the German ear, this "u" sound captures the sense of darkness. For example, in the drama *Iphigenie auf Tauris*, it is the key sound in all those bleak sections which speak of the curse, of "Blut" and "Fluch." In the poem, this "u" sound is particularly eloquent when conjoined with the consonant of "w," the leading consonant of German question particles such as "warum," "was," "wie." In this sense, the opening word "warum," with its sound pattern of "a" and "u" and their associated meanings, prefigures the fabric of the entire poem. Indeed, one could argue that the poem is an extended elaboration on the one question: "Warum?"

Overall, the form of the poem combines stillness with agony. There is the calm of five regular stresses, but the lines vary in length, and there are the recurrent questions: the twice repeated "warum" in the first stanza, and the two questions of "was" and "wie" in the third stanza:

> Sag', was will das Schicksal uns bereiten?
> Sag', wie band es uns so rein genau? (25–26)

> [Say, what does destiny have in store for us?
> Say, what bound us so utterly together?]

The painful paradox is that these questions know the answer, know that the presence of this love is based on absence, on lack of fulfillment. This clarity of perception is central to the opening stanzas, their recurrent terms of cognition, of seeing, perceiving, such as "tiefen Blicke," the verbs "schauen," "sehen," and "spähen." The tragedy, yet also the uniqueness of this love, is precisely that the lovers are denied the bliss of illusion: they know, comprehend. The pain of this knowingness is such that in stanza three the lyrical voice flees into a vision:

> Ach, du warst in abgelebten Zeiten
> Meine Schwester oder meine Frau. (27–28)

> [Ah, you were in times gone by
> My sister or my wife.]

This vision of a former union unfolds in the fourth stanza:

> Tropftest Mäßigung dem heißen Blute,
> Richtetest den irren Lauf,
> Und in deinen Engelsarmen ruhte
> Die zerstörte Brust sich wieder auf; (33–36)

> [You sent calming drops into my blood,
> You ordered the chaotic course of my life,
> And in your angelic arms the ravaged
> Heart found rest and came to itself.]

These lines suggest the close relationship of brother and sister, and they point forward to *Iphigenie auf Tauris*. The poem enacts a sexual fantasy, and at the same time censors it, sublimates it into spirituality. Erotically charged elements are modulated into motifs of spiritual union, soothing communion. In musical terms, sexual union is the bass line, but the melody is that of spirituality, of platonic love. The key terms of the platonic argument are those of moderation and orientation: "Mäßigung," "richten," "beruhigen." The intermingling of persistent sexual desire and the platonic renunciation is immensely subtle in the closing lines of the fourth stanza:

> Fühlt' sein Herz an deinem Herzen schwellen,
> Fühlte sich in deinem Auge gut,
> Alle seine Sinnen sich erhellen
> Und beruhigen sein brausend Blut. (41–44)

> [Felt his heart swelling against your heart,
> Felt right in your eyes,
> And all his senses were cleansed
> And his pounding blood grew calm.]

Goethe exploits here the difference in meaning between the written and the spoken word: through the abbreviation of the past tense, the verb "fühlt'" comes across as present. Similarly, the verbs "sich erhellen" and "beruhigen" are infinitives dependent on "Fühlte," but they are poised on the point of turning into verbs in the present tense, the would-be presence of erotic union.

The final stanza breaks with the vision, but keeps it as a memory:

> Und von allem dem schwebt ein Erinnern
> Nur noch um das ungewisse Herz
>   [. . .]
> Und wir scheinen uns nur halb beseelet,
> Dämmernd ist um uns der hellste Tag. (45–46; 49–50)

[And of all this only a vague
Memory hovers round the uncertain heart
And we seem to be only half alive,
The brightest day around us feels like dusk.]

The wish dream of union turns the conscious life of the present into a kind of living death. The lovers figure as mere specters, "halb beseelet," even the brightest day is but dusk, "dämmernd ist um uns der hellste Tag." Yet, as so often in Goethe's work, agony finally yields to reconciliation — the poem's conclusion affirms the pain of sexually unfulfilled love:

Glücklich, daß das Schicksal, das uns quälet,
Uns doch nicht verändern mag. (51–52)

[Happy that the destiny that torments us
Cannot in fact change us.]

The figuration of Charlotte von Stein as a soothing force informs the love poetry of this period, the so-called "Lida" poems. Her influence is reflected in clusters of motifs which capture the sense of restraint: there are the recurrent adjectives of "still," "mild," "rein," and verbs to do with calming, ordering: "lindern," and "lösen." Key examples for Charlotte's influence would be "Jägers Nachtlied" (1775–76), "Sag' ich's euch, geliebte Bäume" (1780), and "An den Mond" (1776–78), where Charlotte's calming presence is symbolized in the central metaphor of the moon:

Füllest wieder's liebe Tal
Still mit Nebelglanz,
Lösest endlich auch einmal
Meine Seele ganz.

[You fill again the lovely valley
Softly with shining mist,
You finally come to
Release my soul utterly.]

The motif of "lösen" again highlights the affinity of these poems to *Iphigenie auf Tauris* where, for example, in act 3, iii, tormented Orest is spiritually healed by Iphigenie: "Es löset sich der Fluch, mir sagt's das Herz" (1358).

In the "Lida" poems, then, passion is held in check; but it can break out and when it does, it produces a throwback to pre-Weimar days: for example, "Rastlose Liebe" (Restless Love, 1776), with its exclamation marks and question-marks, hardly differs from the earlier poems.

Wie soll ich fliehen?
Wälderwärts ziehen?
Alles vergebens!
Krone des Lebens,
Glück ohne Ruh,
Liebe, bist du! (15–20)

[How should I flee,
Move towards the forest?
All in vain!
Crown of life,
Joy without peace,
That is what you, love, are.]

Overall, the restraint of the Lida poems figures as a systole in Goethe's creativity, but it is decisive for his subsequent work: passion returns in much heightened form in the diastole of the *Römische Elegien* (1888–90). Here, reflectivity combines with vital energy: spirituality and unrestrained carnality fuse into one. Goethe wrote this cycle after the Italian Journey of 1786–88, which in his own words granted him rebirth, "Wiedergeburt." On his return to Weimar he felt deeply alienated. Relations were further strained when he decided to ignore all social codes and live with his mistress, Christiane Vulpius, a commoner. The *Römische Elegien* trace in symbolically charged scenes the quest of the discontented northern spirit who finally finds fulfillment in Rome. The figure of the beloved Faustina remains unidentified, but in part bears the traits of Christiane Vulpius. The term "elegy," then, does not have the common connotation of solemn lament; rather, Goethe uses the term here technically, to mean a poem written in the "elegiac distich" of alternating hexameters and pentameters. It is important to stress that the collection originally bore the title *Erotica romana* and consisted of twenty-four poems, not just the twenty which are printed in the standard editions and which Goethe published. He realized that he could not hope to publish the first and last poems which were unashamed tributes to the priapic god, to the phallus as the agent of fertility. But he did originally submit the other two poems, one of which describes the joy of undressing the beloved woman and having intercourse on the rhythmically creaking bed of love. And the other is a forthright reflection on the curse of venereal disease with its ability to blight sexual spontaneity and to destroy trust between partners. In the event, Goethe was persuaded not to publish these two poems either. Even so, the twenty poems that did appear caused a very considerable scandal.

In one sense, the Elegies stand as polar opposite to the Charlotte poetry: they are jubilantly anti-Platonic. Not surprisingly, Charlotte von Stein was deeply shocked, although the contemplative mode of the poetry generated by her presence is in fact also an integral part of this cycle: The Elegies celebrate both exuberant sexuality and reflectivity. They are driven by carnality as much as by thought which delights in culture, civilization. This fusion of the physical and the spiritual is crystallized in the very name of the city: Roma is a palindrome: if read backwards, it spells Amor. And so we read in the first Elegy:

> Eine Welt zwar bist du, o Rom; doch ohne die Liebe
> Wäre die Welt nicht die Welt, wäre denn Rom auch
> > nicht Rom. (13–14)

> [A world you admittedly are, oh Rome; yet without love
> The world would not be the world, and Rome would also
> > not be Rome.]

Roma-Amor is the briefest formulation for Goethe's lifelong conviction that without Eros there is quite simply no world. The crucial point of the Elegies is, then, that erotic energy is inextricably interlinked with cultural energy. The joy of personal love is inseparable from the glory of civilization: the beauty of the female body merges with the beauty of cultural creation, Rome's artifacts and the poet's own artifact. His Elegies fuse classical order, the hexameter, and erotic energy. This is the essence of the following extract from the fifth Elegy:

> Und belehr' ich mich nicht, indem ich des lieblichen Busens
> > Formen spähe, die Hand leite die Hüfte hinab?
> Dann versteh' ich den Marmor erst recht: ich denk' und vergleiche,
> > Sehe mit fühlendem Aug', fühle mit sehender Hand.
> [. . .]

> Oftmals hab' ich auch schon in ihren Armen gedichtet
> > Und des Hexameters Maß leise mit fingernder Hand
> Ihr auf den Rücken gezählt. Sie atmet in lieblichem Schlummer,
> > Und es durchglühet ihr Hauch mir bis ins Tiefste die Brust. (7–18)

> [And do I not instruct myself when I glance over the forms
> > Of the enchanting bosom or guide my hand down her hip?
> Only then is it that I understand the marble; I think and compare,
> > See with feeling eye, and feel with seeing hand.
> [. . .]

> Often I have made poetry in her arms
> > And lightly with the tapping finger of my hand
> Have counted the hexameter's beat on her back. She breathes in
> > lovely sleep,
> > And her breath warms me through to the depths of my heart.]

Strikingly, visual and tactile perceptions are synthesized: "Sehe mit fühlendem Aug', fühle mit sehender Hand." Such lines reflect the essence of the cycle which time and again fuses body and mind, physical and mental experience. Among the many symbols of sexuality, the motif of fire stands out. And here we can observe very clearly the interlocking of the physical and the spiritual. In the sixth elegy, flames die down only to flare up again: "neuer und mächtiger dringt leuchtende Flamme hinauf" (34; newer and mightier the brilliant flame thrusts upward). And in the ninth, glimmering ashes are rekindled into "Flammen aufs neue" (8; once again flames). On the erotic level, these are, of course, metaphors for renewed sexual desire and energy. But, the representation of physical experience also harbors a cultural argument: The lovers are linked to the great mythical figures of desire and sexuality in ancient Greece and Rome. The following extract from the third elegy celebrates the rapid move from gaze to desire, from desire to consummation, as the energy of heroic times when gods and goddesses freely submitted to the force of Eros:

> In der heroischen Zeit, da Götter und Göttinnen liebten,
>   Folgte Begierde dem Blick, folgte Genuß der Begierde. (7–8)

> [In the heroic age, when gods and goddesses loved,
>   Desire followed upon the gaze, pleasure upon the desire.]

This sense of uninhibited desire and fulfillment is the hallmark of the cycle, and it is captured in the adjectives "beglückt" and "froh," which are particularly pronounced in the fifth and seventh Elegies. This quality of "froh," the synthesis of physical and spiritual elation, is quite absent in the love poetry centered on Charlotte von Stein.

In short, then, the *Römische Elegien* are driven by the polarity of intense sensuous experience on the one hand and equally intense cultural, intertextual reflectivity on the other. In this sense they prefigure what was to become a dominant theme in acts 2 and 3 of *Faust Part II:* the encounter and fusion of north and south, German spirit and Greek culture. The cycle fuses past and present, nature and civilization, sexual desire and reflectivity; and it is worth recalling that the original conception, with its phallic poems, acted out even more overtly the complex dialectic between primitivism and sophistication, between body and mind, between celebration and cerebration.

The celebration of fulfilled love in the *Römische Elegien* figures as powerful counter-blast to the love poetry of unfulfillment which we have seen in "Warum gabst du uns die tiefen Blicke" and which returns in later poems of grief and loss. In this context, let us turn to the group of poems entitled "Trilogie der Leidenschaft" (Trilogy of Passion, 1823–24). The first two poems are powerful in the urgency of their grief; the third offers a measure of comfort. In the opening poem, "An Werther," the directly biographical sting is manifest. We hear very clearly the voice of the older, maturer poet looking back to the most famous figure of all his early literary creations — Werther, the young man who, in the novel that bears his name, is denied fulfillment in love and commits suicide. The novel became a spectacular best-seller, and hence the opening of our poem conjures up Werther's charismatic status as "vielbeweinter Schatten" (much wept over specter). The poet reflects that Werther died, but that he (the poet) lived on. The trilogy has the term "Leidenschaft" in its title. And its three poems seem constantly to touch, as though they constituted some kind of nerve center, words that are linked by assonance with "Leidenschaft": "Leiden," "meiden," "scheiden." The first stanza of "An Werther" sounds this constellation of sound patterns for the first time:

> Und nach des Tages unwillkommner Mühe
> Der Scheidesonne letzter Strahl entzückt.
> Zum Bleiben ich, zum Scheiden du erkoren,
> Gingst du voran [. . .]. (7–10)

> [And after the unwelcome stress of the day
> The last rays of the parting sun delight.
> I was chosen to stay, you to leave,
> You went ahead. . . .]

The repeated "ei" sounds form a litany of pain. The conclusion is one of lacerating colloquial bitterness, compounded by the suppression of the pronominal subject "du" in the final phrase:

> Gingst du voran — und hast nicht viel verloren. (10)

> [You went ahead — and have not missed much.]

What is particularly hurtful about the line is the fact that the sentiment it expresses is so un-Goethean: far more often than not, Goethe asserts the intrinsic value of living. But the re-appearance of Werther here impels the poet to assure his doomed alter ego that he has not missed much. The next three stanzas sketch in the sequence of life experience as one that goes from promise to happiness to loss. To that notion of loss, of course, Werther, whose "gräßlich Scheiden" made him famous, bears eloquent witness. But the end of the poem invokes Torquato Tasso, the tragic poet in Goethe's play of that name. That play closes with the lines:

> Und wenn der Mensch in seiner Qual verstummt,
> Gab mir ein Gott zu sagen, wie ich leide.

> [And where human beings fall silent in their pain,
> A god granted me to say how I suffer.]

The "An Werther" poem ends with a couplet that clearly echoes those lines, but with certain key modifications:

> Verstrickt in solche Qualen, halbverschuldet,
> Geb ihm ein Gott zu sagen, was er duldet. (49–50)

> [Entangled in such torment, part guilty,
> Let a god grant him to say what he endures.]

The most weighty change is the transformation of the past tense "Gab mir ein Gott zu sagen" to the present optative or imperative "Geb ihm ein Gott zu sagen." The shift in verb form weighs heavily: the poem ends with the wish (no more than that) that the god will not desert the poet, that the lyric utterance will not be stillborn.

To say this much is to highlight the question of poetic intertextuality. By entitling the first poem of the trilogy "An Werther" Goethe clearly demands an intertextual awareness from his public, and, given the prodigious success of his novel, he was hardly asking too much. Moreover, he was clearly aware of the ways in which the Tasso figure was a reconfiguration of the Werther figure (in a famous remark he described Tasso as "ein gesteigerter Werther" [an intensified Werther]).[7] Hence, it is not surprising that, in the long and painful retrospective that opens the "Trilogie der Leidenschaft," the ghost of Werther communes with the ghost of Tasso. Goethe makes the *Tasso* intertext explicit by prefacing the second poem of the trilogy, the "Elegie," with the lines from *Torquato Tasso* to which he has already alluded:

> Und wenn der Mensch in seiner Qual verstummt,
> Gab mir ein Gott zu sagen, was ich leide.

> [And where human beings fall silent in their pain,
> A god granted me to say what I suffer.]

Except that the lines are not quite the lines spoken by Tasso. In the play, Tasso says "wie ich leide," whereas in the prefatory quotation to the Elegy, "wie" has been replaced by "was." What is at issue, then, is not so much the mode of suffering as the sheer irreducible "what" at the heart of the anguish.

The "Elegie" is centrally concerned to recall the bliss of a relationship now ended. The poem has within it a fierce sting of grief which culminates in that extraordinary superlative attributed to the last-and-final kiss:

> Selbst nach dem letzten Kuß mich noch ereilte,
> Den letztesten mir auf die Lippen drückte [. . .]. (51–52)

> [Even after the last kiss you caught up with me again
> And pressed the very last one on my lips.]

The language is on the very brink of the sayable, of grief at the threshold of inarticulateness. What compounds the sense of sheer desperation is the indication that the grief threatens to take back the poetic persona that has been so strongly and reassuringly present throughout the lyric oeuvre. As we have already noted, the intertextual debate with *Werther* and *Torquato Tasso* is couched in a despairing register. And in the stanza beginning

> Ist denn die Welt nicht übrig? Felsenwände,
> Sind sie nicht mehr gekrönt von heiligen Schatten? (31–32)

> [Is not the world still there? Rock walls,
> Are they no longer crowned with holy shadows?]

we hear the voice of the poet reminding himself of one of his familiar and reassuring registers: his persistent sense of the rightness and abundance of natural processes. The stanza ends:

> Und wölbt sich nicht das überweltlich Große,
> Gestaltenreiche, bald Gestaltenlose? (35–36)

> [And does not the greatness above the world
> Arch itself, now rich in form, now formless?]

The final line particularly, with its perception of morphological dynamics, is deeply Goethean. Yet in this context of grief and dereliction not even the Goethean registers can help any more; rather, they function as some kind of dreadful act of self-parody. As the first line of the final stanza puts it with heartbreaking simplicity:

> Mir ist das All, ich bin mir selbst verloren [. . .]. (133)

> [I have lost the all, I have lost myself.]

Some of the most moving testimonies of grief in the "Elegie" are those that stay close to the colloquial, as in the line just quoted. One thinks also of:

> Da bleibt kein Rat als grenzenlose Tränen. (114)

> [There is no help but endless tears.]

And there are those stinging shards and fragments of lines:

> Und zwar durch sie! (66)

> [And in fact all her doing!]

Perhaps most vivid of all is the throw-away after the imagined speech of consolation attributed to the girl:

> Du hast gut reden, dacht ich [. . .]. (103)
>
> [It is all very well to talk, I thought.]

Such linguistic stabs acquire especial force given that the poem also works with more exalted registers of grief (and there is a regularity to the meter, rhyme and stanzaic form that produces a sense of dignity, of measured, even decorous utterance). Yet all the high style cannot keep at bay those lines that embody the sheer inexpressibility of human loss. It is only in the final poem of the Trilogy — "Aussöhnung" (reconciliation) — that a measure of comfort is found: in the healing power of music. The first line echoes the proverbial saying "Leidenschaft schafft nur Leiden" — that is: the very word indicates that passion brings pain: "Die Leidenschaft bringt Leiden" (passion brings sorrow). Yet the excess of pain, deriving from the sense of the hours that have evaporated "überschnell" is answered by the miraculous abundance of music — "durch und durch," "überfüllen," "überreich." The "Trilogie der Leidenschaft" ends, then, on a concilia-tory note. But, given the force of what has gone before, the comfort, when it is offered, seems a shade precarious.

The insight that precariousness, tentativeness even, is enough to live by informs one of Goethe's notable love poems from his final years, "Der Bräutigam" (The Betrothed Man, 1824). The poem moves through twenty-four hours, from one midnight to the next. With the exception of two lines, the tenses are in the past throughout the first three stanzas. The poem begins with paradoxes: it is midnight, the body sleeps but the heart is awake and the love it feels converts night into day. Then day comes, but, to the poet, it might just as well be night. The paradoxes are clarified in the second stanza. Day takes the poet away from his beloved; hence, the evening hours are welcomed when the two of them can be together. Yet in the third stanza an all-important shift occurs as the two lovers, watching the setting sun, hope for its return the next day. Until this point in the poem, the contrast between day and night has been heavily loaded emotionally and evaluatively. Day has been alien, unwelcome, because it decrees separation, whereas night has brought them together. Yet now that simple opposition (so beloved, incidentally, of Romantic poets) is transposed, initially with the welcoming of the returning sun, and then, more fully and thoughtfully, in the final stanza.

Once again, at midnight, the self moves, in a dream, to the threshold of the girl's room. The poem is entitled "Der Bräutigam." The lovers are not yet married; the poem is about love before its physical consummation, love at the threshold. The final stanza is in the present tense; and it is a present that is full of desire, of expectation. The poem ends with the lines:

O sei auch mir dort auszuruhn bereitet,
Wie es auch sei, das Leben, es ist gut.

[O let it be granted to me to rest there, too,
However it may be, life, it is good.]

The first of these two lines expresses the wish that the poet and his beloved will be allowed to lie together, will become truly and completely lovers. The second line modifies the subjunctive "sei" from a wish into the "sei" of the concessive mode — "wie es auch sei" — however it may be. And we note how the little word "auch," too, is modified in its force. In the first line (O sei auch mir) it is the "auch" of "me as well," of the wish that he may also lie where she lies. Yet in the second line, the "auch" figures in the standard form of the concessive phrase in German. These two tiny modifications move the sentiments in the closing stanza of the poem from a conditional to an unconditional acceptance of the goodness of life. That is to say: the attitude that prevails throughout the first two and a half stanzas of the poem is one that affirms only one facet of life — the time spent together with the girl. Yet the closing cadence of the poem implies a progression, a growth process, in the poem. As we move from past midnight to present midnight, the attitude that subdivides life into acceptable and unacceptable forms of experience modulates into an acceptance of the process as a whole. As noted, in the last two lines of our poem, the "sei" of wish becomes the "sei" of concessive statement — "whatever may be" — and finally becomes the present indicative — "es ist gut." The final line of the poem

Wie es auch sei, das Leben, es ist gut

is a small miracle. It is often quoted out of context as a sign of Goethe's yes-saying to life. Of course, it is an act of affirmation. But without the context of the poem, without the tentative, patient movement towards that affirmation, without the weight of conquered negation that precedes it, it can sound banal. Yet in the poem it is anything but banal. It is wonderfully resonant in its very colloquial immediacy. The line itself, as an instance of the German language, is utterly implicated in everyday speech patterns. It would feel immeasurably different if Goethe had written:

Wie das Leben auch sei, es ist gut.

But the use of the "es" twice, whereby the indefinite "es" becomes the specific pronoun referring to "das Leben," generates a sense of slight hesitation, of searching before the final affirmation is made.

Goethe's love poetry has taken us into the realm of nature poetry on the one hand and of philosophical poetry on the other. "Der Bräutigam" is less a poem about desire and the social institution of marriage than it is about general patterns of expectation and fulfillment in human living. And on this account it takes us, by way of conclusion, to those poems in which Goethe explores processes of human reflectivity.

It must be stressed that Goethe's philosophical poetry is not the poetic expression of a given, pre-existent philosophical system; rather, it is poetry that explores processes of thinking about human experience. Constantly, he suggests that, in human affairs, thinking is not only an abstraction from, but also a specification and intensification of, human experience. Let us begin with "Auf dem See" (On the Lake, 1775). The poem opens with a stanza in which the "ich" expresses and celebrates closeness to nature. The governing images are those of mother and child; the poet sucks nourishment from nature, is held at the breast, the wave rocks the boat as though it were a cradle. And yet, the second stanza disrupts that umbilical closeness between nature and the human self: the rhythm and rhyme scheme change as dreams return to haunt the poet. The poet's gaze, having tracked upwards at the end of the first stanza, following the shape of the mountains, now sinks downwards, perhaps in a fit of abstraction and pensiveness. The inner life seems to disturb the integrity of the self. But the dream does not have the last word: the last two lines of the middle stanza return the poet to the present world. Yet the reconnected self is of a different kind. The final stanza is all one sentence:

> Auf der Welle blinken
> Tausend schwebende Sterne,
> Weiche Nebel trinken
> Rings die türmende Ferne,
> Morgenwind umflügelt
> Die beschattete Bucht,
> Und im See bespiegelt
> Sich die reifende Frucht.

> [On the wave a thousand
> Floating stars twinkle,
> Soft mists drink in
> The towering distance round about,
> The wings of the morning wind fly
> Around the shadowed bay,
> And in the lake is mirrored
> The ripening fruit.]

The sentence captures three facets of the natural landscape, all of them metaphorical expressions of the interaction of different orders of being: wave and stars, conjoined in the notion of light emanating from water, mist and distant mountain tops brought together in the metaphor of drinking, wind that wings its way round the bay. And finally, there is the ripening fruit mirrored in the lake. Particularly noteworthy is the fact that, in the final stanza, the "ich," so assertively present in the first stanza (ich, mich, unsern, unserm), has disappeared altogether. Yet, of course, the human self is, by implication, there at every turn, not least in the metaphors that so richly assert the ceaseless interplay of natural agencies. Put simply, nature is much more present than in the first stanza. In the first stanza nature is the comforting mother, so close as to be felt rather than seen, to be embraced rather than perceived. By the final stanza — hence the reference to "die reifende Frucht" — the poet has, as it were, grown up, and nature is in focus as a realm seen in its own right, although seen through the metaphorically creative lens of human perception. The somewhat breathless syntax of the opening stanza — the "Und" in the first line almost suggesting a child's rushed narrative — gives way to surer forms of articulation. The agency of this transition in the poem is the resurgence of old dreams and their rejection in the name of the here and now. Our poem, as its title indicates, is, in terms of its foreground statement, a glimpse of a journey by boat across a lake. But, much more importantly, it expresses processes of emotional and cognitive maturation, from self-centeredness to world-centeredness.

Precisely that process of growth continues in the later poetry. It is, for example, at the heart of "Um Mitternacht" (At Midnight, 1818), which gives us, in its three stanzas, glimpses of three different stages of a human life. The first stanza concerns the little boy, who, in his particular "midnight experience," comes to feel his smallness (klein, kleiner Knabe) with especial urgency. He has to pass, on his way to his father's house, close to the graveyard (his father is a clergyman); and he notices the overwhelmingly insistent beauty of the stars. The particular significance of the experience is not spelt out — rather we hear the little boy's wonderment:

> Stern am Sterne
> Sie leuchteten doch alle gar zu schön:
> Um Mitternacht.

> [Star upon star
> They yet shone far too beautifully:
> At midnight.]

But we may conjecture that the importance of the experience has to do with a moment when a young person finds himself, perhaps for the first time, asking philosophical questions about death (the eeriness of the church yard at midnight) and about the scale of the universe (the splendor of the night sky). The second stanza, in its different way, focuses on a cognate experience later in life when we see the lover meeting and parting from his beloved. (The coexistence of "gehend, kommend," of arrival and leave-taking irresistibly recalls "Willkommen und Abschied.") The stanza acknowledges the sheer power of the experience — "mußte, mußte, weil sie zog" (had to go, had to go because she pulled me) — and speaks of constellations in the sky (as in the first stanza).

Gestirn und Nordschein über mir im Streite [. . .].

[Clustered stars and northern lights above me in conflict.]

The import of the experience is not clearly explicated. But once again we can conjecture (just as the poem itself does). Perhaps the self of the lover finds himself asking whether his life is constituted of uncontrollable, intense experiences, or whether there is a measure of coherence and purpose to be discerned in what happens. Hence the "coming and going" of earthly experience; hence the warring principles in the night sky: the clear-cut constellation (Gestirn) on the one hand, and the diffuse haze of the northern lights (Nordschein) on the other. And finally we come to the old man's experience; one in which the implicit motivating force of the poem's theme — thought ("der Gedanke") — comes clearly to the fore. Thought is linked with the calm, steady light of the moon; and it articulates the midnight experience, one poised delicately and knowingly between past and future, between where the human self has come from and where it is going to. Our poem has a refrain which also provides its title. Midnight, at particular junctures, can be a moment of acutely felt transition; and the refrain "Um Mitternacht" marks and makes the transition from stanza to stanza. The poem concerns those moments in a life where the activation of the thinking, reflecting self produces a moment of transition, of maturation and growth. The poem is less about the specific thoughts that the human self has than about the process of thinking as such, a process that is interwoven with human living. Hence, the syntax in the poem is wonderfully loose, tentative, questing. What matters both to the poem and to the sentient life which it invokes, is not the conclusions reached but the search for them.

Precisely that energizing presence of thoughtfulness is at the heart of "Selige Sehnsucht" (Blessed Longing, 1819), the last poem which we wish to consider in any detail. It begins and ends by announcing — and then affirming — the value and importance of a mystery, a mystery that can, it seems, only be conceptualized in terms of paradoxes:

Das Lebendge will ich preisen,
Das nach Flammentod sich sehnet.

[I want to praise that living being
That longs for death by fire.]

Precisely that incommensurability of the living principle in quest of death by fire means that the mystery will not be accessible to the crowd. The three stanzas that follow spell out the paradox by means of patterns of light and dark and light and heavy. The second stanza explores the act of procreation from which all life flows and by means of which all life re-creates itself. As the sexual ardor cools there is, we learn, another kind of feeling that manifests itself, a "fremde Fühlung" which is linked to the light of a candle flame. The third stanza concerns the journey undertaken by the self who responds to the strange feeling and to the call of the candle flame. It is a journey away from the physical consummation of the night of love — into a new kind of union, a higher union, but one that is still driven by the intense authority of erotic desire ("neu Verlangen"; "höhere Begattung"). And in the fourth stanza that journey in quest of higher experience ends, shockingly, with the death of the butterfly in the candle flame. The moment of extinction is powerfully captured in the rhyme-pair "gebannt/verbrannt" which, as the only masculine rhyme (that is, a rhyme that is constituted by stressed syllables) in the first four stanzas, generates brutal authority. If we look back on the sequence of stanzas two to four we find that we have a series of pictures that suddenly come into focus at the end of the fourth stanza when the indefinite "du" is identified as a "Schmetterling." And that image, of course, takes us back to our opening stanza, to the longing for death in flames. Yet, from the philosophical tenor of that opening statement — "das Lebendige" — and from the fact that stanzas two to four are all couched in the "du" form, which implies a generality in respect of human experience, we realize that our poem is not essentially about the animal world but is, rather, about the human capacity for intense experience, experience of both body (the sexual coupling) and mind (the higher union). The philosophical implications are spelt out in the final stanza, which returns to the mystery (the unspecified "es" of the first line of the poem) now formulated as a "das" which prefigures the formulation of the all-important formula to come:

> Und so lang du das nicht hast,
> Dieses: Stirb und werde!
> Bist du nur ein trüber Gast
> Auf der dunklen Erde.

> [And as long as you have not grasped
> This: Die and become!
> Then you are only a sad guest
> On the dark earth.]

This, then, is the wisdom that is so difficult of access; and it has to do with notions of experiential dynamic and change, with processes in which the emergence of new from old entails many intermediate deaths. It cannot be too strongly stressed that the force of "Stirb und werde!" is not other-worldly. Rather, it has to do with the transformatory and self-transformatory law of this-worldly experience; it is a law of ceaseless dying and becoming. Not that thereby actual, physical death is denied (the force of "verbrannt," as we have seen, makes sure that no such denial is allowed). But the poem is ultimately about death not as the antagonist of life but as part of life lived at the greatest pitch of intensity. The butterfly has a central symbolic function: its life cycle enacts the most spectacular series of transformations, of dying and becoming, from egg to caterpillar (larva) to chrysalis (pupa) to winged creature, to say nothing of its spectacular and deathly love affair with the light. This, then, transferred to the human subject as a property of his or her self-understanding, is the law that truly acknowledges our ceaselessly changing being in the world. In a wonderfully colloquial moment

> Und so lang du das nicht hast

Goethe urges us to "get it," to get the point. This, then, is philosophy not as an academic discipline, not as an exercise in austere abstraction, but as a form of thinking-as-experience. And it offers the possibility of dealing with the transience of human life:

> Bist du nur ein trüber Gast
> Auf der dunklen Erde.

By definition all mortal beings are but guests on the earth; none of them lasts for ever. But without an understanding of the process of "Stirb und werde!," the transitory self is "trüb" — unenlightened and melancholy. Understanding the law of dying and becoming is no mere matter of wise observation; rather, it is a force that energizes and quickens. Hence the insistence throughout the poem on the "du"; hence the seeming elitism of the dismissal of "die Menge." The wisdom at issue in this magnificent poem is not a matter of some corporate panacea. Rather, it has to do with each person's sense of experiential truth and value.

"Selige Sehnsucht" confronts the facts of transience and death, but not ultimately to lament the limitations that constrain human life; rather to find an understanding of those limitations that does not blight the human sense of fulfillment in worldly living. The poem "Dauer im Wechsel" (Continuity in Change, 1803), for example, spells out fully the conditions of transience, but only then to find in the human capacity for self-consciousness the promise of "Unvergängliches" (permanence) — although, paradoxically, self-consciousness is the agent that compounds that very law of transience by giving human creatures the awareness of their own mortality. In the poem "Im ernsten Beinhaus wars" (In This Somber Mortuary, 1827) the experience of confronting the skeletal relics of human beings produces not *a memento mori*, but rather a celebration of life. Human life entails a constant interplay of mind and matter; even the material remains of a great personality will bear witness to that interplay:

> Wie sie das Feste läßt zu Geist verrinnen,
> Wie sie das Geisterzeugte fest bewahre.

> [how it allows solid things to merge into spirit,
> how it can solidly preserve the creations of the spirit.]

For Goethe human mortality is central to human reflectivity. He confronts death; and he sees in death not only finitude and termination but also the temporality of all that we are, do, and know. But that temporality, rightly understood, can quicken, perhaps even inspire, us.

3: Narrative Fiction

GOETHE WROTE PROSE FICTION throughout his life; and, as we shall see, he explored the full range of narrative possibilities. In this context, we need to remember that, for much of the eighteenth century, prose fiction in general, and the novel in particular, had to fight hard to achieve respectability. Once the battle was won, the spoils of victory were prodigious: the novel became, and it continues to be, the dominant expression of modern bourgeois culture. And to this process Goethe was a key contributor.

Admittedly, the German novel is not exactly a force to be reckoned with in the company of great European novel fictions, at any rate not before the closing decades of the nineteenth century. For the most part, the running is made in the eighteenth and nineteenth centuries by the English and French novel traditions. The English novel begins early to register the shock waves of mercantile modernity and thereby to assert the possibility that bourgeois consciousness is worthy of treatment in the epic mode. Richardson discovers in the epistolary novel the appropriate form for the drama of intense, beleaguered subjectivity; at the more robust end of the spectrum, Fielding justifies the modern novel as a form of comic epic in prose, and other writers join him in not only asserting but demonstrating the combination of entertainment value and weighty human concern that can quicken the pages of the modern novel (Defoe, Smollett). It is a potent legacy whose presence can be sensed in the major achievements of the subsequent generation of writers: Jane Austen, Dickens, the Brontës, George Eliot. The French novel of the eighteenth century also registers the potent energies of a new cult of feeling (Rousseau, Laclos). After the cataclysm of the French Revolution that voice of inwardness modulates into the urgent articulation of socio-political modernity, which, in novelistic terms, leads to particular attention being paid to the workings of social materiality and, by extension, of psychology (Stendhal, Flaubert), often with quasi-scientific pretensions to dispassionate accuracy (Balzac, Zola).

In this illustrious company, it has to be acknowledged, the German novel is something of a Cinderella. It is informed, as are its European contemporaries, by a bad conscience in respect of the popular forms of narrative art: adventure stories, romances, and so on. It too seeks to lift the rattling good yarn into some condition of thematic weight and seriousness. One feature is particularly characteristic of the German situation:

certain key advances in terms of the novel genre are accompanied by important theoretical responses to those advances. Wieland's novel *Agathon* (first edition, 1767) is at the heart of Blanckenburg's famous essay on the genre, *Versuch über den Roman* (1774). Goethe's *Wilhelm Meisters Lehrjahre* (1795–96) captures the sophisticated exegetical attention of Friedrich Schlegel with his essay *Über Goethes Meister* (1798) and of Hegel in his *Ästhetik* (1818–28). We shall return later in this chapter to a discussion of the insights of both Schlegel and Hegel. At this stage, we simply want to register two issues. One is that, although the modern European novel came of age in the course of the eighteenth century and realized its full potential in the course of the nineteenth, it had to wait a very long time until it found any sustained and profound theoretical analysis and discussion — arguably until Henry James wrote the "New York Prefaces" in the first decade of the twentieth century. The signal exception to this historical rule occurs in Germany where Schlegel's and Hegel's insights into the modern novel as a genre are absolutely epoch-making in their textual perceptiveness and historico-cultural sophistication. And it is noteworthy that both of them are, in effect, spelling out the theoretical implications inherent in Goethe's *Wilhelm Meister* project. The second issue concerns the dimension of reflectivity in the German novel. Precisely that reflectivity makes the German novel somewhat peripheral to the broad tradition of European novel writing in the nineteenth century. That corpus, as we have already indicated, subscribes broadly speaking to the narrative aim that we know as realism, a project that entails full acknowledgement of the force of social materiality in human affairs. The novels within this tradition depict forms of experiential disenchantment, as the untried young protagonist is forced to compromise with the demands of social practicality. In Germany, by contrast, the novel sustains a more inward and thoughtful mode and thus generates what one might call a narrative of reflectivity. To this latter enterprise Goethe's fiction, as we shall see, is entirely central.

One form this reflectivity takes, in Goethe's hands, is the ability to explore various narrative modes: many of his works operate with processes of embedding and re-contextualizing narrative statements, so that the text as a whole becomes a self-thematizing and self-commenting universe of discourse. For example, *Werther* consists of the one-way letters of the protagonist to his friend Wilhelm, of the extensive report of the "Herausgeber" or editor figure, of a lengthy section of Macpherson's *Ossian* that is incorporated because Werther has translated the work, and he and Lotte read the translation together. *Die Wahlverwandtschaften* includes an interpolated novella entitled "Die wunderlichen Nachbarskinder." *Wilhelm Meisters Lehrjahre* includes poems, songs and maxims, a pietistic memoir, and in *Wilhelm Meisters Wanderjahre* we find a bewildering array of eleven interpolated novellas or short stories housed within an "archival" framework, one that stresses the arbitrary nature of the plot of the novel. There is something virtuosic about this variety; Goethe constantly makes an issue of, and asks us to reflect on, matters of narrative focus, of structuration and contextualization, of texts and meta-texts.

All this may sound both rarefied and forbidding, poles apart from the vivid sense of socio-psychological particulars that fill the pages of Dickens or Balzac. Yet it is not as bloodless as it sounds. In respect of *Die Wahlver-wandtschaften,* Goethe spoke of his aim as being "sociale Verhältnisse und die Konflikte derselben symbolisch gefaßt darzustellen"[1] (to portray social circumstances and the conflicts between them in symbolic concentration). To a degree, this applies to his prose work in general. Goethe as narrator does have a lively sense of society, but it is not society defined as material-ity, as streets, houses, furnishings; rather it is society defined as mental fur-niture, as the signs and tokens, the assumptions and symbols of social sig-nification. Goethe frequently explores the inwardness of his characters, but not as a realm exempt from or alternative to society. On the contrary, society is shown to function as a system of elaborate semiotics. The char-acters all live in, by, and for, certain images and pictures; and precisely this repertoire of signification is the point of confluence for private and public concerns. Hence, the Goethean narrative, which works in terms of "sym-bolic grasping" of social experience (the "symbolisch gefaßt" of his comment on *Die Wahlverwandtschaften*), explores the socio-psychological specificity of his characters' lives. As socialized creatures, the characters make cultur-ally derived symbols of their experience. Goethe invites us to be self-conscious as readers in order that we may be able to register the role of literary, especially narrative, forms in the self-understanding of modern subjectivity. When we attend to the implications of the epistolary novel, of the novel of theatrical life, of the novel of adolescence, of the pietistic auto-biography, of the novel of marriage and adultery, of the novel as a commu-nity of stories, we are inquiring into more than narrowly literary matters. Rather, the literary mode is the correlative of certain kinds of socio-psycho-logical self-definition and self-understanding on the part of the characters.

Let us now turn to Goethe's narrative art. Because we want to discuss his novels in one group, we shall begin by looking at the shorter prose and at the epic of modern life *Hermann und Dorothea.* The first text that concerns us is the story which Goethe entitled simply *Novelle* (1828).

It is, in some ways, a strangely stilted story, stilted both in its events and in its characters. The setting is contemporary with the time of writ-ing, the early nineteenth century, and we find ourselves in a small German principality. The recently married prince leaves with his courtiers on a long-awaited hunt. His young wife is left behind, attended by an uncle and Honorio, a young equerry. There is a discussion of plans to restore an old castle, making it a site safe for recreational purposes. The three figures ride toward the castle, crossing the market place of the town where wild animals are on display in cages. They rest above the old castle, only to find their peace violently disturbed. A puff of smoke appears in the market place, and the Princess recalls a previous, terrifying fire of which she has heard frequent accounts from the uncle. In the confusion two of the wild animals have escaped; the tiger appears and runs in panic up the hillside. Honorio shoots the tiger. The lion takes refuge in the old castle. But violence is not necessary. The young boy, part of the family in charge of the wild animals, calms the frightened animal by playing his flute and singing. On this image of order restored the story closes.

Most commentators have felt that *Novelle* works with a movement from order into violence and back into order. The exposition, for example the depiction of the market place, stresses the harmony of the social world, and we end with a vision of harmony that embraces the animal world, the social world, and (in the song of the boy) the divine world. Moreover, as various hints indicate, Honorio is in love with the Princess; and, in the course of the tale, he learns to overcome what could be a socially and psychologically disastrous infatuation. Yet the story's treatment of Honorio's passion is tantalizingly understated; there is remarkably little individual psychology for us to go on. And this is because Goethe's narrative is a masterpiece of subtextual statement. In a profusion of subtle links, parallels, and echoes, the text sketches in its true theme: the dark side of the socialized, repressed, imagination of civilized men and women: fantasy images alert us to the undercurrents of violence, sadism, blood-letting. The story makes clear that the hunt is occasioned neither by concerns of security nor by the need for food, but simply by the desire for sport. This recreation is, in short, an act of war, a "Kriegszug" (HA 6, 492) against the peaceful animals of the forests. Similarly, the wild animals displayed in the cages are not wild; long captivity has made them docile. But, as the uncle points out, the people who go to the side shows want to see not what is before them, but what is depicted in the posters advertising the attractions — one of which shows a tiger about to maul a black man. Yet even the uncle is not proof against the disturbing phenomenon which he so acutely diagnoses because one of his favorite anecdotes is of the earlier fire on the market place. The result is that, when a second fire breaks out, the Princess can see only terrifying images, both of the fire and of the wild animals. The tiger that runs toward her is frightened, not vicious; but in her mind's eye she registers the violent image from the poster. By giving chase, Honorio angers the animal. He kills it and offers the Princess the hide in an archetypal gesture of male prowess. And the Princess recalls his skill in cavalry sports and tournaments; he is particularly adept at impaling the mock-up head of a black man as he gallops past. The reference to the black man recalls the poster of the tiger. The story is remarkable for the density of its subtextual statement; and in the process it explores the mentality of socialized men and women.

At the end of the tale, the narrator quotes the lament of the mother for the dead tiger and apologizes that he can only offer an approximation to that piercingly natural language: "Vergebens würde man sie in unsern Mundarten übersetzen wollen; den ungefähren Inhalt dürfen wir nicht verfehlen" (504; In vain would one seek to translate it into an everyday speech; but we may not conceal the approximate import). Here, the narrator clearly aligns himself with the discourse of "our" awareness; and it is, of course, the discourse of social order, social repression. The narrative voice, too, is part of the problem which the text is concerned to explore. Hence, the narrative subtext embodies the socio-psychological subtext, which is the true theme of *Novelle*.

A masterpiece of its kind, *Novelle* also has a certain exemplary force by virtue of its title. Initially Goethe planned to call the story "Die Jagd" (The Hunt). But finally he decided on the simple generic designation *Novelle*. In a famous remark to Eckermann, he sketches in the implications: "denn was ist eine Novelle anders als eine sich ereignete unerhörte Begebenheit?" (744; for what is a novella if not an unheard-of event that has actually occurred?). The observation has all the hallmarks of a casual aperçu. But it has achieved an almost canonical status within German literary scholarship. It is, and we shall return to the issue at the end of this chapter, characteristic of Goethe that he had an extraordinarily acute sense of generic issues. That is to say: single-handedly he contrived to explore the expressive and formal possibilities of modern fiction, and, in this case, of the modern novella, both in the tale itself and in the title he gave it. The sketch of a definition which he offers draws marvelously economic attention to a particularly suggestive constellation: the story combines the intimation of the exceptional (wild animals on the loose in early nineteenth-century Germany) with an assertion of general applicability (sich ereignet), which indicates that the laws of familiar material and social causality are respected. There is, in other words, nothing magical about Goethe's story. It is neither a ghost story nor a fairy tale (as we shall see, he wrote both of those). Rather, the exceptional moment crystallizes the mentality of everyday living and experiencing.

If we look at the early cycle of tales entitled *Unterhaltungen deutscher Ausgewanderten* (Conversations of German Emigrants, 1795), we can see Goethe exploring the possibilities of the "Novelle" form. He takes the governing structural model — a frame narration housing a series of stories — from Boccaccio's *Decameron*. In Boccaccio, a group of young people flee from the plague in Florence and retire to a country estate where, by the process of telling and listening to tales, they reinstate a social and discursive order that has been destroyed by the chaos in the town. Goethe transposes this generic constellation to the modern world. The threat to order and civil society is now the French Revolution. Once again the telling of tales is seen to have an educative force. And the stories told, which thematize the interplay of order and chaos, range from simple ghost stories to moral tales, which explore the capacity for self-control vested in mature men and women, to an extended fairy tale. None of these tales are, in our view, in the same league artistically as *Novelle*. But they show us Goethe worrying at, and experimenting with, the possibilities of the short prose form; they show him constantly interrogating and thematizing modes and forms of narration.

Goethe's best known, and for generations of readers throughout the nineteenth century best loved, response to the French Revolution was the verse epic *Hermann und Dorothea* (1797). It depicts, in the mode of Homeric narrative, the arrival in a small German market town of refugees fleeing from the turmoil of the French Revolution. The son of the inn-keeper, Hermann, embarked on an errand of mercy, comes across a young woman, Dorothea, who, as best she can, is looking after an older woman who has just given birth. He gives them all the food and clothing that he has with him. Later he seeks out the young woman again to offer further help. The contact between them ripens into love and the story closes with their engagement. The virtuosically handled epic form serves two functions. One is to dignify the people and the doings of the small town, to make them, not in spite of, but because of, their marginality to the earth-shattering events across the border, worthy of narrative treat-ment in the grand manner. The other is to generate an affectionate, on occasion mocking, irony. Take, for example, the depiction of the engage-ment in the final canto. In the following lines one hears both a validation of the moment of family ritual, and, in the bracketed third line, which mentions the father's pudgy hand, more than a hint of humor:

> Eilig faßte darauf der gute verständige Pfarrherr
> Erst des Vaters Hand und zog ihm vom Finger den Trauring
> (Nicht so leicht; er war vom rundlichen Gliede gehalten)
> Nahm den Ring der Mutter darauf und verlobte die Kinder.
>
> (HA 2, 238–41)

> [Swiftly thereupon the good and wise clergyman
> Seized the father's hand and took the wedding ring from his finger
> (No easy matter, for it was trapped in that limb's roundness)
> He then took the mother's ring and solemnized the engagement.]

A moment such as the bracketed interpolation partakes of a strand of irony which delights in the clashing of dignified epic registers on the one hand with a world of pipes, slippers, and garden gnomes on the other. Admittedly one sometimes wonders if the text does not occasionally produce moments of involuntary humor, as, for example, in the extraordinary line:

Da versetzte der Vater und tat bedeutend den Mund auf.

(Canto 5, 108)

[Then the father replied and opened his mouth significantly.]

In any event, a mixture of genial irony and high seriousness sustains *Hermann und Dorothea*. The upshot is a work that is, for present-day readers, part appealing and part inaccessible. Yet there are deeply memorable moments. One is to be found on the very last page of the epic. Dorothea, as the engagement is being solemnized, explains why she already has an engagement ring on her finger. It was given her by a young man who went to Paris to support the revolution, but he was imprisoned and killed. Dorothea recalls his last words to her, words that acknowledge the world-historical change wrought by the French Revolution and link that sense of change to a larger perception of the mutability of all things:

Nur ein Fremdling, sagt man mit Recht, ist der Mensch hier
auf Erden:
Mehr ein Fremdling als jemals, ist nun ein jeder geworden.
Uns gehört der Boden nicht mehr; es wandern die Schätze;
Gold und Silber schmilzt aus den alten heiligen Formen;
Alles regt sich, als wollte die Welt, die gestaltete, rückwärts
Lösen in Chaos und Nacht sich auf, und neu sich gestalten. (269–74)

[One says rightly that human beings are but strangers here
on earth:
More a stranger than ever before has everyone become.
The ground belongs to us no longer; fleeting are the treasures;
Gold and silver melt and trickle from their ancient, sacred forms;
Everything is on the move, as though the shaped and ordered world
Were going to dissolve back into chaos and night, and be
made again.]

Hermann und Dorothea houses this sense of radical disturbance within Germany's small-town conservatism, and is deeply grateful for the latter. Yet, even so, the shock waves cannot be fully contained. The reported words of the young idealist are unforgettable, particularly his warning to Dorothea never to forget the fragility that inalienably is part of the human lot in the modern world:

Aber dann auch setze nur leicht den beweglichen Fuß auf;
Denn es lauert der doppelte Schmerz des neuen Verlustes. (286–87)

[But then set your agile foot down only lightly;
For the double pain of a new loss is waiting.]

Much of *Hermann und Dorothea,* both metrically and thematically, plants
solid, perhaps all too solid, feet in the soil of German sturdiness. But moments such as those quoted bring a measure of differentiation, even perhaps an undertone of reflection and questioning, into Goethe's otherwise
so comforting small-town epic.

By contrast, when we move to *Werther* and *Die Wahlverwandtschaften,*
we find ourselves in an unstable world. Both novels are animated by a de-
termination to explore the workings of human passion and to find the appropriate narrative-cum-generic correlative of this broad theme. *Die Leiden
des jungen Werther* (1774, second version 1787, to which we shall refer in
our analysis) is a novel in letter form, and the following may serve as a
representative example:

> Verzeihen Sie mir diese Vertraulichkeit! O [. . .] Sie können auch
> Menschen, die nichts als natürliche Menschen sind, lieben und Bruder
> nennen. Ich bin Ihr Bruder! Ich fühl' es, daß ich's bin! . . . Könnte ich
> nur drei Wochen bei Ihnen sein! Aber ich fühl' es voraus, Sie würden
> mir zu lieb werden. Ich würde im eigentlichen Sinne vor Liebe krank
> werden; und sterben, wenn ich Sie wieder verlassen müßte. (HA 6, 561)

> [Forgive me this intimacy! You can also love people who are nothing
> but natural people and call them brother. I am your brother! I feel
> that I am! . . . If only I could spend three weeks with you. But I al-
> ready feel in advance that you would become too dear to me. I
> would, in the truest sense of the word, fall sick because of love, and
> die if I ever had to leave you again.]

One instantly recognizes the Werther tone and the Werther sentiments;
there is the frequent recourse to hyperbole; the assertion of feeling as the
supreme organ of cognition (Ich fühl' es, daß ich's bin, Aber ich fühl' es
voraus); the sense of excess which threatens to bring self-extinction in its
wake (vor Liebe krank werden; und sterben). The letter is typical of Werther.
But it does not, in fact, come from the novel; it was written by the forty-
year-old Wieland to Lavater in 1776. Perhaps this glimpse of the epistolary
culture of the age can help to explain why *Werther* was an extraordinary
best-seller, in fact the first to issue from Germany. The primary cause of its
phenomenal success was the extent to which it was so utterly attuned to the
contemporary discourse of *Empfindsamkeit,* with its stress on the supreme
truthfulness of the heart. It was a culture within which the writing and receiv-
ing of letters played a significant role. The Werther style was as much part
of the common currency of social life as are the abundant descriptions of
streets, houses, rooms that fill the pages of a Balzac or Dickens novel.

The novel, as its title proclaims, is about one figure — Werther — and about his anguish. The events extend from May 1771 to December 1772. He is a gifted young man who has little chance of finding a fulfilling career. He falls in love with Lotte, a young woman who is already engaged to a man by the name of Albert. He becomes obsessed with her; his gloom deepens, and finally he shoots himself. The name itself is unusual; all the other principal characters are given Christian names — Lotte, Albert. But Werther has simply his surname; and it implies some kind of value or "Wert." Precisely what this value might be is something that will haunt us throughout the novel. At the beginning Werther is alone; but, far from being oppressed by the lack of human society, he rejoices in his rapturous connectedness to the natural world around him. The letter of 10 May reads:

> Eine wunderbare Heiterkeit hat meine ganze Seele eingenommen, gleich den süßen Frühlingsmorgen, die ich mit ganzem Herzen genieße. Ich bin allein und freue mich meines Lebens in dieser Gegend, die für solche Seelen geschaffen ist wie die meine. Ich bin so glücklich, mein Bester, so ganz in dem Gefühle von ruhigem Dasein versunken, daß meine Kunst darunter leidet. Ich könnte jetzt nicht zeichnen, nicht einen Strich, und bin nie ein größerer Maler gewesen als in diesen Augenblicken. Wenn das liebe Tal um mich dampft, und die hohe Sonne an der Oberfläche der undurchdringlichen Finsternis meines Waldes ruht, und nur einzelne Strahlen sich in das innere Heiligtum stehlen, ich dann im hohen Grase am fallenden Bache liege, und näher an der Erde tausend mannigfältige Gräschen mir merkwürdig werden; wenn ich das Wimmeln der kleinen Welt zwischen Halmen, die unzähligen, unergründlichen Gestalten der Würmchen, der Mückchen näher an meinem Herzen fühle, und fühle die Gegenwart des Allmächtigen, der uns nach seinem Bilde schuf, das Wehen des Allliebenden, der uns in ewiger Wonne schwebend trägt und erhält; mein Freund! wenn's dann um meine Augen dämmert, und die Welt um mich her und der Himmel ganz in meiner Seele ruhn wie die Gestalt einer Geliebten — dann sehne ich mich oft und denke: Ach könntest du das wieder ausdrücken, könntest du dem Papier das einhauchen, was so voll, so warm in dir lebt, daß es würde der Spiegel deiner Seele, wie deine Seele ist der Spiegel des unendlichen Gottes! — Mein Freund — Aber ich gehe darüber zugrunde, ich erliege unter der Gewalt der Herrlichkeit dieser Erscheinungen. (HA 6, 9)

> [A wonderful serenity has taken possession of my whole soul like the sweet spring mornings, which I enjoy with all my heart. I am alone and rejoice in my life in this area, which is made for such souls as mine. I am so happy, best of my friends, so utterly submerged in the feeling of gentle existence that my art suffers from it. I could not

now draw — not one single stroke — and yet I have never been a greater painter than in these moments. When the lovely valley steams around me and the high sun rests on the surface of the impenetrable darkness of my forest and only individual rays steal into the inner sanctuary and I then lie in the high grass by the tumbling brook and, closer to the earth, thousands of different grasses catch my attention; when I feel closer to my heart the teeming of the little world between the stalks, the infinite, impenetrable forms of the worms and grubs and insects and feel the presence of the Almighty who made us in his image, the rustling of the all-loving one who carries and keeps us hovering in eternal bliss; my friend! when the dusk falls upon my eyes and the world around me and the sky rest fully in my soul like the form of a beloved — then I am overcome by yearning and think: Ah, if only you could breathe onto the paper everything that lives so fully, so warmly within you, that it might become the mirror of your soul just as the soul is the mirror of the infinite God! — My friend — but I am overwhelmed by all this, I succumb to the power of the glory of all these phenomena.]

We note the constantly asserted reciprocity between Werther and nature, the rapturous expressions of likeness, kinship, and wholeness: "gleich" and "ganz" are key words. Yet inseparable from this splendor is an intimation of danger, of an experiential energy so great that it threatens to overwhelm the expressive capacity and coherence of the self. Werther finds it difficult to draw; he is aware of being engulfed by a force that he cannot contain. The seeds of the disaster are, then, present from the beginning. But even so, the great sentence that dominates the letter, with its "wenn . . . wenn . . . dann . . . dann" pattern, is wonderfully expressive. Borrowing from particular forms of contemporary rhetoric (and specifically from the homiletic or sermonizing tradition), Werther's outpouring rises magnificently to the challenge of finding words for the tumult within him. But, as we follow the sequence of the letters, we witness a pattern of degeneration and decline. The letters, initially at any rate, are addressed to a friend; but increasingly we lose all sense of interpersonal communication. The traffic flows all one way; and the result is desperate claustrophobia. We could trace a number of themes throughout the novel: Werther and nature, Werther and love, Werther and religion, Werther and art. Common to all four strands is a process of ever greater disintegration as Werther slides into a paranoid condition. His inability to make compromises, to find some kind of sustaining balance between self and world means that increasingly he tries to make the world in his own image, or discounts it entirely. There is something all-or-nothing about Werther. Increasingly he forfeits any sense of the contours that contain and, by containing, define the self. Ominously, in the letter of 24 July of Book 1, he writes: "alles schwimmt und schwankt so vor meiner Seele, daß ich keinen Umriß packen kann" (41; everything so swims and floats before my soul that I can get hold of no outlines). The dreadful self-absorption of Werther's mind blights his relationship to everything outside himself, to the extent that only those experiences are admissible that corroborate the self. His religiosity turns into a near-blasphemous identification of himself with Christ. The same holds true of his relationship to Lotte. Clearly she is very much drawn to him; but one particular remark is most telling: "Ich fürchte, ich fürchte, es ist nur die Unmöglichkeit, mich zu besitzen, die Ihnen diesen Wunsch so reizend macht" (103–4; I fear, I fear, it is only the impossibility of possessing me that makes this wish so appealing to you). Perhaps Werther is in love with love rather than being in love with another person who is genuinely perceived as other. *Werther* is one of the most intense psychological novels ever written. It culminates, with unforgettable cruelty, in a botched suicide. Werther in his last days spends more and more time envisaging and creating the scenario for a noble, decorous, beautiful death. But the reality of his dying is anything but that; it is hideous.

Werther's name, as we have noted, implies value. The prefatory statement from the editor which opens the novel refers to poor Werther, and invites compassion. All of which raises with particular urgency the question of what we are to make of him. At one level, our answer will no doubt be framed in psychological terms, and so far our discussion of the novel has proceeded along such lines. We register both the intensity and the monstrosity of the uncompromising self, the self that will live only in the authority of what its own heart is and knows. Yet we can also hear the character of the protagonist as one that expresses an intense philosophical dilemma: that of the acutely self-aware, self-reflective spirit who is in quest of simple, integral, unifying experience. When, for example, Werther writes of the sheer beauty of Lotte dancing, he describes a body and a consciousness in perfect union:

> Tanzen muß man sie sehen! Siehst du, sie ist so mit ganzem Herzen und mit ganzer Seele dabei, ihr ganzer Körper *eine* Harmonie, so sorglos, so unbefangen, als wenn das eigentlich alles wäre, als wenn sie sonst nichts dächte, nichts empfände; und in dem Augenblicke gewiß schwindet alles andere vor ihr. (24)

> [You have to see her dancing! You see, she is so caught up in it with her whole heart and her whole soul; her whole body one single harmony, so carefree, so unselfconscious as though that were everything, as though she had no other thoughts or feelings; and, beyond all doubt, in that moment everything else pales into insignificance.]

As many commentators have registered, the image of the dancer at one with the dance constantly recurs in nineteenth-century European literature as the palpable physical expression of a desperately longed-for ontological wholeness.[2] Precisely that glimpse of wholeness of being contrasts brutally with Werther's sense of having to live in fragmented and fragmenting self-awareness:

> Wenn Sie mich sähen, meine Beste, in dem Schwall von Zerstreuung! Wie ausgetrocknet meine Sinne werden! Nicht *einen* Augenblick der Fülle des Herzens, nicht *eine* selige Stunde! nichts! nichts! Ich stehe wie vor einem Raritätenkasten und sehe die Männchen und Gäulchen vor mir herumrücken, und frage mich oft, ob es nicht optischer Betrug ist. Ich spiele mit, vielmehr, ich werde gespielt wie eine Marionette und fasse manchmal meinen Nachbar an der hölzernen Hand und schaudere zurück. (65)

> [If only you could see me, best of my friends, in the wastes of distraction. How dried up my senses become. Not *one* moment of fullness of the heart, not *one* blessed hour! Nothing! Nothing! I stand as though before a freak show and see the little men and horses pass before me, and I often ask myself whether it is not an optical trick. I play along — or rather I am played along like a marionette and sometimes I take my neighbor by his wooden hand — and I recoil in horror.]

At such moments, the center of this remarkable novel is by no means the Eternal Triangle, which would imply that, if only Lotte had been available to Werther, everything would have turned out well: rather, the text traces the displacing force of human self-consciousness.

Part of our uncertainty as to how we are to judge Werther derives from the particular formal organization of the text. As we have noted, the bulk of the novel consists of Werther's letters. Crucially, they constitute not a dialogue but a monologue; and this is the precise formal correlative of his psychological sickness. But as Werther's mood darkens there is, as a simple matter of plausibility, the need for an editor figure to step in to order Werther's often incoherent, fragmented, and undated final jottings. At one level the "editor" is a dispassionate onlooker, someone who, for example, gives an account of Werther's suicide, who reports events as facts occurring in a world of outward cause and effect. When the novel shifts us from Werther's letters to the narrative of the editor, the effect is both shocking and liberating. We leave the claustrophobia of Werther's self-absorption, and we enter a world of palpable human and social interaction. At this level of structural statement, then, the text passes judgment on Werther as we move from inwardness to outwardness. Yet the editor is anything but a strident or censorious judge; rather, he is deeply sympathetic to Werther. In the brief prefatory note, he allows us to hear a number of responses, and many of them, as we have already noted, serve to commend Werther to us. He introduces himself as the assiduous compiler of Werther's letters, thereby legitimating both himself as documentary agent and the authenticity of the text that follows (that is to say: the fiction is that these are genuinely the letters that Werther wrote). But the documentary mode gives way to a more assertive, buttonholing one: we are told that we will be grateful to have this record of Werther's temperament because we will not be able to deny him our tears and admiration.

> Was ich von der Geschichte des armen Werther nur habe auffinden können, habe ich mit Fleiß gesammelt und lege es euch hier vor, und weiß, daß ihr mir's danken werdet. Ihr könnt seinem Geist und seinem Charakter eure Bewunderung und Liebe, so seinem Schicksale eure Tränen ihm nicht versagen.
>
> Und du, gute Seele, die du eben den Drang fühlst wie er, schöpfe Trost aus seinem Leiden, und laß das Büchlein deinen Freund sein, wenn du aus Geschick oder eigener Schuld keinen nähern finden kannst. (7)

> [Whatever I have managed to locate that has to do with the story of poor Werther I have collected most zealously and I put it before you here knowing that you will be grateful. You cannot deny his spirit and his character your admiration and his destiny your tears.
>
> And you, good soul, who feel the same pressures as he did, draw comfort from his suffering and may this little book be your friend if, because of fate or your own shortcomings, you can find no closer one.]

The plural mode of address — "Ihr" — then contracts to singular — "du" — as the individual reader is urged to make this little book his or her friend, although a note of warning is sounded about allowing the book to replace all other human contact. This is a magnificently economical and complex preface, which invites us constantly to shift our ground, and to be aware that we are doing so. The "little book" is, as it were, pressed into our hands, but it comes with a health warning. We are urged both to identify with Werther and to keep him at arm's length.

Precisely that disquieting ambivalence is at the heart of Goethe's great novel. *Werther* remained an uncomfortable text for Goethe throughout his life. He never read from it in public; his own responses to the Werther figure range from the censorious to the justificatory. Moreover, the events in the novel were, and were known to be, scandalously close to real-life events (involving Goethe himself and a young woman by the name of Lotte Buff who was engaged to a man called Kestner). At one level Goethe was, of course, fully justified in resenting prurient questions as to "where he got his novel from." At another level, he knew that the suggestion of indiscretion was part of the book's power. (It does, after all, depend centrally on the fiction of personal, private letters being made public. Moreover, for the details of Werther's catastrophic end Goethe drew on the much talked-about suicide of a young man by the name of Jerusalem; he even went so far as to request an account of that suicide from none other than Kestner himself, and used whole sections of Kestner's account in the text of *Werther*). Goethe's own relationship to Werther was, then, nothing if not ambiguous; and some of that ambiguity is transferred to us, the readers.

It is also noteworthy that he wrote two versions of the novel. The first, of 1774, is the more passionate and immediate; the second, of 1787, is more understated in tone, and is more sympathetic to the Albert figure (Kestner). Yet, in our view, Goethe's attempt to redress the balance of sympathies makes matters more, rather than less, complex. And the complexity generates the shifting ground of our relationship to Werther. The later version generalizes the issues more, whereas the first version stays closer to a fiercely individual and specific focus. The second version, for example, introduces the "Bauernbursch" figure, a young farmhand who loves his mistress, a widow, and believes himself to be encouraged by her. When he discovers he has a rival, he kills him. That Werther identifies with the young man and even seeks to support him before the judicial authorities is a measure of his sickness. At the same time this little social cameo suggests that the issue of passion denied an outlet has broader socio-cultural implications than simply one young man's emotional inadequacy. The kindness of the widow to her employee is misunderstood as a sexual invitation; but the implication is that such kindness is so rare that it can lend itself to misinterpretation. Similarly, although he is a solipsistic figure, Werther's life and death are not bereft of a social dimension. He is an intelligent, gifted, lively young man of bourgeois upbringing; and he is unable to find any social activity worthy of his talents. We should not forget that The American Declaration of Independence, which speaks of the individual citizen's right to the "pursuit of happiness," is contemporary with *Werther*. In one crucial incident he is snubbed by various aristocrats for outstaying his welcome at a dinner party. In part because he cannot express himself socially, he tries to write a self into being through his letters — just as he tries to write a loving self into being to make up for the lack of an actual relationship. Above all else — and here we reach the last strand of statement in this extraordinarily sophisticated novel — he is an intensely literary person and persona. Not that he is, in any professional sense, a creative writer: he is, and remains, too much of a dilettante for that. But he is deeply aware of literariness as part of his being and experience. When he and Lotte first become acquainted, they share the experience of a thunderstorm by invoking the name of the major contemporary poet, Klopstock, whose famous poem "Die Frühlingsfeyer"

(The Celebration of Spring) contained a much-admired evocation of a thunderstorm. At the end of his life, Werther, in his stage-managed suicide, leaves Lessing's play *Emilia Galotti* open on his desk. His literary predilections move in the course of the novel from Homer to Ossian. He translates the latter; and he and Lotte read that translation with intense emotion. In other words: *Werther* is a novel about a culture in which secular literature acquires cult status; and it is therefore deeply appropriate that it, too, had the spectacular distinction of becoming a cult book. In a quite uncanny way — not least because Goethe had a remarkable sense of the epistolary novel as the appropriate form for this particular juncture in the history of his culture — *Werther*, as text, thematizes and prefigures its own success. And that dimension of self-consciousness compounds our sense of the text's destabilizing energy. To this day, *Werther* has lost none of its power to engage and unsettle its readers.

Albeit in very different ways, as we shall see, *Die Wahlverwandt-schaften* (The Elective Affinities, 1809) is also a novel text that can play havoc with its readers. The events with which the novel is concerned all take place on the estate of Eduard, a minor aristocrat, and his wife Charlotte. The action begins when they decide to invite two friends to join them on the estate: the Hauptmann (Captain), a gifted man who is unable to find employment for his many practical talents, and Ottilie, a beautiful young orphan who is Charlotte's niece, and who is finding it difficult to make headway at school. Gradually, erotic entanglements develop: Eduard and Ottilie fall helplessly in love, and Charlotte and the Captain, although less explosively, find themselves irresistibly drawn together. In the volatile and highly charged climate of unfolding emotional involvement a fatal disturbance intrudes upon the act of love-making that occurs one night between husband and wife (Charlotte and Eduard). In the actual experience of intercourse each partner is thinking of the absent, and desired, lover. The result is a child who, though the genetic product of Charlotte and Eduard, bears unmistakable features of the Hauptmann and Ottilie. Matters remain suspended in fateful irresolution while both the Hauptmann and Eduard are away from the estate. But, as the foursome come together again, matters come to a head. Ottilie has a passionate meeting with Eduard by the lake. When she tries to return to the house by rowing across the water, she loses her balance and the child is drowned. In her that catastrophe produces the irrevocable decision not to proceed any further in the relationship with Eduard. She cannot deny her feelings for him; but she does deny her own right to bodily existence, and she starves herself to death. Eduard is heartbroken and dies soon afterwards. The two of them are buried side by side.

Die Wahlverwandtschaften is a deeply allusive and elusive text. At one level it is about passion and nothing else; it is a love tragedy in which, to an extent that the characters themselves only dimly apprehend, subterraneous currents of emotion and desire carry all before them. At another level, it is a forbiddingly and ferociously cerebral novel. The upshot is utterly paradoxical: an abstract novel about visceral experience.

It may be helpful to start by spelling out the levels of statement at which the events unfold before us. At one level, we seem to be concerned with things that are, at the very least, mysterious, if not magical, and imply the workings of some supernatural force. In any event, we are confronted by a profusion of unexplicated patterning. Eduard and Ottilie have complementary migraine headaches and her handwriting becomes uncannily similar to his. Ottilie can intuitively accompany Eduard's utterly erratic flute-playing. There is the goblet with the entwined initials E and O, the fact that Eduard planted the plane trees on the day of Ottilie's birth, and Ottilie's seemingly miracle-working powers after her death. Yet parallel to these weighty intimations of the mysterious we have a whole strand to the novel that conveys the existence of — and validates — the human capacity for self-control, for moral choice, for (to put it at its most modest level) common sense. Much of the implication of destiny and fate is associated with the love of Eduard and Ottilie; whereas Charlotte and the Hauptmann, although they too are overtaken by feelings that they can neither understand nor control, live and oblige themselves to live in a world of explicit moral choices, of consciousness and conscience. Once we heed this cognitive dimension, we find ourselves both aware of and, perhaps, offended by Eduard's headlong propensity to make every incident, scene, object, utterance symbolic of his ineluctable destiny to love Ottilie. And finally, there is a level of thematic statement which has to do with nature, nature both within and outside the human sphere. All these three levels of thematic statement — the supernatural, the moral, and the natural — partake of and derive from sustained patternings within the statement of the novel text. By any standards, *Die Wahlverwandtschaften* is over-endowed with possible significations. It is both concerned with the claustrophobia of life on a small estate, and it is itself a fiercely claustrophobic text. Alone the cluster of names speaks volumes: the women characters are called Char*lotte* and *Ott*ilie; and the Hauptmann's name is Otto — and this was Eduard's name as a child. Small wonder that the child is called Otto. The name itself is a palindrome, and, like all patterns in the novel, demands to be read both forwards and backwards. Added to which, the initials of the four main characters (as they are usually named in the novel, and in the order of their appearance in the narrative) spell E-C-H-O. At times one begins to wonder if one is not, in fact, reading a conundrum, an experiment, rather than a novel. But, infuriatingly, the text outflanks us here and suggests precisely this possibility. In a remarkable opening gesture — "Eduard, so nennen wir einen reichen Baron . . ." (HA 6, 242;

Eduard, so we shall call a rich baron) — we sense that we may be in the realm of conjecture and contingency. It is almost as though we are being invited to enter a narrative universe that begins "let us assume that there is a rich baron. . . ." Moreover, the title of the novel is echoed, mirrored, discussed, thematized in the text, as we shall see. There is cerebration, knowingness at every turn, then; but it does not seem to clarify or explain, still less control, events. There is only a hall of mirrors before us — and, insofar as we are prepared to enter the text — all around us.

How do we find our point of entry into the text? There are a few pages of exposition before all four characters come together, before the E-C-H-O constellation comes into being. Once we have negotiated that conjectural, opening sentence, we seem to be on relatively safe ground. We might even be in the world of Jane Austen novel as husband and wife move around their property. Discussion initially centers on the estate, but then turns to the possibility of inviting the Hauptmann to join them. Charlotte is unwilling to change the balance of their lives. But Eduard presses the case, arguing that both of them are mature, self-aware people, and that, by that token, they are equal to handling the changes in emotional temperature and chemistry that might ensue. But his wife responds: "das Bewußtsein, mein Liebster, ist keine hinlängliche Waffe, ja manchmal eine gefährliche für den, der sie führt" (248; Consciousness, my dearest, is no adequate weapon — indeed sometimes a dangerous one for the one who wields it). This is one of those moments where, by implication, the theme and manner of the novel interlock. As events will show, consciousness is not proof against emotional turmoil. Moreover, we the readers will find that we are reading a highly self-conscious novel, that, on frequent occasions, we are aware of our own role as interpreters, as decoders of the signs and portents and parallels with which the novel is so liberally endowed. But we too find it difficult to achieve clarity and stability of understanding; our attempts at second-guessing the text are strangely inconclusive. In a sense, we might say that *Die Wahlverwandtschaften* means too much for its own — and for our — good.

The Hauptmann is invited to join Eduard and Ottilie; and it is the resulting threesome that one evening discusses the notion of "Wahlverwandtschaften" (elective affinities), processes of bonding and re-bonding in chemistry. At issue is the possibility that a particular compound can be fractured by the appearance of a third substance which then bonds with one of the previously conjoined substances — almost as though some kind of choice were being exercised. At one level, the discussion amongst the three friends genuinely does concern recently discovered chemical processes.[3] At another level, the characters ceaselessly make metaphorical links between the behavior of chemical substances on the one hand and the chemistry of human attraction on the other. And, as soon as one formulates the matter in this way, in terms of "human chemistry," one asks oneself whether this, too, is a literal or metaphorical statement. Are men and women subject to the laws of material reality in the same way as the chemical substances are? If so, what is the force of "Sitten und Gesetze" (272; customs and laws) in the human sphere? Are they merely more complex forms of material processes, or do they truly bespeak a dimension of experience in which men and women have at least a measure of cognitive and ethical autonomy? Throughout their discussion, the characters traverse the metaphorical minefield of their topic. Charlotte at one point likens the chemical substances not just to "Blutsverwandte" (blood relatives) but to "Geistes- und Seelenverwandte" (273; relatives in mind and soul); but then she also insists on the all-important differences between a chemical experiment on the one hand and the complex choices of human behavior on the other:

> Diese Gleichnisreden sind artig und unterhaltend, und wer spielt nicht gern mit Ähnlichkeiten! Aber der Mensch ist doch um so manche Stufe über jene Elemente erhöht, und wenn er hier mit den schönen Worten Wahl und Wahlverwandtschaft etwas freigiebig gewesen, so tut er wohl, wieder in sich selbst zurückzukehren und den Wert solcher Ausdrücke bei diesem Anlaß recht zu bedenken. (275)

> [These discussions of likeness are charming and entertaining, and who does not delight in playing with similarities? But human beings are, after all, located several rungs higher than those elements; and if they have here been a shade casual in their use of the beautiful words choice and kindred by choice, they would be well advised to examine their own conscience and to consider, in this context, the value of such terms.]

Here we touch the central issue. Charlotte warns against thoughtlessly playing with analogies: crucially, human beings are creatures who discriminate, who reflect (bedenken), who make and act upon distinctions. Yet she herself has warned against placing great trust in the human capacity for reflectivity and self-consciousness. Thinking, it would appear, merely compounds the complexity. The rest of the novel offers a dialectically open view of the presence and absence of cognitive autonomy in human affairs.

Ottilie enters the novel, and the seemingly ineluctable agency of human attraction takes hold: it works not just through material agencies but also through mental processes. In the extraordinary scene of spiritual adultery, where husband and wife, Eduard and Charlotte, have intercourse but are spiritually unfaithful to each other, Goethe explores the complex role of mental processes, of images and fantasies in human eroticism. The remarkable scene invokes the notion of "rights" — conjugal rights, the rights of bodily immediacy, the rights of moral and institutional commitments; but it also acknowledges the power of image-making in human desire:

> Eduard war so liebenswürdig, so freundlich, so dringend; er bat sie, bei ihr bleiben zu dürfen, er forderte nicht, bald ernst bald scherzhaft suchte er sie zu bereden, er dachte nicht daran, daß er Rechte habe und löschte zuletzt mutwillig die Kerze aus.
>
> In der Lampendämmerung behauptete die innere Neigung, behauptete die Einbildungskraft ihre Rechte über das Wirkliche. Eduard hielt nur Ottilien in seinen Armen, Charlotten schwebte der Hauptmann näher oder ferner vor der Seele, und so verwebten, wundersam genug, sich Abwesendes und Gegenwärtiges reizend und wonnevoll durcheinander. Und doch läßt sich die Gegenwart ihr ungeheures Recht nicht rauben. Sie brachten einen Teil der Nacht unter allerlei Gesprächen und Scherzen zu, die um desto freier waren als das Herz leider keinen Teil daran nahm. Aber als Eduard des andern Morgens an dem Busen seiner Frau erwachte, schien ihm der Tag ahnungsvoll hereinzublicken, die Sonne schien ihm ein Verbrechen zu beleuchten; er schlich sich leise von ihrer Seite, und sie fand sich, seltsam genug, allein, als sie erwachte. (321)

> [Eduard was so charming, so friendly, so insistent; he pleaded to be allowed to stay with her, he did not demand, now seriously, now jestingly he sought to persuade her, he never thought to invoke his rights and finally, exuberantly, he extinguished the candle.
>
> In the half light of the lamp, inner inclination, the imagination asserted its rights over the real. Eduard held only Ottilie in his arms, Charlotte saw, sometimes closer, sometimes more distant, the captain before her mind's eye, and so it was that, magically enough, absent and present entities mingled charmingly and blissfully. And yet the present will not allow its immense rights to be usurped. They spent part of the night with all kinds of talk and joking, which were the freer because their hearts were not involved. But when Eduard awoke on his wife's breast the following morning, it seemed to him that the morning was looking in ominously, the sun seemed to him to be illuminating a crime; he crept quietly away from her side, and, strangely enough, she found herself alone when she awoke.]

Consciousness would seem to make possible both human choice and also human craving and fantasizing. Late in the novel, after the death of the child, Ottilie decides to go no further in the relationship with Eduard. In her diary we see her struggling to find her own understanding of herself, of her place in the world. When she decides to assert herself, she repeats the phrase "Ich bin aus meiner Bahn geschritten" (462, 476; I have strayed from my path). It is her one great moment of reflectivity and self-analysis in the novel; it is also a supreme moment of moral choice and self-assertion.

Yet it is also accompanied by the relentless process of starving herself to death. We find ourselves caught between two understandings of her behavior at this juncture — and, by extension, between two views of human affairs. On the one hand, we have the clear sense that human self-consciousness enables the workings of free will and moral choice; and on the other, that human self-consciousness can be largely, if not entirely, controlled by compulsive behavior, by self-loathing and, in this particular case, by something very close to anorexia.

Die Wahlverwandtschaften is, then, a novel that generates questions rather than answers. The role of the novel's title speaks volumes: there is no other novel text in European literature whose title is so thoroughly discussed within the novel itself. Yet precisely that climate of intense discussion and reflectivity produces density — rather than clarity — of statement. In other words, the notion of "elective affinities" is not the interpretative key to the text; rather, it is its theme. At the end of the novel, the narrator describes how Eduard and Ottilie lie next to one another in the chapel; and we read:

> heitere, verwandte Engelsbilder schauen vom Gewölbe auf sie herab, und welch ein freundlicher Augenblick wird es sein, wenn sie dereinst wieder zusammen erwachen. (490)

> [Serene, kindred images of angels look down upon them from the vault and what a friendly moment will it be when they in some future life awake together.]

For the last time, a key term from the novel's title — "verwandt" — is sounded. We find ourselves asking in what sense the lovers are "related" to the angels. Perhaps we might hazard the suggestion that their love was one molded by a mysterious, even numinous, destiny, that there is something transcendental, sacred even, about them? But we can also take a much more reductive view and recall that the young architect who restored the chapel fell in love with Ottilie, and, hence, the angels all bear her features and are pictorially "verwandt." Even aesthetic creativity in the service of religious belief is not, it seems, proof against the inroads of human desire.

When Charlotte resists the applicability of "elective affinities" to human affairs, she urges that "der Mensch" — "mankind" — should think carefully (recht [. . .] bedenken) what the implications of such an analogy are. The novel itself makes such "carefully thinking" readers of us all; but without allowing us to reach certain and, by that token, reassuring conclusions. The narrative voice is, for example, an infuriatingly oblique presence: at times, it is probing and perceptive in the evaluative and interpretative comments made; at other points it is tantalizingly reticent and unhelpful. In consequence, we feel ourselves urged to interpret, but are very much left to our own devices. As a novel of passion, *Die Wahlverwandtschaften* may not be the most exciting read in world literature. But we know of no other narrative text that is profounder in its ability to generate questions about the cognitive implications of human desire — or profounder in its ability to engage us as novel readers in that density of textual implication which is the correlative of the novel's theme.

Thus far we have been highlighting the philosophical implications of *Die Wahlverwandtschaften,* treating the text as some kind of experimental model of the philosophical workings of human desire. But the characters involved in this experiment cannot, in the last analysis, abstract themselves — or be abstracted by us as readers — from the particular historical and social context of their lives. And, viewed under this aspect, the experiment emerges as the expression of lives that are curiously aimless, bereft of any truly engaging social activity. The opening to the novel suggests that there is something fussy and ultimately sterile about Eduard and Charlotte's way of life. As members of the minor aristocracy, they aspire to be architects of the world around them, but their attempts at finding renewal in their listless domain are doomed. This extends even to the figures who come from a different (bourgeois) social world and are in quest of a fuller life: the Hauptmann, and, most particularly, Ottilie. There is a considerable darkness to the novel as the agency of death lurks everywhere. The significations of both the religious and the aristocratic universe atrophy at every turn. Nature at times assumes a vengeful aspect and resists the manipulations of man and woman. The energy driving the plot forward seems to be some kind of malignant fatality that carries everything and everybody before it and decrees the doom of a whole way of life, a doom that in one way or another affects all those who are, or become, part of its ambience. The philosophical profundity of the novel interlocks with its somber social diagnosis: those who experiment with life rather than living it may uncover all manner of mysteries in the domain of human cognition; but those mysteries, once unleashed, can take a terrible toll of lives bereft of any fulfilling activity.

The conjoining of philosophical and historical issues is also characteristic of the great narrative project which occupied Goethe throughout his life — the sequence of novels centered on the figure of Wilhelm Meister, to which we now turn. The first novel of that sequence, *Wilhelm Meisters theatralische Sendung* (Wilhelm Meister's Theatrical Mission,[4] written between 1777 and 1785) is, for most readers, the most engaging. It is a splendid novel of adolescence and concerns a young man who seeks fame and fortune in the theatre. There is much social and psychological realism in the ironic narrative mode which acknowledges both the idealism and the immaturity of the eager young man, both the excitement and the tawdriness of the theatre. Goethe never published the novel. Rather, he left it as a fragment, and then returned to it, deriving from it the first five books of *Wilhelm Meisters Lehrjahre* (Wilhelm Meister's Apprenticeship, 1796). We shall say more about the whole theme of the theatre under the heading of the later novel. But we wish to stress here several achievements of the earlier version. Predominantly, they have to do with its realistic energy. The novel opens with a cameo portrait of the frustrations and tensions within the bourgeois family. It is largely because of the desire to escape these constrictions that Wilhelm turns to the theatre. In the *Lehrjahre* this opening phase of socio-psychological portrayal is cut altogether, and as a result the novel is robbed of much of its social specificity:

> Es war einige Tage vor dem Christabend 174– als Benedikt Meister Bürger und Handelsmann zu M—, einer mittleren Reichsstadt, aus seinem gewöhnlichen Kränzgen Abends gegen acht nach Hause ging. Es hatte sich wider die Gewohnheit die Tarock Partie früher geendigt, und es war ihm nicht ganz gelegen, daß er so zeitlich in seine vier Wände zurückkehren sollte, die ihm seine Frau eben nicht zum Paradies machte. Es war noch Zeit bis zum Nachtessen, und so einen Zwischenraum pflegte sie ihm nicht mit Annehmlichkeiten auszufüllen, deswegen er lieber nicht ehe zu Tische kam als wenn die Suppe schon etwas überkocht hatte. (MA 2.2, 9, and HA 8, 487)

> [It was a few days before Christmas 174– when Benedikt Meister, citizen and merchant of M—, a medium-sized free city, returned home towards eight in the evening from his usual convivial circle. Contrary to custom, the game of tarock had ended earlier, but it did not really suit him to return to his four walls, which his wife did not exactly transform into paradise. There was still time before supper; and she was not in the habit of filling such hours with pleasure — and for this reason he did not like to get home before the soup had already slightly boiled over.]

It is a splendid opening — vivid and immediate. One notes the rueful, vernacular irony of "eben nicht zum Paradies" and "nicht mit Annehmlichkeiten." Hence, the father will do anything to avoid arriving home early (the "es war ihm nicht ganz gelegen" is a delightful touch of wry understatement). From all this one senses vividly how and why Wilhelm, as a young person starved of affection and good humor at home, will set his heart on a career in the theatre.

We have already noted that this opening section is completely excised from the *Lehrjahre*. And even where the passages are retained, sometimes they are just slightly diminished in stylistic force. Take the following example, which reports children's delight in the pleasures of things illicit and forbidden. We give below the text of the *Theatralische Sendung;* the interpolated brackets contain the changes that are made to the passage in the *Lehrjahre:*

> Die Kinder haben in einem wohleingerichteten und geordneten Hause [in wohleingerichteten und geordneten Häusern] eine Empfindung wie ungefähr Ratten und Mäuse haben mögen, [;] sie sind aufmerksam auf alle Ritze und Löcher, wo sie zu einem verbotenen Naschwerke [Naschwerk] gelangen können; sie genießen's mit einer verstohlenen wollüstigen Furcht, und ich glaube, daß dieses ein großer Teil des kindischen Glücks ist. [genießen es mit einer solchen verstohlenen wollüstigen Furcht, die einen großen Teil des kindischen Glücks ausmachen]. (MA 2.2, 16)

> [Children have, in a well-appointed and orderly house [in well-appointed and orderly houses], the kind of feeling which rats and mice probably have, [:]they keep their eyes open for any gaps and holes where they can have access to a forbidden delicacy, they enjoy it with a secret voluptuous terror, and I think this is a major part of childhood joy [enjoy it with that kind of secret and voluptuous terror which constitutes a major part of childhood joy].]

The later text does, admittedly, retain a good deal of the vivacity of the original. But it is more intent on moving into a generalizing mode (even though, in the *Lehrjahre,* the glimpse of Wilhelm's childhood comes from Wilhelm himself as he recounts the story of his early years to the beloved, but sleeping, Marianne). Indeed, it is central to the purpose of the later novel that Wilhelm's experience becomes socio-culturally representative as the expression of the quest of the bourgeois self for a role within a society that is still dominated by aristocratic culture. To this representative end some of the immediacy of the *Theatralische Sendung* is sacrificed.

The novel of Wilhelm's theatrical aspirations dominates the first five books of the *Lehrjahre,* as we have noted. What then follows is an interpolated manuscript, the "Bekenntnisse einer schönen Seele" (Confessions of a Beautiful Soul), in which a woman gives her account of how she came to find fulfillment in a religious calling. In the final two books of the novel Wilhelm becomes more and more associated with the so-called "Turmgesellschaft" (Society of the Tower), a progressive secret society made up of both aristocratic and bourgeois members who seek to further a variety of social projects, reconciling the particularity of the individual's gifts and temperament with the sustaining wholeness of the Society as a broad community. Moreover, the ethos of the "Turmgesellschaft" seeks to acknowledge both the virtues of the aristocratic appreciation of style and aesthetic semblance and the bourgeois belief in hard work and practical achievement. The sequence of events which, it has to be admitted, is not the most arresting aspect of the novel, is a strange mixture of the episodic and the providential. Natalie, to whom Wilhelm becomes betrothed at the end of the novel, is a shadowy figure. She is associated with images that mean a great deal to him — with his grandfather's art collection, with a compassionate figure who is represented in the picture of the ailing son of the king, and with the so-called "beautiful Amazon," who helps Wilhelm and the theatrical troupe after they have been attacked by robbers in Book 4. This benign agency seems to be watching over Wilhelm. But the benignity also has its ruthless side. Wilhelm becomes deeply attached to two figures: Mignon the waif, and the Harper (as it turns out, he is her father, but the union from which Mignon comes is incestuous). They are touching, forlorn creatures; the words they speak and the songs they sing all express homelessness and longing. They embody the possibility that pathology and disarray can have an immense poetic appeal; but both figures are written out of the novel at the end. In the "Saal der Vergangenheit" (hall of the past) where Mignon's funeral takes place, the key motto is "Gedenke zu leben" (HA 7, 540; be mindful to live) — an inversion of the traditional injunction to be mindful of death. But neither Mignon nor the Harper can be mindful to live or can further life in others. The poetry of their being is inseparable from their doomed condition. And the whole thrust of the plot, while its episodic profusion does not allow Wilhelm himself to have much sense of being master of his own destiny, yet conspires to protect and fulfil him, to fit him for life. His apprenticeship years may feel eventful; but in the last analysis they are sheltered, and Mignon and the Harper have to be edited out.

The first five books constituting the so-called *Theaterroman* show Wilhelm extending his personality in a great number of ways. Most obviously, the enrichment is social; he leads a bohemian life and comes into contact with many people whom polite society tends to shun. (This is particularly true of his sexual experience: it is noteworthy how often forms of androgynous encounter cross his path.) He also extends himself imaginatively by playing out various roles, by learning to explore possibilities within himself that might otherwise go unacknowledged. Moreover, the theatre is part of the whole conceptual texture of the novel because it obliges Wilhelm to reflect on the relationship between idea and reality, between reflecting and doing. All these issues culminate in Wilhelm's involvement with Shakespeare's *Hamlet,* a play with which he becomes obsessed. At the end of the *Theaterroman* Wilhelm is enriched and more mature than he was. And yet he drifts away from the theatre; there is no spectacular repudiation. It is simply that he has outgrown a necessary but circumscribed phase of his life.

The "Bekenntnisse einer schönen Seele" that follow introduce Wilhelm to a life of concentrated inwardness. Not that this is asserted as an unequivocal value; but it propels Wilhelm toward that greater concern for ideas and ideals that will characterize his dealings with the "Turmgesell-schaft." Yet curiously, even in that final phase of the novel, Wilhelm's development is tentative rather than forthright. He is admitted to the membership of the Society of the Tower, he is allowed to browse in the archive in which the various stories of the development and growth processes of individual members of the Society are stored. Yet he feels none the wiser. At times he can even be irritated by the Society's fondness for maxims and pithy sayings. A mere three pages from the end of the novel he laments his lack of any sense of clarity and wisdom. That everything culminates in a happy ending has more to do with good fortune than with any sureness of understanding on Wilhelm's part.

Given the fact that our hero has difficulty in making sense of his own experiences, it is understandable if we, too, as readers are left perplexed. But at least certain aspects of cultural and philosophical context can give us a measure of comprehension. In an all-important discussion with his bourgeois friend Werner, Wilhelm explains some of the socio-psychological parameters of his experience, and in the process he makes an all-important distinction between the "Bürger" and the "Edelmann":

> Wenn der Edelmann durch die Darstellung seiner Person alles gibt, so gibt der Bürger durch seine Persönlichkeit nichts und soll nichts geben. Jener darf und soll scheinen; dieser soll nur sein, und was er scheinen will, ist lächerlich oder abgeschmackt. Jener soll tun und wirken, dieser soll leisten und schaffen; er soll einzelne Fähigkeiten ausbilden, um brauchbar zu werden, und es wird schon voraus-gesetzt, daß in seinem Wesen keine Harmonie sei noch sein dürfe, weil er, um sich auf *eine* Weise brauchbar zu machen, alles übrige vernachlässigen muß. (HA 7, 291)

> [If the nobleman through the deployment of his person says every-thing, the bourgeois says nothing through his personality — and is meant to say nothing. The former may and should be seen; but the latter is supposed only to be, and what he wants to be seen to be is risible and tasteless. The former should undertake certain activities and should achieve an effect. The latter should work hard and pro-duce something. He should develop individual capacities in order to be a useful member of society, and it is not generally assumed that there is — nor should there be — any harmony in his being because he, in order to be usable in one particular way, has to neglect all the other possibilities.]

Wilhelm is, as it were, in quest of a bourgeois role for himself, but does not quite know where to find it. Precisely because of his uncertainty, his life expresses many forms of bourgeois culture — and they are cen-trally part of the historicity of the *Lehrjahre*. The second half of the eighteenth century in Germany was an age passionately concerned with the need to found a national theatre; and the discovery of Shakespeare was a powerful force in the energizing of cultural debate at the time. Moreover, Pietism particularly provided a discourse of intense inwardness, both religious and psychological. This element of personal self-scrutiny and self-expression contributed to a culture in which diaries, letters, memoirs were particularly in favor. The secret society was an institution that was germane to both social and cultural life in Goethe's Germany; one thinks, for example, of the various sub-groupings within late eighteenth-century society: the Freemasons, the Illuminati, the many orders and brotherhoods, both progressive and sinister. (One needs only to contrast Mozart's *The Magic Flute* (1791) on the one hand with the novels of the Marquis de Sade on the other to sense the full spectrum of the issues involved: secrecy could be the emblem of humane initiatives but also of exultant perversity.) The point we are after is a simple one, but it is easily overlooked: Goethe's *Wilhelm Meisters Lehrjahre* embodies and takes issue with late-eighteenth-century social and cultural life in ways and to an extent that are not self-evident to novel readers nowadays.

Moreover — and this is the final point that concerns us — *Wilhelm Meisters Lehrjahre* is an absolutely central text in the evolution of the modern German novel, not least because for many practitioners of and commentators on the novel it acquired the status of a canonical Bildungsroman. This genre has often been claimed to be the chief German contribution to the European novel. At one level it is a narrative that is close to the concerns of European realism, addressing as it does the psychological and social rites of passage of an adolescent as he (and most usually it is a "he") makes his way through the adult social world, seeking to find a place for himself. What, however, is particular about the German Bildungsroman is that the issues are framed less in terms of practicality than with a view to a philosophically differentiated definition and exploration of the interplay of self and world. In the *Lehrjahre,* Wilhelm's sense of his own path through experience is of an urgently individuated process: "mich selbst, ganz wie ich da bin, auszubilden, das war dunkel von Jugend auf mein Wunsch und meine Absicht" (290; to develop myself, just as I am, has always been, albeit obscurely, from my youth my goal). Within this self-definition Goethe's novel is remarkable in its scrupulous understanding of the complex and largely diffuse processes of individual development and growth. What Wilhelm himself does not understand is comprehended by the novel itself: namely that he partakes of a certain general, and by that token exemplary, stature. At one level he stands for the particular endowment of the human species, for adolescent humankind and the growth processes through which it necessarily passes on its way to adulthood. And at another level, Wilhelm is representative of his culture, of the quest of the bourgeois subject to make its way in the post-aristocratic social world. Wilhelm may, in a number of ways, be unremarkable. But it is that ordinariness that makes him, and the novel in which he figures, deeply representative of late eighteenth century bourgeois culture in Germany. The tentativeness is part of the novel's truth. The project of human perfectibility is, admittedly, in evidence; but it depends for its realization in the context of an individual life on a whole range of psychological, social, and existential factors. And, above all else it depends on good fortune rather than rational, goal-directed thinking.

Wilhelm Meisters Wanderjahre (1821 and 1829) is, as its title implies, a kind of continuation of the earlier text. (The governing metaphor is, of course, that of the guild structure of professional training which decreed the sequence of apprentice, journeyman, and master.) The notion of journeying is omnipresent in the *Wanderjahre*. Wilhelm, now married to Natalie, has agreed to the injunction of the "Turmgesellschaft" to stay no more than three days under one roof. Hence, the whole ethos of the novel is not one of possession, stability and certainty, but rather of movement, change, pluralism. And the novel sustains this ethos not only thematically but also formally by moving back and forth between various discursive and narrative worlds. We have short tales or *Novellen,* we have letters, papers of various kinds, maxims. And there is no clear principle of superordination or subordination. There are three story lines that tend to re-appear in the novel and are, by that token, more constitutive of the total narrative work than are the self-contained tales. We have the evolving relationship between Wilhelm and his son Felix, a relationship that culminates in a scene where Wilhelm, having learnt the skills of a "Wundarzt" (surgeon), is able to save his son from the consequences of an accident. We have the unfolding love between Felix and Hersilie; and there is another love story involving Leonardo and Nachodine. But, apart from occasional moments, none of this is handled with any particular urgency or intensity. Indeed, in one sense *Wilhelm Meisters Wanderjahre* is largely uninterested in storytelling as an absorbing process of sustained chronological and psychological interest. Characters come into and go out of focus for no particular reason. They tend to appear and disappear. Sometimes they are key agents in a story, sometimes they are peripheral figures in somebody else's story, sometimes they are narrators. There is, then, in the *Wanderjahre* a profusion of narrative processes in evidence; but not much story telling that generates substantial characters or substantial events. For this reason the exceptions to the rule are particularly noteworthy. The tale "Der Mann von fünfzig Jahren" (The Man of Fifty Years) has powerful moments of experiential authority: in particular, it explores the theme of aging, and the attempt to hide aging by the use of make-up. There is also the account Wilhelm sends to Nathalie of one of his earliest and profoundest boyhood experiences. He recalls how he went swimming with a boy of his own age, the son of a fisherman. The sexual charge is unmistakable, and expresses itself powerfully in the moments of shared nakedness:

> Als er sich heraushob, sich aufrichtete, im höheren Sonnenschein sich abzutrocknen, glaubt' ich meine Augen von einer dreifachen Sonne geblendet: so schön war die menschliche Gestalt, von der ich nie einen Begriff gehabt. (HA 8, 272)

> [When he worked himself free and sat up in order to dry himself in the high sunlight, I believed that my eyes had been dazzled by a triple sun — so beautiful was this human form of which I had previously had no inkling.]

The erotic intensity is unchecked by their subsequent clothed condition:

> Schnell angekleidet standen wir uns noch immer unverhüllt gegeneinander, unsere Gemüter zogen sich an, und unter den feurigsten Küssen schwuren wir eine ewige Freundschaft. (272)

> [having quickly slipped into our clothes, we yet still stood unconcealed before each other. Our temperaments drew us together — and amidst the fieriest of kisses we swore eternal friendship to each other.]

The moment of childhood love is, however, short-lived. In an appalling accident, the fisherman's son, who has been fishing for crabs, is drowned, together with four other boys. The bodies are recovered; and one very small boy, who has collected the crabs, brings the precious harvest back to the adults with eerie conscientiousness. Such moments of narrative energy are unforgettable; but they are, it has to be said, very rare. They serve primarily to remind us of a traditional narrative universe that we seem to have left far behind us. For the most part, the *Wanderjahre* is sustained by narrative pluralism, by ongoing narrativity with little or no human substance being acknowledged along the way. We seem to be, in many ways, close to Flaubert's notion of the "livre sur rien." We have an editor figure. Yet his function is not (as in, say, *Werther*) to authenticate the text we are reading, to intensify the suggestion that we are concerned not with invented but with genuine material. Rather, the editor confirms the fundamentally textual nature of the universe in which we find ourselves. In consequence, we are asked not to surrender to the mimetic power of fictions, but to read and re-read as active participants, as co-makers of the archive which we have entered. In a sense the *Wanderjahre* believes in the human community as an aggregation of stories, of attempts to convert experience into discursivity of various kinds. And the novel ends "Ist fortzusetzen" (MA 17, 714) — "to be continued." It is worth reflecting on

this phrase. It is familiar to us as the "to be continued" of serial publication. But the normal form in German is "Fortsetzung folgt." This implies
that there is a finite continuation, and, by implication, a final explanation
and closure of the story we are reading. In other words, the standard formula addresses traditional notions of excitement, involvement in the
story, a desire to know how everything works out in the end. But the
Wanderjahre is situated in a different textual universe, one in which narrativity, discursivity is a ceaseless process, one sustained without any foreclo-
sure in prospect.

There is, then, no master narrative in the *Wanderjahre,* to which all
the component parts are subservient. There is only a pluralism of texts.
And even those which look conceptually authoritative — like, for example, the maxims — merely thematize the question whether, in a universe
of texts, there can be any privileged, meta-textual realm, one that stands
outside and stabilizes the textual profusion. The answer is "no." Maxims
are as much texts as any others. All of which brings the *Wanderjahre* close
to a post-modern universe of pan-textuality. Yet one hesitates quite to
make that claim, not least because there are tendencies in the novel which
resolutely pull in the opposite direction. The *Wanderjahre* is a text that is
strenuously, even didactically, concerned to understand and to evaluate
the modern condition; issues such as overpopulation and migration (a
socio-economic inflection of the old motif of "Wandern") are discussed,
as are the relative merits of old and new forms of economic activity (much
concern is, for example, expressed about the position of handicrafts such
as spinning and weaving, which are threatened by the advent of new
technology). The various virtues and drawbacks of the Old and New
Worlds, of Europe and America, are extensively debated. There is a measure of historically diagnostic energy to these concerns; the theatre, we recall, has resolutely been rejected in favor of an ethos of hard work and
deference (these values are central to the "Pädagogische Provinz"). Precisely that didactic thrust is responsible for the half-heartedness of much
of the narration which condemns passion as an aberration. (The two exceptions which we have mentioned are remarkable precisely for acknowledging the truth of intense feeling.) There is, then, a didactic project at
the heart of the *Wanderjahre,* yet it constitutes only one strand within
the novel fiction. The other strand is one of high, almost playful, self-
consciousness and generates a genially ludic quality. At one level, as is implied by the novel's subtitle "Oder die Entsagenden" (or the Renun-
ciants), every effort is made to affirm the values of restrained and
conditioned living; at another, self-limitation is overtaken by the belief in
forms of ironic self-transcendence. The upshot is a novel that stylistically
and thematically falls between two stools, and in the process forfeits any
sense of real narrative animation.

This may seem harsh as a judgment. And we want, in conclusion, to moderate that harshness by suggesting that, if we take the *Wanderjahre* not so much as a novel text in its own right but as part of the larger *Wilhelm Meister* project, then it acquires both cogency and interest. Let us recall a point that we made earlier: from the closing decades of the eighteenth century, there is in Germany, with the work of Friedrich Schlegel and Hegel, a remarkably precocious flowering of sophisticated novel theory. Common to both their theoretical concerns is the need to explore and explicate the essential ambivalence of the modern novel as a genre. For Schlegel, the novel mediates between the prosaic imperative to chronicle events and circumstances on the one hand and the achievement of high, self-reflexive, almost encyclopedic spirituality on the other. Hegel, too, is exercised by the interrelationship of prose and poetry, be-tween the unyielding force of bourgeois circumstances on the one hand and the poetry of the young person's aspirations to make a better world on the other:

> Diese Kämpfe nun aber sind in der modernen Welt nichts weiteres als die Lehrjahre, die Erziehung des Individuums an der vorhanden-en Wirklichkeit, und erhalten dadurch ihren wahren Sinn. Denn das Ende solcher Lehrjahre besteht darin, daß sich das Subjekt die Hörner abläuft [. . .].
> [. . .] Der Roman im modernen Sinne setzt eine bereits zur *Prosa* geordnete Wirklichkeit voraus, auf deren Boden er sodann in seinem Kreise — sowohl in Rücksicht auf die Lebendigkeit der Begebnisse als auch in betreff der Individuen und ihres Schicksals — der Poesie, soweit es bei dieser Voraussetzung möglich ist, ihr verlorenes Recht wieder erringt.[5]

> [Now these struggles are, in the modern world, nothing but the ap-prenticeship, the education of the individual at the hands of existing reality, and they acquire their true meaning through this process — because the end of such an apprenticeship is that the subject gets licked into shape. [. . .]
> [. . .] The novel in its modern sense presupposes a reality that is al-ready configured as *prosaic,* on whose foundations it then, within its experiential realm — in respect of both the liveliness of the events and of the individuals and their destiny — endeavors to re-conquer the lost rights of poetry, insofar as this is, given the context, at all possible.]

This is a remarkable commentary, embracing as it does both the theme and the mode of the modern novel. Fascinatingly, for both Schlegel and Hegel the key novel text was Goethe's *Wilhelm Meisters Lehrjahre.* We, however, have the advantage of both of them because we can survey the whole *Wilhelm Meister* project, from the *Theatralische Sendung* to the *Wanderjahre*. And when we take stock of that project, we are struck by the fact that Goethe has, in exemplary form, produced a narrative trilogy that summarizes the possible modes of the modern novel: from the socio-psychological realism of the *Sendung* on the one hand to the self-reflexive ironies of the *Wanderjahre* on the other. Hegel and Schlegel both manifestly sensed the extent to which Goethe was able in his fiction to acknowledge both the materiality and the mentality of the modern world; the novelist was, as it were, both story-teller and philosopher. Similar claims have been advanced for Goethe's narrative achievement by such key twentieth-century theoreticians of the modern novel as Bakhtin and Lukács. Perhaps this fact can help us to gauge the scale of Goethe's achievement as a writer of prose fiction. In the constant reworking process of the *Meister* project he found generic expression for the various forms of modern narrative subjectivity. The rewriting process itself, the sense of a shifting dynamic of signification was utterly central to his diagnosis of the modern. Goethe's *Meister* project is a key witness to the rise of the modern novel — not least because it has its own novel theory built into it, thanks to its consistently self-thematizing narrative mode. Moreover, as we have sought to show, Goethe produced three undoubted masterpieces — *Werther, Die Wahlverwandtschaften,* and *Novelle,* masterpieces that are not simply erratic individual achievements, but also have a certain generic stature. *Werther* is one of the supreme epistolary novels of European literature, *Die Wahlverwandtschaften* is a key text in the company of nineteenth-century novels concerned with adultery, and the *Novelle,* if only by virtue of its title, lays claim to being generically exemplary. The confluence in Goethe's creativity of a life-long interest in narrativity on the one hand, and on the other, with a readiness to experiment with the emergent generic possibilities of modern prose fiction is a signal achievement. Goethe is not widely acknowledged as one of the canonical — that is, indispensable — makers of modern fiction. It is time he was, because, like so few other great writers, his narrative practice also is his narrative theory.

4: Drama

COMPARED WITH HIS great contemporaries Schiller and Kleist, Goethe does not strike one as a born dramatist. That is to say: he does not resolutely seek to define worldly experience in terms of endlessly proliferating moments of conflict. Indeed, many commentators have suggested that his was a primarily lyrical talent, one that found its finest expressivity in eavesdropping on the flux of mood and thought that constitutes the inwardness of the individual self.[1] In this sense, there is something monologic about his voice. Yet the range and variety of his achievement in the dramatic mode is impressive. In a revealing remark of March 1775, he commented that he would perish if he did not write plays.[2] Later he became involved in both the institutional and artistic management of the theatre in Weimar. In the original performance of his *Iphigenie auf Tauris* he played the part of Orestes, and in 1827, he described *Torquato Tasso* as bone of his bone and flesh of his flesh.[3] In other words, there can be no doubt that he needed the theatre as an imaginative space in which he could work at the problems that troubled him. And, looking at his dramatic oeuvre as a whole, one can discern certain recurring preoccupations. One is the need to body forth in language and action the dynamic of the human self. His comprehension of that bodying forth is anything but solipsistic; in his dramas he richly and circumstantially depicts the context — historical, political, cultural, personal — within which his protagonist has to live. In that process, Goethe worries at an issue which is, no doubt, at one level a perennial debate within human experience, but which, at another level, is a particularly urgent dilemma raised by modern culture: how to negotiate the clashing imperatives of order, containment, morality on the one hand, and of vitality, energy, freedom on the other. It is admittedly true to say that Goethe's vision is not as uncompromisingly tragic as that of many of his contemporaries, mainly because he saw polarity, the dynamic interaction of opposed principles not as a destructive force, but as the creative heartbeat within human experience. Yet, by definition, that tenet of polarity was also generative of dramatic configurations and confrontations. Moreover Goethe was fond of endowing his central characters with a powerful range of imaginative and imagined energies and of exploring their function within a world of practical imperatives and hard-nosed choices.

Goethe's earliest plays turn on the challenge posed by emotional, usually erotic, energy to the regulatory expectations of the social and moral order. *Die Laune des Verliebten* (1767) is a pastoral play, written when Goethe was a student in Leipzig: Eridon, the male lover, has to learn to be less judgmental in his dealings with the claims of sexual desire generally and, specifically, in his treatment of Amine his beloved. The comedy *Die Mitschuldigen* (1769) is much more probing in its analysis of socio-moral order and of threatening disorientating energies. The play centers on the seemingly secure life of an innkeeper and his family. But patterns of restlessness make themselves felt from the start. The setting, an inn, is a space where security and rest interact with the open roads of adventure; and the action takes place in one turbulent night, the time when the inadmissible erupts. Sophie, the innkeeper's daughter is entrapped in an unhappy marriage to Söller, an obsessive gambler. In the course of one particularly turbulent night, her former admirer Alcest appears and endeavors to re-activate her feelings. The disturbance passes; Sophie heeds the demands of the social and moral code. But the happy ending, like her marriage, is a shade precarious.

The anarchical potential that is the mainspring of *Die Mitschuldigen* comes into its own in the short verse play *Satyros* (1773). The appearance of Satyros as incarnation of primitive energies disturbs the people who wish to maintain their allegiance to the piety and morality of the hermit. Yet finally the lure proves too strong; they turn their back on decency and celebrate their new god — until they see what the principle of raw energy means when acted out in interpersonal terms: Satyros is discovered trying to rape one of the respected women of the community. They are outraged and expel him. But not before a good deal of damage has been done.

At times, Satyros's language is close to some of Goethe's finest lyric poetry — for example when he describes the dynamism of creation:

> Und die Elemente sich erschlossen,
> Mit Hunger ineinander ergossen,
> Alldurchdringend, alldurchdrungen. (HA 4, 301–3)

> [And the elements opened themselves up,
> Poured greedily into each other,
> Driving everywhere, driven everywhere.]

The handling of active and passive participles in the final line recalls the poem "Ganymed." What are we to make of such overlaps? At one level, there is clearly not a little self-ironization at work whereby some of the cherished concerns of Goethe's early work are called into question by being shown to be, as it were, transferable from Satyros to Ganymed and back again. Yet the Satyros figure does also touch on a register of primitivity that was undoubtedly part of Goethe's creative temperament: One thinks of the suppressed sections of the "Walpurgisnacht" in *Faust I*, of the original conception of the *Römische Elegien* with its priapic poems, of the provocative license in respect of sexual attitudes in the "Venezianische Epigramme." Precisely those elements that bid defiance to established definitions of seemliness can be traced again in the two early dramas *Mahomet* (1773) and *Prometheus* (1774), both of which extend the discourse of rebellion to the relationship between the human subject and the divinity.

Within the early dramatic oeuvre, Goethe's most differentiated exploration of the attraction and the weakness of the uncompromisingly self-assertive, titanic subject is *Götz von Berlichingen* (1773). The play is a key document of the Sturm und Drang; in a number of ways. Stylistically it is clearly a product and an expression of the great love affair with Shakespeare which was central to the release of the imagination in eighteenth-century Germany. *Götz* is loosely structured; it is a kind of filmic chronicle play which moves swiftly across a dizzying array of social classes and groups. It is, then, programmatically defiant of French neo-classical aesthetics with their stress on adherence to the three unities. Moreover, it is a play couched in vivid, varied, racy prose. Hence, it is part of a strategy for renewal of the national literature: it replaces the conventions of French neo-classical drama by creating a panorama of early modern German history, and it elevates forms of everyday, even dialect speech, into the vehicle for literary expression. At times, this includes, in Shakespearean fashion, explicit crudity, as, for example, in the famous line: "Er aber, sags ihm, er kann mich im Arsch lecken" (As for him, tell him he can kiss my arse) (which proves still too much for the Hamburger Ausgabe [HA 4, 139]). In thematic terms, too, *Götz* is an all-important document of German literature of the 1770s: it seeks to explore the national past in order to find there the basis for the regeneration of the contemporary world. As we shall see, there are a number of ways in which *Götz* reads late eighteenth-century Germany through early sixteenth-century Germany, and vice versa. Finally, the stress placed in the play on the values of energy and freedom and especially on the figure who lives life to the full, the "Kraftkerl," is typical of the Sturm und Drang.

The play tells of the decline of Götz von Berlichingen, one of the most charismatic of the Imperial Free Knights of the Holy Roman Empire. The events of the drama depict a process which begins by showing us Götz as a splendidly vigorous, assured man. He is utterly secure within his world, and extracts his friend Weislingen from the clutches of the princes and bishops and everything that they stand for. Yet by the end of the play, he is a broken, exhausted, despairing figure who has no fight left in him. It is a curious progression in many ways; somehow it feels as though it must extend over many years, but, in terms of the specifics of the action and plot line, it can only cover a few months. What, then, produces this strangely telescoped downfall of Götz? Not physical suffering, not a moral or spiritual crisis (he is no Schillerian hero in the mould of Karl Moor in *Die Räuber* who comes to understand, and to judge himself for, the error of his ways). Rather, Götz fades away because he and those like him are obsolete, are doomed by the processes of historical change. However much the play upholds the existential splendor of Götz, and however much it grieves over his demise, it also pays full attention to the movements and tendencies in the historical and political world that decree his end.

Herder had drawn Goethe's attention to Justus Möser's essay "Von dem Faustrechte" (1770). It was a discussion of the fourteenth century, of the time when the Holy Roman Empire was dominated by a great number of Imperial Free Knights who, within a structure of largely nominal allegiance, underpinned by direct access to the Emperor, were literally a law unto themselves: they made and put into practice the laws that obtained inside their tiny domains. Goethe sets his drama in a later period — the early sixteenth century — when precisely that way of life was under threat. He does not invent the Götz figure; there was a real-life original, who lived from 1480 to 1562 and who, toward the end of his life, wrote an account of his life and times, paying particular attention to his involvement in the Peasants Revolt that occurred in the immediate aftermath of the Reformation. Goethe transforms the figure; his Götz becomes the representative of the obsolescence of such Free Knights and all they stand for. In Goethe's play, the emperor cannot tolerate the ethos of pluralism and particularism within which Götz, Selbitz, and those like them thrive. He is mindful of the omnipresent threat of Turkish aggression. Hence, he needs to maximize political and military unity and to this end he uses as his agents the princes, bishops, and the nobility who administer much larger territories than do the Free Knights. There is also the attempt to create a new climate of centralist, bureaucratic rule, with which the princes, bishops and nobles are more than happy: it gives them the chance, in the name of serving the needs of the emperor, to crush the obdurate individualism of the Free Knights. *Götz von Berlichingen* may not be the profoundest drama of German literature; but it does express a genuine sense of a particular historical juncture that defines the dramatic action.

How, then, is this historical and political analysis conveyed? At one level it can be heard in scenes of overt discussion and debate such as in act 1 where there is an extended set-piece confrontation between Götz and Weislingen. Götz upholds "den Wert eines freien Rittersmanns, der nur abhängt von Gott, seinem Kaiser und sich selbst" (HA 4, 90; the realm of a free knight who owes allegiance only to God, his Emperor, and himself). Weislingen puts the case for greater administrative unity:

> Wenn nun auf der anderen Seite unseres teuren Kaisers Länder der Gewalt des Erbfeindes ausgesetzt sind, er von den Ständen Hülfe begehrt, und sie sich kaum ihres Lebens erwehren: ist's nicht ein guter Geist, der ihnen einrät, auf Mittel zu denken, Deutschland zu beruhigen, Recht und Gerechtigkeit zu handhaben, um einen jeden, Großen und Kleinen, die Vorteile des Friedens genießen zu machen? (91)

> [If now on the other hand the lands of our dear Emperor are exposed to the tyranny of our traditional foe, and he needs help from the various estates but they can scarcely maintain themselves, is it not then a good spirit that urges them to think of ways and means to calm Germany, to administer right and justice in order to allow everybody, great and small alike, to have the chance of enjoying peace?]

To Götz this whole strategy, conceived to bring greater orderliness and calm into the affairs of the Empire, is anathema because he sees in it nothing but power politics. Moreover, all his instincts rise in revolt against what he perceives as the bureaucratization and administrative abstraction of modern life:

> Nun ergehn Verordnungen über Verordnungen, und wird eine über die andere vergessen; und was den Fürsten in ihren Kram dient, da sind sie hinterher und gloriieren von Ruh und Sicherheit des Reichs, bis sie die Kleinen unterm Fuß haben. Ich will darauf schwören, es dankt mancher in seinem Herzen Gott, daß der Türk dem Kaiser die Waage hält. (91)

> [Now decree upon decree is issued and one by one they are forgotten. And whatever suits the princes, they pursue it and they glory in the peace and security of the Empire — until they have brought everyone to heel. I would swear that many in their hearts thank God that the Turk creates a balance of power with the Emperor.]

Certainly what we see in the very next scene, set in the Bishop's palace at Bamberg, confirms Götz's accusations. We witness frivolity, self-serving machinations of all kinds, and mounds of paper everywhere. Yet, when the bishop speaks of the emperor's wish "das Reich zu beruhigen, die Fehden abzuschaffen, und das Ansehen der Gerichte zu befestigen" (96; to calm the Empire, to put an end to feuding, and to strengthen the reputation of the courts), we do not merely hear the voice of class interest and self-seeking. Equally, the emperor's brief appearance in act 3 makes clear that he feels he has no alternative but to confine Götz, Selbitz and their like to their estates so that they keep the peace; but he also has great affection and respect for them:

Ich möchte die Leute gerne schonen, sie sind tapfer und edel. Wenn
ich Kriege führte, müßten sie mit mir zu Felde. (122–23)

[I would wish to spare these people. They are courageous and noble.
If I were to take up arms, they would have to join me in the field.]

Götz is radically out of sympathy with the modern world; he perceives
everything as part of a conspiracy directed against him and the values by
which he lives. He loathes and distrusts paper. He recalls to Sickingen in
act 3 how he once received instructions on paper as to how he should
conduct himself in a military campaign:

da legt er mir einen Zettel aus der Kanzlei vor, wie ich reiten und
mich halten sollt; da warf ich den Räten das Papier wieder dar und
sagt: ich wüßt nicht darnach zu handeln, ich weiß nicht, was mir
begegnen mag, es steht nicht im Zettel, ich muß die Augen selbst
auftun und sehn, was ich zu schaffen hab. (126)

[Then he puts a piece of paper in front of me which came from the
chancellery saying how I am supposed to ride out and conduct myself. So then I threw the paper back at the counselors and said that I
could not behave accordingly. I cannot know what will come along;
it is not written on a piece of paper. I must keep my eyes open and
see for myself what I have to do.]

The little domain that Götz administers is not run by bureaucratic edict;
on the contrary, everything has the immediacy and intimacy of family life.
Yet, however admirable this ethos is, it can scarcely be extended to the
governance of an empire, particularly in view of the threat of foreign aggression. In that historical context, then, Götz and those like him are
deeply conservative figures. They defend their little, intimate, pre-modern
worlds against what they see as the baleful inroads of alien forces — and
the play makes us understand why. But it also makes us understand the
fact that, and the reasons why, they are doomed. For Götz, the analysis is
entirely simple; he sees decline all around him. The Emperor is "die Seele
eines so krüppligen Körpers" (141; the soul of such a crippled body). At
the end of act 4, Götz links the sickness of the Emperor with his own
dwindling vitality: "Unsere Bahn geht zu Ende" (156; our path is reaching its end). As in his later drama *Egmont,* so here Goethe offers a precise
and critical illumination of the nemesis awaiting those who seek to define
and to defend political roles in terms of personal, largely instinctual values. In the closing scenes of the play, the register of lament becomes ever
stronger. Here, one notes that Götz even loses the undivided simplicity of
his psyche that has been hitherto so much the hallmark of his way of life.
His tendency to reflect on himself seems part of the eroding weakness
that he feels both around him and inside him:

Georg ist tot. — Stirb, Götz — Du hast dich selbst überlebt, die
Edeln überlebt. (175)

[Georg is dead. Die Götz, you have outlived yourself, outlived your
noble company.]

Both the sentiments expressed here and the mode of their expression
presage imminent doom. This is crystallized in the figure of young Georg:
typically, at the start of the play he figures as a youth in a suit of armor
which is too big for him. In the course of the play he does grow into the
warrior's role, but only to die before Götz. In this sense, the closing
scenes turn on the larger historical perspective whereby Götz becomes
obsolete. His one child, Karl, enters a monastery rather than continue in
his father's footsteps. The issue of heirs, of "Nachkommenschaft" dominates the last few speeches of the play, and we shall need to return to it in
due course.

The figure of Karl shows up one of the particular strengths of Goethe's
drama: it comprehends historical change as a complexly varied and omnipresent process. History is at issue not simply at the obvious junctures of
grand historical debate, but also in more understated signs and portents.
We have noted Götz's aversion to the tendency towards bureaucratization
within the Empire. That tendency is present not only in public affairs, but
also in his own family. Karl is, in a way that baffles and saddens his father,
an extraordinarily bookish child. In act 1 the boy recites his lessons to his
father with great pride:

Jaxthausen ist ein Dorf und Schloß an der Jaxt, gehört seit zweihundert
Jahren den Herrn von Berlichingen erb- und eigentümlich an. (88)

[Jaxthausen is a village and a castle on the Jaxt and has belonged for two
hundred years to the masters of Berlichingen as their dynastic property.]

But this form of words strikingly lacks spontaneity of identification. As
Götz ruefully remarks, "Er kennt wohl vor lauter Gelehrsamkeit seinen
Vater nicht" (88; For pure learnedness he does not know his own father). And he recalls that when he, Götz, was at that age he knew all the
rivers and paths on the estate by a process of physical exploration, long
before he knew any of their names. It is a touching little cameo scene between father and son. Götz registers, and is a shade troubled by, the fact
that the boy is going to have a cooked, rather than a raw, apple for pud-
ding. "Schmeckt so besser" (88; tastes better like this), as Karl says.
Clearly his father sees matters differently, and perhaps senses that the implications of the book learning and cooked apples extend well beyond
their immediate context. Weislingen is touched by the boy, and wishes
Götz great joy. And in one of the finest, proverbially tinged, lines of the

play Götz expresses his doubts as to what is to come: "Wo viel Licht ist, ist starker Schatten — [. . .]. Wollen sehen, was es gibt" (88; Where there is much light there is also strong shadow. We shall see what comes about). At the end of the play Elisabeth asks if she should send Lerse to fetch Karl from the convent where he is (presumably both for his safety and his education) accommodated. Götz replies in words which recognize the difference between their generational (and psychological) temperaments: "Laß ihn, er ist heiliger als ich, er braucht meinen Segen nicht" (175; Let him be; he is holier than I am. He does not need my blessing).

A further level of differentiation in respect of the play's historical argument is provided by the complex forms (and thematizations) of the multiple symbolisms that surround Götz's person. The play opens with two peasants at an inn, and they exchange stories of Götz's prowess: "Erzähl das noch einmal vom Berlichingen!" (74; Tell again the story about Berlichingen). The "noch einmal" points up a key theme in the play: that of (political and other) myth-making. Götz is seen by many as the symbol for independence of spirit, naturalness, resistance to the centralizing tendency of the Empire. We hear his symbolic identity being acknowledged in the scene with Bruder Martin, who is in fact the young Martin Luther. When he sees the iron hand, he realizes that he is talking to Götz, and he knows of the accretions of legend that accompany that figure:

> Es war ein Mönch bei uns vor Jahr und Tag, der Euch besuchte, wie sie Euch abgeschossen ward vor Landshut. Wie er uns erzählte, wie Ihr littet und wie sehr es Euch schmerzte, zu Eurem Beruf verstümmelt zu sein, und wie Euch einfiel, von einem gehört zu haben, der auch nur eine Hand hatte und als tapferer Reitersmann doch noch lange diente — ich werde das nie vergessen. (82)

> [There was a monk with us some time ago who had visited you when your hand was shot off near Landshut. As he told it, you suffered a great deal and it hurt you greatly to be mutilated in your work. And then it occurred to you that you had heard of somebody who had only one hand and who still managed to serve long and well as a knight. I will never forget that.]

The repeated "wie" tells us that the story of Götz's wounding has a legendary dimension. Hence Bruder Martin's delight at meeting the great man; hence his injunction to the young Georg — "Folge seinem Beispiel" (82; follow his example) — which applies equally to the image of St. George, which he gives the boy, and to the image of Götz, which he has just helped to nourish by telling again the story of the heroic loss of the hand. At such points, Goethe as dramatist thematizes the notion of political charisma. It prefigures the term, which is now in common parlance, as defined by Max Weber: for purposes of political analysis, in particular of legitimation of authority in modern society, he contrasts the term which derives from a theological context and denotes a sign of grace, with legal and bureaucratic forms. Something of that contrast can be heard in Goethe's play. In this context, we should recall the full title of the play: *Götz von Berlichingen mit der eisernen Hand: ein Schauspiel* (Götz von Berlichingen with the Iron Hand: A Play). In other words, the play incorporates the central symbol into its title. And that symbol, as we shall see, is a strangely volatile thing in the range of meanings which it can generate.[4] The human hand is heavily invested with symbolic meaning in a whole variety of contexts: it is a greeting, a symbol of faith, of contracts, of one's own particular identity, of the interplay between self and world, of mediating activity, and so on. Yet in Götz's case the symbol is rendered problematic because the physical particularity on which it rests is a mutilation of the integrity of the body. It is also, of course, a symbol of the ability of a heroic personality to overcome the mutilation. It is, then, a noble scar, an honorable wound. But it is also an inert thing, a denial of warmth and physicality. It is also a redoubtable weapon. And, for Bruder Martin who will kiss it, it is "mehr wert als Reliquienhand, durch die das heiligste Blut geflossen ist, totes Werkzeug, belebt durch des edelsten Geistes Vertrauen auf Gott" (81; worth more than the hand of some saintly relic through which the most sacred blood has flowed; a dead thing brought alive by the most noble spirit's trust in God). The iron hand, then, is a symbol of Götz's public role. And in its very ambivalence it captures much of his political significance in the play. It stands for his way of life, sustained as it is by "Faustrecht," as upheld by Möser's essay. In this sense the iron hand betokens strength, immunity to pain, but also a diminished, wounded condition. It can also suggest the potent ways in which even something or someone dead can continue, as symbol, to exert potent political influence. Examples might range from "John Brown's body lies a-moldering in its grave, but his soul goes marching on" to the famous slogan "Che lives."

The ambivalent force of the symbol itself — and of the whole process entailed in someone's having to live with a nexus of symbolizations attached to their very person — is captured in a dream which Götz reports in act 1 when he is reunited with Weislingen:

> Mir war's heute nacht, ich gäb dir meine rechte eiserne Hand, und du hieltest mich so fest, daß sie aus den Armschienen ging wie abgebrochen. Ich erschrak und wachte drüber auf. Ich hätte nur fortträumen sollen, da würd ich gesehn haben, wie du mir eine neue lebendige Hand ansetztest. (99–100)

[I dreamt last night that I gave you my right iron hand and that you held me so fast that it came away from its fastening, as though broken. I was frightened and woke up because of it. I should have continued to dream and then I would have seen how you fitted me with a new hand.]

Later, in act 4, Götz, betrayed by Weislingen and in great danger, will recall that dream, but without the happy ending. And suddenly the destroyed hand is part of the doom that crowds in upon him from every side:

Er sagte mir Treu zu, und hielt meine rechte Hand so fest, daß sie aus den Armschienen ging, wie abgebrochen. Ach! Ich bin in diesem Augenblick wehrloser, als ich war, da sie mir abgeschossen wurde. (151)

[He swore loyalty to me and held so firmly on to my right hand that it came away from its fastening, as though broken. Ah I am in this moment more defenseless than I was when my hand was shot away.]

Here, we hear somebody crushed by the weight of the symbol that he has and is. It is part of the pain that floods the final scenes of the play: Götz becomes increasingly aware of his symbolic role in contexts that increasingly militate against his ability to play that role. He even becomes an onlooker at his own self and at his own symbolic persona:

Suchtest du den Götz? Der ist lang hin. Sie haben mich nach und nach verstümmelt, meine Hand, meine Freiheit, Güter und guten Namen. Mein Kopf, was ist an dem? (173)

[Were you looking for Götz? He is truly gone. They have mutilated me bit by bit, my freedom, my goods, my good name. And as far as my mind, what does that matter?]

It is an extraordinary speech, in which Götz speaks of his own decline as a process of dismemberment. At one point he even sees his own ailing body as the negation of all those metaphors of natural vitality which have been so much part of his own self-understanding and of his contemporaries' understanding of him:

Die Bäume treiben Knospen, und alle Welt hofft. Lebt wohl, meine Lieben; meine Wurzeln sind abgehauen, meine Kraft sinkt nach dem Grabe. (174)

[The trees grow buds and the whole world hopes. Fare well, my dears, my roots have been cut away, my strength declines into the grave.]

At the end of the play Götz sees himself as the symbol of an anachronism. And yet, of course, this is not the last word. Götz may, in his despair, see himself as being dismembered, but there is also the process of remembering which is potently at work in the play and which was central to its reception in eighteenth century Germany. That remembering has crucially to do with the issue of symbolization. We have already commented on the theme of "Nachkommenschaft" (or lack of it), which comes to the fore at the end of the play. When Götz is confined to his estate, Elisabeth says:

> So schreib doch deine Geschichte aus, die du angefangen hast. Gib deinen Freunden ein Zeugnis in die Hand, deine Feinde zu beschämen; verschaff einer edlen Nachkommenschaft die Freude, dich nicht zu verkennen. (155)

> [So write down the story which you have already begun. Put into your friends' hands a witness that will shame your enemies. Give to your noble successors the joy of knowing you properly.]

The original Götz did indeed write his autobiography. But Goethe's Götz cannot do so. Yet the theme of the legacy to posterity sounds powerfully in the last two speeches of the play:

> MARIA: Edler Mann! Edler Mann! Wehe dem Jahrhundert, das dich
>   von sich stieß!
>
> LERSE: Wehe der Nachkommenschaft, die dich verkennt! (175)

> [MARIA: Noble man! Noble man! Woe unto the century that
>   rejected you!
>
> LERSE: Woe unto the successors who fail to know you properly!]

The chief agent, of course, that ensures that subsequent ages will not fail to know Götz is Goethe's drama. Not only did it, as it were, put Götz and his world on the map for Goethe's contemporaries, it has continued to do so for subsequent generations of readers. Thereby it has played a crucial role in that symbolization and image-making process that is central, as we have seen, to the play's very theme. It is still performed, often as an open-air historical pageant; and for many German schoolchildren it is their first introduction to the drama of their national history, to that process whereby history and fiction intermingle, both in the "then" of the represented era and in the "now" of the artistic representation.

That dialectical debate between then and now can be seen in sharp focus if we consider the play's import for Goethe's contemporaries. As we have seen, one of the chief thematic preoccupations of the play is with Götz's claim to be, in political terms, a largely autonomous agent, answerable only and directly to the Emperor. In this sense he stands for the value of subjectivity; his is a selfhood that acknowledges no other arbitration of right and wrong than that offered by the promptings of his own heart and mind. And the contrastive example of this kind of selfhood is to be found in the figure of Weislingen. He is somebody who is at the mercy of every mood and whim that takes hold of him. He is inconstant, fickle, volatile. At any given moment he is true to what he knows and feels to be the case, but that feeling and knowing can change direction from moment to moment. When he is in Götz's world, away from the bishop's palace, he feels that he has been restored to his true self:

> Götz, teurer Götz, du hast mich mir selbst wiedergegeben, und, Maria, du vollendest meine Sinnesänderung. Ich fühle mich so frei wie in heiterer Luft. (101)

> [Götz, dear Götz, you have given me back myself, and, Maria, you complete my change of heart. I feel as free as in the balmy air.]

The identification of freedom with clear air recalls key metaphors from Götz's speeches. Yet where Götz finds constancy of being and purpose in the freedom that he espouses, Weislingen finds only instability. When he speaks, in the passage quoted above, of his "Sinnesänderung," we hear a possible double meaning. In Weislingen's case, the state of mind depends crucially on the state of the senses. And although at any given moment the import of his sense experience is total — "Ich fühle nichts, als nur daß ich ganz dein bin" (98; I feel nothing but that I am wholly yours) — all the intensification of language and being (nichts, nur, ganz) does not generate certainty and integrity. Adelheid will pronounce a devastating diagnosis when she says: "So seid Ihr ein Chamäleon?" (112; So are you a chameleon?); and she supremely will be able to manipulate Weislingen. She is fully aware of her own sexual attractiveness and is able to exploit it to the full, to use the senses to dominate the person. The presence, then, of Weislingen and Adelheid in Goethe's drama contributes to a debate about the energy and the limitations of subjectivity as a value. At one level, that debate functions in philosophical terms, as we have seen. At another level, it has cultural-historical import. A figure such as Weislingen is, in a sense, an anachronism in the world of the early sixteenth century. His persona as emotional chameleon has, if anything, to do with the subjectivism of late eighteenth-century German culture. When he speaks, we hear shades of Goethe's other subjectivist figures — Werther, Clavigo, for example. Götz contrasts two forms of subjectivity: that of Götz, where the proud assertion of the autonomous self goes hand in hand with a way of life that is active, resolute, purposive, energetic; and that of Weislingen who is moody, unfocused, labile, and ultimately ineffectual. Götz uses history, then, as a field of force in which past and present engage in urgent debate. That past may be over and done with; but the authority of the way of life which it enshrines lives on and provides a critique of the "Nachkommenschaft" that follows it.

In two plays of the 1770s Goethe continues his reckoning with the modern subjectivist self. Both *Clavigo* (1774) and *Stella* (1775) have a male protagonist who is emotionally and cognitively unstable, whose capacity for loving is as intense as it is wayward. Both plays offer some kind of critique, philosophical and moral, of the condition of anchorless subjectivity, but ultimately both plays succumb to the indirection that is their theme. Yet with *Egmont* (1775–87) we encounter a drama that, like *Götz*, both contextualizes the wayward self in historico-political terms and finds a genuine differentiation of philosophical argument. In some ways, as we shall see, *Egmont* is an untidy drama; and this is in part due to its protracted genesis which extended from 1775 to 1787. The Goethe who put the finishing touches to the play had spent over ten years at the court in Weimar; hence the play's Sturm und Drang theme of rebellion against oppression had become somewhat alien to him. But Goethe's uncertainty about his youthful drama was to prove ultimately enriching, because the play thereby acquired a critical, indeed self-reflexive, dimension. In other words: the text both celebrates and criticizes the figure of Egmont. It is both monument and critique; it attends scrupulously to the whole process of image-making as part of the political world. It is theatre about the theatre of politics.

It tells of the oppression of the Netherlands in the late sixteenth century by the Spanish crown. The tolerant Regent Margarete von Parma is replaced by the Duke of Alba. He proceeds to subdue the people by arresting and executing their leaders. Oranien foresees this danger and decides to leave the capital. He pleads with his friend and ally to do the same, yet Egmont is determined to remain in Brussels. The play ends with his imprisonment: his execution is imminent, although in the final moments Egmont is granted a glorious vision of freedom.

Perhaps the best way into the play is to begin with the responses of one of its most perceptive — and earliest — critics: Schiller. The particular points he raises and the implications of his objections have continued to inform Egmont criticism ever since. Schiller had three principal reservations about the play. First: he objected to the static quality of the portrayal of Egmont; we hear constantly of Egmont's greatness, but we hardly ever see him in action. Second: he felt that the play aspired to, but lacked, the stuff of tragic greatness: for example, in his view, the love scenes between Egmont and Klärchen, while appealing, were not sufficiently weighty to sustain a tragic drama. Third: he objected to the ending of the play which he saw as a "Salto mortale in eine Opernwelt"[5] — a spectacular, but unjustified leap into a kind of quasi-operatic transfiguration.

Beyond any doubt, the ending of the play does pose real difficulties. It offers a validation of the protagonist not just in personal and existential terms but also as some kind of political martyr; whereas the Egmont shown in the play often seems alarmingly cavalier in his relationship to practical politics. And we are given no suggestion that Egmont comes in any thoroughgoing sense to understand his political failings, to judge himself in the way that a Schillerian hero would. Moreover, Klärchen is a touching and appealing figure; but one wonders by what right (other than Egmont's love for her) she can appear in the final tableau as the human face of liberty. It is interesting to recall at this stage that Schiller, at Goethe's invitation, wrote a stage version of the play. He makes a number of alterations, most particularly he changes the status of the apotheosis at the end. In Schiller's version, it is confined to Egmont's consciousness. It functions therefore not as a glorifying tableau in which we share, but as the wish-dream of a condemned man, as a moment of self-justification. In fact, that tendency is not absent from the Egmont we see throughout Goethe's play. In act 1, Margarete comments: "Sein Gewissen hat einen gefälligen Spiegel" (HA 4, 382; his conscience is an easygoing mirror), for instance. What Schiller's version does, interestingly, is to heighten the play's latent potential as a critical reading of its protagonist. But it removes much of the complexity of Goethe's project. For reasons that we shall seek to spell out in due course, Goethe was right to restore the original text after Schiller's death, including the offending final scene.

It is noteworthy that Egmont does not appear at all in act 1 of the play. Yet he is omnipresent as an image, a symbol within the consciousness of his people. He is first named as a yardstick for superb marksmanship. In the opening archery competition, Ruysum praises the skills of one contestants: "Er schießt wie sein Herr, er schießt wie Egmont" (371; he shoots like his master, he shoots like Egmont). And a few moments later we hear from Soest of the immense attractiveness of Egmont:

> Warum ist alle Welt dem Grafen Egmont so hold? Warum trügen wir ihn alle auf den Händen? Weil man ihm ansieht, daß er uns wohlwill; weil ihm die Fröhlichkeit, das freie Leben, die gute Meinung aus den Augen sieht [. . .]. (372)

> [Why is the whole world so well disposed to Egmont? Why should we be prepared to care for him in every way? Because you can see it at once that he wishes us well; because gaiety, freedom, good will shine out of his eyes.]

Throughout act 1, we sense the omnipresence of the image-making process in respect of Egmont. Even as a child, Klärchen was, we learn, in thrall to the "Bild vom Grafen Egmont" (387; image of Count Egmont). The power of that image extends throughout the play. At the beginning of act 5, Klärchen will seek to inspire the people to resist the Spanish oppression:

Bleibt! Bleibt und drückt euch nicht vor seinem Namen weg, dem
ihr euch sonst so froh entgegen drängtet! — Wenn der Ruf ihn
ankündigte, wenn es hieß: "Egmont kommt! Er kommt von Gent!"
da hielten die Bewohner der Straßen sich glücklich, durch die er
reiten mußte. (435)

[Wait! Wait and do not turn away from his name, which you always
used to crowd around. When the cry went up, when it was said "Egmont is coming! He is coming from Ghent," then people would think
themselves lucky to live on the streets through which he would pass.]

And, even in the heart of the enemy camp, Ferdinand, the son of Alba,
has been touched from his earliest years by the magic of Egmont's image:

Du bist mir nicht fremd. Dein Name war's, der mir in meiner ersten
Jugend gleich einem Stern des Himmels entgegenleuchtete. Wie oft
hab ich nach dir gehorcht, gefragt! (448)

[You are not a stranger to me. It was your name that in my first flush
of youth shone upon me like a star within the heavens. How often
did I listen for news of you, did I ask about you!]

This potent force of image-making affects the very mode of representation: Schiller was quite right to sense that there is something operatic
about the play. Many of the most memorable moments are occasions on
which Egmont spells out his own nature to us, and they almost feel like
arias. One notes three such moments in act 2 when Egmont takes issue
with his Sekretär:

Es dreht sich immer nur um den einen Punkt: ich soll leben, wie ich
nicht leben mag. Daß ich fröhlich bin, die Sachen leicht nehme,
rasch lebe, das ist mein Glück; und ich vertausch es nicht gegen die
Sicherheit eines Totengewölbes. (399)

[It always comes down to the same point: I am supposed to live in a
way that I do not want. That I am carefree, that I take things casually, that I live at a fast pace — that is my joy. And I will not exchange it for the security of a mausoleum.]

And:

Und wenn ich ein Nachtwandler wäre, und auf dem gefährlichen
Gipfel eines Hauses spazierte, ist es freundschaftlich, mich beim
Namen zu rufen und mich zu warnen, zu wecken und zu töten? (399)

[And if I were a sleepwalker and were walking on the dangerous
ridge of a roof, would it be a kindness to call me by my name — to
warn, awaken, and kill me?]

And:

> Wie von unsichtbaren Geistern gepeitscht, gehen die Sonnenpferde
> der Zeit mit unseres Schicksals leichtem Wagen durch; und uns
> bleibt nichts, als mutig gefaßt, die Zügel festzuhalten, und bald
> rechts, bald links, vom Steine hier, vom Sturze da, die Räder
> wegzulenken. Wohin es geht, wer weiß es? (400–401)

> [As though driven by invisible spirits, the sun horses of time rush
> forward pulling the fragile chariot of our destiny. And we have no
> choice but to hold on to the reins for dear life and to try to steer the
> wheels to the right, to the left, away from that stone, from that
> abyss. Where ultimately we are headed for, who can know?]

All three "arias" have common ground in their proud assertion of the
need to live fully and dangerously. Egmont knows only the virtue of living in the headlong energy of minute-by-minute intensity. He is associated with the horse as symbol of natural beauty and vitality, and there are
frequent echoes of the figure of Apollo. They are in evidence, for example, in the image of the charioteer, in references to the color of gold and
to the bow and arrow: Egmont, we learn in act 1, is a superlative archer,
and in the final scene the goddess of freedom hands Egmont a bunch of
arrows.

Such powerful symbolizations conspire to endow Egmont with a significance that points beyond the human sphere. But we should not forget
that the play also embeds him in a set of arguments that articulate the
human sphere, understood as both a moral and a social realm. One example has to do with the temporality of human existence. Egmont, as we
have noted in our discussion of his three set piece "arias," believes in living exclusively in the present. Yet recurrently, we encounter passages in
the text which challenge Egmont's philosophy by expressing a very different kind of consciousness: the awareness of the continuum of past, present, and future. In act 1, Machiavell reminds Margarete that she has
often reproached him with being a reflective, intellectual spirit rather than
a man of resolute action in the present:

> Ihr sagtet oft im Scherze: "Du siehst zu weit, Machiavell! Du solltest
> Geschichtsschreiber sein: wer handelt, muß fürs Nächste sorgen."
> Und doch, habe ich diese Geschichte nicht vorauserzählt? Hab ich
> nicht alles vorausgesehen? (378)

> [You have often said in jest: "You see too far, Machiavelli! You
> should be a historian; but whoever is active must care about immedi-
> ate things." And yet, did I not predict this history? Did I not foresee
> everything?]

The theme sounds again in a very different — on this occasion, erotic — context in the following brief exchange:

MUTTER: Wie wird's in der Zukunft werden?

KLARE: Ach, ich frage nur, ob er mich liebt; und ob er mich liebt, ist das eine Frage? (385)

[MUTTER: What will the future bring?

KLARE: Oh I am only bothered about whether he loves me; and can there be any doubt that he does love me?]

Klärchen rejects all notions of past and future; to her, the immediate truth of her and Egmont's love for each other is all that matters. In the political sphere Vansen, in his wish to stir up unrest, invokes the past in order to destabilize the present:

So seid ihr Bürgersleute! Ihr lebt nur so in den Tag hin [. . .]. Ihr fragt nicht nach dem Herkommen, nach der Historie, nach dem Recht eines Regenten; und über das Versäumnis haben euch die Spanier das Netz über die Ohren gezogen. (391)

[That is the way you are, you solid citizens. You live each day as it comes. You do not ask about origins, about history, about the rights of a Regent. And because of this failure the Spaniards have been able to pull a net over your heads.]

When Egmont arrives he puts a stop to all disquiet by asserting that the present reality offers enough fulfillment for the honest citizen. "Ein ordentlicher Bürger, der sich ehrlich und fleißig nährt, hat überall so viel Freiheit, als er braucht" (394; An orderly citizen who supports himself honestly and decently has everywhere as much freedom as he needs). As these examples suggest, the play offers conflicting views of life: it allows Egmont to express the beauty and intensity of a life lived in repudiation of "Sorge," that anxious condition that holds in check any surrender to the present by endless disquiet about the future. But the play does not leave Egmont's philosophy unchallenged; rather, it acknowledges the importance of seeing the present in temporal context, of knowing that present living derives from past experiences and will have future consequences. In terms of his philosophy of life, then, Egmont is called into question. And the questioning is even more urgent in political terms. Schiller's reservations about Egmont's behavior as protagonist in the political sphere are pertinent, and, crucially, they are echoed in the play itself: Goethe himself generates the critical perspective that Schiller spells out. On frequent occasions the play reminds us that Egmont is no metaphysical principle, no Apollo, but rather a privileged figure in a precisely evoked historical and social world. He is (and he never forgets it) a member of the Order of the Golden Fleece, and is by that token answerable only to the King and to God. He is proud of these traditional rights, guaranteed by the former Emperor Charles V. Many of the freedoms he claims for himself — his right to be his own man, to live according to the promptings of his own nature and temperament — derive from his privileged aristocratic rank. Like Götz, he is no revolutionary. And, given the conservatism of his people, he can legitimately claim to represent them. The crowd in the opening scene have a very clear sense of hierarchy. They trust their political rulers, Egmont, the Regent Margarete, Oranien; and the scene ends on the unanimous chorus "Sicherheit und Ruhe! Ordnung und Freiheit!" (377; Security and Peace! Order and liberty!). The concept of freedom is, then, securely housed within an allegiance to peace and quiet. And these same citizens, at the beginning of act 2, distance themselves from the violent behavior of the iconoclasts.

All this is to indicate the extent to which Egmont is deeply embedded in a social world in which he plays an entirely central role and which he claims (often rightly) to understand. But, as a number of hints suggest, the political situation is changing: Unrest and civil disobedience is mounting in the provinces; the Spanish crown is losing patience; Margarete the Regent knows that she is under pressure. Every indication is, then, that the King sooner or later will move to oppress the Netherlands. And precisely this changing situation reveals the inadequacy of Egmont's political awareness. He is so reluctant to contemplate change that he tends to deny that any changes are occurring. And this reluctance to heed the demands of the political situation is compounded by the cherished, and cultivated, casualness of his behavior and life-style. In act 2, we see Egmont dealing with administrative chores; his methods are easy-going in the extreme to the despair of his punctilious secretary. The scene ends, as we have noted, with those aria-like speeches which have everything to do with Egmont's temperament, and nothing to do with practical affairs. The act closes with the superlative scene between Egmont and Oranien which serves to highlight the extent of Egmont's political naiveté.

Oranien begins by referring to their recent audience with the Regent, and is intensely concerned to get a sense from her behavior of any straws blowing in the political wind. But for Egmont, such signs as there are — for example the Regent's coolness of manner — are not political indicators, but merely personal traits, aspects of Margarete's temperament and of woman's moodiness. By contrast, Oranien is the professional politician, fascinated by the chessboard of the power game: "ich stehe immer wie über einem Schachspiele und halte keinen Zug des Gegners für unbedeutend" (403; I always stand as though surveying a chessboard and I never regard any move of my opponents as insignificant). His fear is that the Spanish King will invade the Netherlands and, in order to minimize all chance of rebellion, will capture the most influential of the local leaders, Egmont and Oranien. At this point, Egmont does listen to his friend's words, but only to repudiate them. He argues that it would be a tactical error for the King to proceed in this way because it would drive an ultimate wedge between the Netherlands and Spain. But Egmont is wrong to dismiss as unthinkable — "Sie können nicht wollen" (404; They cannot want that) — what is swiftly accomplished by Alba. He is wrong to assume that the arrest of himself and Oranien will immediately produce a popular uprising. As the final act shows, the people are frightened and cowed. Oranien's tactics are right: that he and Egmont should leave the capital, should go into the provinces, there to organize resistance as a form of guerrilla warfare. To this course of action Egmont is implacably opposed. He does not mind fighting for his people in open warfare; but the idea of a campaign that involves not soldiers but families is anathema to him. Oranien presses his case:

> Wir sind nicht einzelne Menschen, Egmont. Ziemt es sich, uns für Tausende hinzugeben, so ziemt es sich, uns für Tausende zu schonen. (405)

> [We are not individual people, Egmont. If it can be right for us to sacrifice ourselves for thousands, then it can also be right for us to save ourselves for thousands.]

To which Egmont responds with an existential, rather than a political, argument:

> "Wer sich schont, muß sich selbst verdächtig werden." (405)

> [Whoever saves himself must end up distrusting himself.]

It is a moment that expresses the full extent of Egmont's political naiveté. And it weighs heavily — as does the exchange, a few lines earlier, in which Egmont rejects a fact simply because he does not want it to be true:

ORANIEN: Alba ist unterwegs.
EGMONT: Ich glaub's nicht.
ORANIEN: Ich weiß es. (404)

[ORANIEN: Alba is on his way.
EGMONT: I do not believe it.
ORANIEN: I know it.]

At the end of the scene, Oranien takes his leave of his friend with tears in his eyes because he knows Egmont is doomed. He urges him to think again; but that is not Egmont's way of doing things:

Daß andrer Menschen Gedanken solchen Einfluß auf uns haben! Mir
wär es nie eingekommen; und dieser Mann trägt seine Sorglichkeit in
mich herüber. — Weg! Das ist ein fremder Tropfen in meinem
Blute. Gute Natur, wirf ihn wieder heraus! (407)

[That the thoughts of other people can have so much influence upon
us. I would never have thought it. And this man transfers his anxie-
ties to me. Away with all that! That is an alien drop in my blood. Nature, in your goodness, get rid of it.]

Egmont is bemused that other people can have influence on him. He rejects the concerns that Oranien has voiced. And, crucially, he rejects them
not on political grounds but because they are, as he sees it, utterly foreign
to his very being. Once again, notions of existential or natural integrity
are uppermost in his mind, and not considerations of political import. All
of which is not to deny that Egmont is a potent political force in the lives
of his people; nor is it to deny that in many respects he has an inborn in-
stinct for politics, for example, how to handle a crowd. But he is utterly
reluctant to concern himself with tactics, with the nuts-and-bolts of practical leadership. And in the rapidly shifting ground of the world in which
he finds himself, he is tested and found wanting. And for his naiveté, as
the closing phase of the drama shows, he will pay with his life.

Some of that naiveté, a kind of willed ignorance about his own political persona and responsibilities, can be heard in the scene that ends act 3.
Egmont has heeded Klärchen's wish and gone to visit her in the full
splendor of his public rank, including the Order of the Golden Fleece.
Klärchen, overwhelmed by the presence in her arms of a figure whose
name is constantly on everybody's lips, asks if he truly is "der große Egmont" (414; the great Egmont). To which he replies in the negative. He
sits, she kneels before him, looking up at him; and in a long speech he explains that the public Egmont is a travesty of his true self, is hemmed in
by the constant pressures of public office and obliged to move through an
alien world. Whereas, by contrast, the true Egmont is the man before her:

der ist ruhig, offen, glücklich, geliebt und gekannt von dem besten
Herzen, das auch er ganz kennt und mit voller Liebe und Zutrauen
an das seine drückt. Das ist dein Egmont. (415)

[he is calm, open, happy, loved and known by the best heart, which
he also knows well and with full love and trust presses to his. That is
your Egmont.]

The declaration is touching; it is music to Klärchen's ears. And yet one
has to remember that these words are spoken by a man arrayed in the full
regalia of his public office. Egmont's words may disavow his persona as
political figure; but his appearance belies that disavowal at every turn. The

adoring girl worships both the lover and the great leader of his people. Egmont's repudiation of his public selfhood is as naive as so much of his resistance to Oranien's pleas for a new kind of tactics.

Our analysis thus far has been concerned to show that there is a considerable discrepancy between the specific individual whom the play puts before us and the image to which he gives rise. At the end of the play, Egmont is executed; yet before his death he sees (and in Goethe's version we too see) a vision that justifies him as a martyr for the cause of the Netherlanders' freedom. As we have already noted, the apotheosis validates him not only existentially but also politically. His last words are spoken (in his imagination) to the serried ranks of his people, including women and children. He seems to have forgotten his earlier objections, in the scene with Oranien, to a campaign of civil unrest that would entail the presence in the firing line of "Bürger [. . .] Kinder [. . .] Jungfrauen" (405; Citizens . . . children . . . maidens). His last words claim exemplary political status for himself: "fallt freudig, wie ich euch ein Beispiel gebe" (454; fall joyously and follow my example). The closing cadence of the drama is triumphant, and is underpinned by music (most of us will think, of course, of Beethoven's superb incidental music to the play). Yet all this, to recall Schiller's strictures, operatic splendor seems utterly at variance with the complex, critical illumination of Egmont which the play has provided. How are we to make sense of this discrepancy?

Perhaps the key step is to acknowledge the discrepancy for what it is: a significant, thematically meaningful, discrepancy. We have already registered that Egmont is omnipresent in act 1 precisely because he himself never appears. In short, that omnipresence is rooted in his symbolic function. Whilst that function cannot come into being without the specific person who gives rise to the symbol, it is not dependent for its operation on the presence of that person. Indeed, to repeat an earlier point, the absence of the person, particularly when occasioned through a death that has the interpretative resonance of martyrdom, can intensify the power of the image. As we had occasion to remark in our discussion of *Götz*, the symbol has a particularly powerful role to play in the creation of the "Nachkommenschaft" of the charismatic hero. It is also helpful, in the context of this discussion, to invoke Goethe's comments, in *Dichtung und Wahrheit*, on the role of the daemonic in Egmont. He describes it as "eine der moralischen Weltordnung, wo nicht entgegengesetzte, doch sie durchkreuzende Macht" (HA 4, 570; a power that runs counter to, if it does not actually contradict, the moral order of the world). And he goes on to spell out the troubling incommensurability that obtains between the sheer force of daemonic energy on the one hand and the world of moral responsibility on the other:

Es sind nicht immer die vorzüglichsten Menschen, weder an Geist
noch an Talenten, selten durch Herzensgüte sich empfehlend; aber
eine ungeheure Kraft geht von ihnen aus. (570)

[They are not always the best of people, whether in terms of their
temperament or their talents , and they do not exude kindliness. But
a huge energy emanates from them.]

Here, Goethe highlights the gap between an irresistibly attractive force-
filled persona on the one hand and on the other hand the specific self ex-
isting in the morally defined realm of interpersonal relations. In *Egmont,*
Goethe recognizes both the psychological-cum-moral and the political issues posed by the daemonic. And he sees that, precisely in the latter
sphere, the daemonic is central to the process of image-making. In the
first two acts of the play, there are many references to the iconoclasts, the
"Bilderstürmer." If it can be a political statement to destroy images, then
it can also be a political statement to create them.

What we see in the apotheosis at the end of the play, then, is not a
justification of Egmont the man; rather, it is the symbol of what he has
come to stand for in the hearts and minds of his people. Klärchen, too,
becomes part of the apotheosis at the end, not least because she symbolically signals the transfer of the energies for change from the aristocratic to
the bourgeois class. (It is worth reflecting that Goethe completed Egmont a mere two years before the outbreak of the French Revolution.)
To ask whether the Egmont or the Klärchen whom we see in the drama
have earned this symbolic transfiguration is to miss the point (which is
precisely where Schiller fell down). Ultimately, Goethe's *Egmont* reflects
and reflects critically on processes of imagining and symbolization in human affairs, above all in the political sphere. They are, of course, problematic processes in all sorts of ways; yet they are extraordinarily powerful:
they may be intangible, but they can impact on tangible circumstances. In
one of the most moving utterances of the entire play, Egmont, taking his
leave of Ferdinand, says:

[. . .] du verlierst mich nicht. War dir mein Leben ein Spiegel, in
welchem du dich gerne betrachtest, so sei es auch mein Tod. Die
Menschen sind nicht nur zusammen, wenn sie beisammen sind, auch
der Entfernte, Abgeschiedne lebt uns. (450)

[You will not lose me. If my life was a mirror in which you loved to
look at yourself, may my death be that also. People are not only close
when they are together; even distant or absent people live in us.]

Surely, all of us know what he means. And precisely that theme of the operative force of our imaginings will concern us in *Iphigenie auf Tauris,* to
which we now turn.

It is the first drama which Goethe wrote at the court of Weimar, and it displays the features which one associates with the notion of neo-classicism: the play spurns outward action and theatrical effect; there are very few stage directions. The sense of calm is further underpinned by an essentially monologic structure — eruptions into real dialogic tensions are very rare. In other words: *Iphigenie* embodies "Verinnerlichung": the text centers on the realm of the psyche, on consciousness and conscience. This inwardness did not prove popular: Johann Jakob Bodmer spoke for many when he uttered his sheer sense of boredom. He resented being bombarded by long speeches and moralizing maxims: "Man erzählt da in Monologen, die Personen antworten einander in Sentenzen" (HA 5, 410; People talk in monologues and they respond to each other in maxims).

The play reworks Euripides' *Iphigenie in Tauris*. Goethe was the first to transplant Greek drama onto the German cultural scene, just as, with *Götz*, he had been the first to transplant the Shakespearean mode onto the German stage. The mythological background plays an important part. Iphigenie's ancestor, the Titan Tantalus, challenged the Olympian gods by testing their omniscience. Outraged, the gods threw him into the underworld, Hades, and placed a curse on his descendants — an unending cycle of strife and carnage. This curse also haunted Iphigenie's family. Her father, King Agamemnon, setting sail for Troy, was ready to sacrifice her to the goddess Diana; but she saved Iphigenie and transported her to Tauris, there to serve as her priestess. Meanwhile the curse continued: On his return from Troy, Agamemnon was killed by his wife Klytemnestra, and she in her turn was murdered by Iphigenia's brother, Orestes.

This is roughly the point where the play starts. On Tauris, Iphigenie rejects King Thoas's marriage proposal, and in anger he reinstates the custom of human sacrifice. Orestes arrives with his friend Pylades. Orestes, murderer of his mother, suffers from mental torment. The oracle of Apollo, brother of Diana, has promised salvation if the image of the sister is returned to Greece. Orestes and Pylades interpret "sister" as a reference to Apollo's sister, that is, the holy statue of Diana, and prepare to steal it. They need Iphigenie's help, but she insists on truthfulness and tells Thoas of the impending theft. At the point of deadly crisis, Orestes suddenly perceives the real meaning of the oracle: "Schwester" refers not to Diana, but to Iphigenie. King Thoas finally gives his blessing and the Greek party leaves.

Like *Egmont*, the play had a protracted genesis. The first version, in prose, was performed at the Weimar court in April 1779. Goethe played the role of guilt-ridden Orestes. In psychological terms, this can be seen as a kind of self-therapy, for behind the figure of the beloved sister Iphigenie there is Charlotte von Stein. Indeed there are overt links to the poem "Warum gabst du uns die tiefen Blicke." Goethe immediately started to translate the prose version into verse: he stressed the criterion of stylistic harmony during this period, and he finished the second version in Rome, 1787. Schiller was impressed. He saw the play as the very embodiment of the Winckelmann ideal of Greek art, of calm and dignity. By 1802, however, he had profound misgivings; above all, he objected to the lack of theatrical vitality — and to the fact that the curse on Orestes only figures in psychological terms, that the mythological furies, agents of revenge, are absent. By 1827, Goethe himself acknowledged the problem, as we shall see.

Yet since the nineteenth century, Iphigenie is part of the German literary canon: it is seen as *the* monument to the ethos of Enlightenment, to the ideal of "Humanität," enlightened humaneness. The play links with Kant's essay "Was ist Aufklärung" (1784), with his *Kritik der praktischen Vernunft* (1788), and it anticipates the norms of truth and truthfulness which inform his essay on the "Vermeintliches Recht, aus Menschenliebe zu lügen" (Presupposed Justification for Lying with a Philanthropic Purpose, 1797). Here, Kant defines lying as a crime against one's own person and humanity. The vision of an enlightened humanity dominates these decades: it also informs, for example, Gotthold Ephraim Lessing's *Nathan der Weise* (1779), and Schiller's theoretical writings, in particular *Die ästhetische Erziehung des Menschen* (1795), which stresses our capacity to be "Mensch," human and humane. Mozart's opera *Die Zauberflöte* (1791) equally hails the force of truth and love, and so does Beethoven's *Fidelio* (1806), with its simple statement: "Es sucht der Bruder seinen Bruder / Und kann er helfen, hilft er gern" (The brother looks for his brother, / And if he can help, he helps gladly).

Even these days, the figure of Iphigenie ranks as the symbol of moral emancipation. Such critical consensus is rather unique — indeed the play is unique within Goethe's overall work. We have touched on the problems which beset the glorification of Egmont: with the figure of Iphigenie no such problems arise. No critic doubts her status as a symbol; skepticism only arises in respect of the play's resolution. Ever since Schiller, many have argued that the victory of a humane morality is too easy, that the objective world poses no real threat, that the play avoids tragic conflict.

Despite such reservations about the ending, the first question must be: why is this play essentially so persuasive — as persuasive as its protagonist who heals Orestes from madness and who persuades him and Thoas to choose the path of enlightened morality. The play's classical calm and lyrical beauty cannot in itself be sufficient explanation: this kind of beauty also informs *Die natürliche Tochter* (1803), yet here it goes hand in hand with processes of deception and delusion. We would argue that the integrity of both the play and its protagonist rests on the fact that it centers on a woman — the only woman in the play, and a woman of particular provenance. Up to act 5, Iphigenie figures, in terms of practical action, as powerless and therefore innocent. In the past, her life was at the mercy first of her father, then of Diana, and finally Thoas. Now, as priestess, Iphigenie has only one authority, that of the word: "Ich habe nichts als Worte" (863; I have nothing but words). Moral integrity is, then, based on disempowered femininity. Iphigenie has nothing to lose and nothing to gain — hence her language is free from the contagion of self-interest. Only by being isolated from the theatre of action, can Iphigenie unambiguously embody the voice of conscience, morality. In 1827 Goethe told Eckermann that only women figures can serve as vessels of morality, of "Idealität" — male figures are far too compromised by their involvement in practical reality. (HA 5, 428).

This gendering of morality is of course deeply problematic. On the one hand, one can argue that it privileges woman over man, that, in *Iphigenie,* it prefigures modern feminism, its commitment to pacifism.[6] On the other hand, the doctrine of woman's spiritual superiority is of course in danger of reinforcing her marginality. In the following, we want to show how Goethe's play turns this very marginality into a challenge to the dominant center of male culture and power.

Iphigenie starts out as a bundle of contradictions. She has not chosen the contemplative life, and, in the opening scene, she resents her lack of active freedom. The inactive life is woman's lot:

> Ein unnütz Leben ist ein früher Tod;
> Dies Frauenschicksal ist vor allen meins (115–16)
>
> [A useless life is an early death;
> Woman's lot is supremely mine.]

Subsequently, she repeatedly bemoans the restrictions of woman's life. Yet, despite all this, she yearns time and again for the order of patriarchy. She longs back to Agamemnon, her real father, and she calls Thoas her "zweiter Vater" (second father). How do we account for these contradictions? The answer may lie in her dual cultural origins: she has grown up in a patriarchal feudal system governed by her father, the King and by Zeus, the divine king presiding over the Olympian gods. She serves this system even now as a priestess on Tauris. These cultural roots explain her respect towards the gods and her father — despite the fact that the gods have cursed her family and that her father was ready to kill her. But Iphigenie is also a descendant of the Titans, of Tantalus. The Titans ruled the earth until they were overthrown by the Olympian gods, and the concept of hierarchy had been utterly alien to them. It is these Titanic origins which increasingly emerge in Iphigenie. They make themselves felt whenever she rebels: when she refuses to marry Thoas, and above all when she rebels against the power of the Olympian gods. This power is crystallized in the iron fate, the "ehern Band," which they have imposed on the house of Atreus. Iphigenie's rebellion erupts in act 4, v. Here, she faces the fact that, in the interest of Orestes, she is forced to deceive Thoas, to lie; and she interprets this betrayal of her morality as yet another coercion imposed by the gods: "Soll dieser Fluch denn ewig walten?" (1694; Should this curse forever prevail?) It is at this point that the Titan in her rebels and challenges the authority of the Olympian gods:

> O daß in meinem Busen nicht zuletzt
> Ein Widerwillen keime! Der Titanen,
> Der alten Götter tiefer Haß auf euch
> Olympier, nicht auch die zarte Brust
> Mit Geiersklauen fasse! Rettet mich
> Und rettet euer Bild in meiner Seele. (1712–17)

> [O that in my heart finally
> No anger should take hold. The deep hatred
> Of the Titans, of the old gods, for you
> Olympians — let it not grasp this tender
> Breast with its predatory claws! Save me
> And save your image in my soul.]

As the last line suggests, the gods can only rescue their "Bild," that is, Iphigenie's continued faith, if they change — change their iron rule and spare her. Her voice of dissent informs the famous song of the Fates — the "Parzenlied" — which immediately follows. Iphigenie recalls it from her childhood. It is a song of human insignificance, echoing the poem "Grenzen der Menschheit" (Limits of Humankind, 1781). Iphigenie was brought up in this very culture. The song speaks of horrendously indifferent gods, and crucially, of an outrageous system of absolutist governance:

> Es fürchte die Götter
> Das Menschengeschlecht!
> Sie halten die Herrschaft
> In ewigen Händen
> Und können sie brauchen
> Wie's ihnen gefällt. (1726–31)

> [Let the race of men
> Fear the gods
> They hold sway
> In their eternal hands,
> And they can use that power
> However they please.]

But in the final stanza comes the decisive sting:

> So sangen die Parzen!
> Es horcht der Verbannte,
> In nächtlichen Höhlen
> Der Alte die Lieder,
> Denkt Kinder und Enkel
> Und schüttelt das Haupt. (1761–66)

> [So sang the Parcae!
> The banished one
> In dark caverns,
> The old man, he hears the song
> Thinks of children and grandchildren
> And shakes his head.]

"Der Verbannte" and "Der Alte" refer to the Titan Tantalus, the rebel. Thinking of future generations, he shakes his head — "Denkt Kinder und Enkel / Und schüttelt das Haupt." This gesture of negation is ambiguous: it can be read as Tantalus' regret at his hubris, as a warning to future generations; but it can also be interpreted as a critical epilogue, an epilogue which in Titanic fashion rejects the absolutist rule of the Olympian gods. Both aspects reverberate in the protagonist as the term "Verbannte" establishes a clear link between banished Tantalus and his banished descendant, Iphigenie; but from this point onward, the element of rebellion comes to the fore: Iphigenie, in the name of emancipation, comes to pit moral autonomy, values of truthfulness and integrity, against traditional authority, against a legacy of iron rule, of violence. In act 5, iii, she summons up the courage to tell the truth, and she explicitly sees this challenge as the female version of male heroism:

> Hat denn zur unerhörten Tat der Mann
> Allein das Recht? Drückt denn Unmögliches
> Nur er an die gewaltge Heldenbrust?
> Was nennt man groß? [. . .] (1892–95)

> [Has then only man the right
> To the unheard-of deed? Is it only he
> Who presses impossible things to his heroic heart?
> What does one call greatness?]

The male heroism of "unerhörte Tat" is denied to woman. Iphigenie's heroic deed is that of moral force. In other words, she feminizes "Tat," feminizes male energy into the power of spiritual strength. She pits the strength of truth against the power of both the gods and Thoas:

                    Wenn
Ihr wahrhaft seid wie ihr gepriesen werdet,
So zeigt's durch euern Beistand und verherrlicht
Durch mich die Wahrheit — Ja vernimm, o König,
Es wird ein heimlicher Betrug geschmiedet, (1916–20)

                    [If
you truly are what you are praised for being,
Then show it by helping me now and glorify
Truth through me. Hear, o King,
A secret deception is being planned.]

We should note here the radical nature of this challenge. The word "wahr-haft" hovers between adjective and adverb: the sentence can mean "If you are truthful, show me" or "if you truly exist, show me." In other words, the lines vibrate with the threat of Iphigenie breaking the contract of faith. In theological terms, this is the most radical moment in the play. The existence of the gods is made to depend on human and humane action. In this sense, the play radicalizes the conclusion of the poem "Das Göttliche":

Der edle Mensch
Sei hilfreich und gut!
Unermüdet schaff' er
Das Nützliche, Rechte,
Sei uns ein Vorbild
Jener geahneten Wesen!

[Let noble humankind
Be helpful and good!
May they tirelessly bring about
That which is useful and right;
Let them be to us a model
Of those intuited beings.]

In other words, true humanity encapsulates and prefigures the divine. It is in this critical spirit that the play re-interprets Greek myth. The oppressive system of gods, of immutable fate, its iron law, is displaced by the law of enlightenment, of reason and morality. In this sense the play partakes of the eighteenth century critique of myth in general — one thinks above all of Voltaire. Goethe's play is, then, not only a debate across the gulf of some three thousand years, but is part of the contemporary agenda of emancipation.

Truth and truthfulness are acted out at three key points: in act 1, iii, Iphigenie tells Thoas of her origins. In act 3, i, Orestes breaks with pretence and tells Iphigenie who he is. His words "zwischen uns sei Wahrheit" (1081–82; between us let there be truth) — a highly distinctive semi-line — stand at almost the exact mid-point of the play. Finally, as we have seen, in act 5, iii, Iphigenie tells Thoas the truth, and she is vindicated. The Gods "oblige" as it were: Thoas listens to the voice of reason.

This brings us back to those critical voices which argue that the victory of reason is far too easy, that the play avoids the test of real, concrete resistance. This may well be the case; indeed it is the ever critical Schiller who prefigures such reservations. In 1802, he speaks of the play's modernity — he calls it "erstaunlich modern" (astonishingly modern) — and he observes that without the real, concrete presence of the furies, the agony of Orestes is but a sham: "Ohne Furien kein Orest" (414–15; no Orestes without furies). Schiller's remarks very much anticipate strands within twentieth-century interpretations. However, one could certainly argue that, although the limitations of German inwardness are manifest, the modernity of *Iphigenie* lies precisely in the abandoning of outward conflict. Particularly on a feminist reading, the text's "Verinnerlichung" emerges as decisively modern, in the following sense: If the play conformed to the drama of outward conflict, action, it would duplicate precisely that drama which has blighted the lives of Iphigenie's ancestors, a drama driven by the male will to power. In choosing the mode of inwardness, Goethe displaces the primitive drama of action, and he replaces it by another kind of drama which we might call feminine: the drama of poetry, of lyrical thought processes. We are asked to heed Iphigenie's pleading — "O höre mich! O sieh mich an" (1190; O hear me! O look at me) — to listen to the poetic constellations and to see their implications. At the very center of the poetic structure, we find the image of a blighted humanity. The struggle between despair and hope is reflected in sustained patterns of antithetical motifs which act out the debate between the determinism of Greek myth and liberation through enlightenment. Motifs of entanglement, entrapment dominate. Metaphors such as "Netz" bespeak a cursed humanity, suffering under the "ehern Band" of iron fate, and yearning for salvation. But equally recurrent is the motif of "retten," of "heilen." Similarly, the force of light is pitted against that of darkness: motifs like "Sonne," "hell," "leuchten," and "strahlen" countermand motifs of doom, such as "dunkel," "Nacht," "Trauerland," and "Tod." Furthermore, the radiance of such adjectives as "rein" and "wahr" countermands the legacy of the curse as reflected in the ominous "u" sounds of "Betrug," "Blut," and "Fluch," and numerous motifs of fluidity are pitted against the deadly fixity of immutable fate: "lösen," and "fließen" countermand patterns of "starr," and "ehern." And, overall, of course, the iambic pentameter, its smooth flow, is set against chaos and discord.

However, this poetic argumentation, in place of outward action, carries of course an inherent risk. In 1827, Goethe told Eckermann that the play-in-performance had always left him deeply alienated, that he could not bear to see the poetic force of the play, its "inneres Leben" struggling to assert itself within an inadequate outward representation (HA 5, 410). This brings us to a related point in answer to Schiller's objection that the absence of the ancient furies is too soft an option: *Iphigenie* as a poetic drama is a highly self-conscious utopian text which overrides by definition the notion of concrete conflict. By "self-conscious" we mean that the utopian text celebrates the victory of reason, but in fact constantly points to its limits. Like Lessing's play *Nathan der Weise* (1779), *Iphigenie* fully admits that the vision of a perfected humanity is no more, but no less than a pointer, a regulative idea, unattainable, yet indispensable as a guide. Numerous elements in the text delimit the utopian vision: the setting, Tauris, is on the margins of the political world, and there are only five characters — no chorus which would generate a public dimension. But more importantly, we find two central visions of harmony which are both strictly limited: In act 3, ii, Orestes has a vision of the underworld; he sees it as a paradise of peace. All his ancestors, friend and foe, are reconciled:

> Sie gehen friedlich, Alt und Junge, Männer
> Mit Weibern, göttergleich und ähnlich scheinen
> Die wandelnden Gestalten. Ja sie sind's,
> Die Ahnherrn meines Hauses! (1271–74)

> [They walk peacefully, old and young, men
> With women; godlike and kindred
> The wandering figures seem to be. It is they,
> The ancestors of my house!]

This vision prefigures the conciliatory ending of the play. Yet this utopian vision is considerably undercut for, at this point, Orestes is still mentally deranged. His vision is poised between delusion and utopian intimation, and one is reminded of Egmont's final dream. In addition, the paradisal scene explicitly excludes Tantalus; the primordial origins of the curse are not extinguished. The second utopian moment comes at the end of the play. Thoas lets Iphigenie, Orestes, and Pylades leave in peace. But this resolution is strikingly reticent. True, Iphigenie's language unfolds into a lyrical aria, but as regards Thoas, Goethe can only give us a minimal musical assurance. At first, Thoas simply replies "So geht" (so go), and after Iphigenie's plea, he moves to "Lebt wohl" (farewell). Within these four syllables, the sound pattern remains constant, but — crucially — it is inverted so that the final stress falls on the notion of blessing of "wohl." This is, of course, a brilliant modulation, but it does not grant the comforting certainty of an extended concluding speech.

In the light of this final reticence, it comes as no surprise that, despite the hopes raised by *Iphigenie,* Goethe was quite pessimistic. On 8 April 1779, he noted in his diary that there is a fundamental gap between reflectivity and action: "Man tut unrecht, an dem Empfindens- und Erkennensvermögen der Menschen zu zweifeln; da kann man ihnen viel zutrauen; nur auf ihre Handlungen muß man nicht hoffen" (It is quite wrong to doubt the capacity of feeling and cognition in human beings; at that level one can expect a lot of them. But one should have no great hopes for their actions). This gap between thought and action preoccupied him throughout his life, and it is only in *Iphigenie* that he found a synthesis. Once his texts re-enter the realm of social reality, the values of "Menschlichkeit" and "Wahrheit" proved untenable. The synthesis breaks up in his next play, *Torquato Tasso.* Here, the voice of truthfulness struggles to assert itself in the discourse of courtly convention.

This play follows hard on the heels of *Iphigenie,* and the two texts are best appreciated in contrast to each other. The original prose version dates back to the early 1780s. The final version, largely finished in Italy, was published in 1790. The mode of "Verinnerlichung" is even more pronounced than in *Iphigenie:* the play turns on a situation rather than action. There are again just five characters, and they move in essentially monologic configurations.

Set in the sixteenth century, the play turns on the conflict between the hyper-sensitive poet Tasso and the ethos of the court, an ethos of restraint, of "Maß" and "Mäßigung." Its representatives are the Duke of Ferrara, Alfons; his sister, the Prinzessin; her friend Leonore; and Antonio, the diplomat. There are only three moments of action. In act 1, iii, Tasso is crowned as the supreme poet. In act 2, iii, the poet is so irritated by Antonio that he draws his sword. This breach of etiquette is punished: Tasso is ordered to stay in his room. Increasingly, he shows signs of paranoia. Finally in act 5, iv, Tasso embraces the Prinzessin. He has good reason to believe that she returns his love, but she recoils, and the courtly circle, horrified, hastily leaves for town. Tasso is left behind, alone with his opponent Antonio. The final scene is poised between catastrophe and hope: Antonio stretches out his hand, as though to cancel out Tasso's hostile gesture of drawing his sword in act 2, iii; and in his final speech, Tasso accepts that suffering and creative energy are for him intertwined:

> Und wenn der Mensch in seiner Qual verstummt,
> Gab mir ein Gott, zu sagen, wie ich leide. (3432–33)

> [And where human beings fall silent in their pain,
> A god granted me to say how I suffer.]

This holds out the hope that the poet may turn catastrophe, the experience of loss, into poetic gain. The tragic element is, then, muted: the play is called "Ein Schauspiel." Yet, as countless critics note, the imagery of the concluding lines is precarious. And external evidence is very negative: as Goethe's audience knew full well, in 1579 Duke Alfons had Tasso imprisoned for seven years, and the poet never recovered his former powers. He died in 1595.

Tasso clearly has aesthetic affinities with *Iphigenie,* yet there is a fundamental thematic difference: *Iphigenie* is centered on the universal moral value of "Menschlichkeit" and "Wahrheit." By contrast, *Tasso* turns on the specific concept of "Sittlichkeit": rooted in "Sitte," in convention, custom, it is a socially constructed moral notion. The play is a sharp sociocultural analysis, and at the center of this analysis is the clash between the individual being and the norms of a particular social world, the courtly "Kreis." This thematic shift accounts for the stylistic difference: in place of lyrical beauty, we now find a cerebral language which negotiates concepts, arguments. Only the voice of the poet regularly soars off into lyrical visions. In the following, we shall focus on this clash between the poet and the court, and we hope to show how the import of the play gradually widens beyond the specific problem of courtly culture and comes to analyze critically the process of civilization, of social integration. It is particularly this latter aspect which makes the play intensely modern and captures the imagination of producers and actors.

First, then, the tragedy of the artistic sensibility. *Tasso* figures as the first "Künstlerdrama" in German. On this level, the play bears strong autobiographical traits: there are clear links between Duke Alfons and Duke Carl August, and between the Prinzessin and Charlotte von Stein. But it is not a direct translation: Goethe was immersed in the practical affairs of the court and yearned for private, creative space. Nevertheless, in 1827, he told Eckermann that the play did express the malaise — "Schmerzliches und Lästiges"[7] (painful and wearisome things) — which haunted his first few years at Weimar. He stressed that the text was still an integral part of himself: "Bein von meinem Bein und Fleisch von meinem Fleisch"[8] (bone of my bone and flesh of my flesh). Furthermore, as pointed out in our discussion of Goethe's poetry, the shadow of Tasso returns in the "Trilogie der Leidenschaft" where it interlinks with the figure of Werther. The play does indeed hark back to the early novel: Tasso and Werther share a highly-strung sensibility that swings from elation to dejection, from proud self-assertion to intense crises of identity. Werther's agony prefigures Tasso's fear of losing himself — "mich zu verlieren" — of being "ein Nichts." Both figures are in danger of losing their sense of identity, but there is a crucial difference: the lynchpin of Werther's identity is the heart, his inner life. By contrast, Tasso yearns to move out of his contemplative life, to be involved in the active life as symbolized by Antonio. Above all: Werther embodies mere sensitivity, whereas Tasso is a supreme artist. He channels his energies into the objective shape of the artifact.

The fraught relationship between Tasso and the court lies at the heart of any interpretation. From the start, the poet is a figure who is part of the establishment, yet also alien to that culture. He repeatedly states that he has found a second home at the court, that its culture sustains his creativity. And yet Tasso refuses to heed the ethos of the court. He regularly seeks refuge in solitude, in "Einsamkeit." In short, then, he figures as a contradictory mix of assimilation and alienation. In the opening scene, the Prinzessin and Leonore try in vain to define his being. He is an elusive figure who oscillates between closeness and distance — "meiden" and "fliehen" are key verbs. As Leonore comments: "Er scheint sich uns zu nahn, und bleibt uns fern" (170; He seems to come close to us, yet he remains distant). Despite his central role at the court, Tasso's individuality defies definition, appropriation by others.

The reasons for this fraught relationship are manifold. As a temperament, Tasso, like his historical original, is mentally threatened. He embodies an individualist subjectivity which is loath to acknowledge the boundaries of social reality. The incompatibility of the courtly world and Tasso's selfhood is crystallized in recurrent patterns: on the one hand there is the courtly ethos, the code of "Kreis," "Gesellschaft," "Maß," "Sittlichkeit," and "Höflichkeit"; on the other, there is Tasso's individualistic energy, in motifs such as "Leidenschaft," "unbeherrscht," and "heftig." In short, his temperament is such that it regularly clashes with the conditions of the objective world.

These personal traits are intensified by Tasso's artistic genius. This poet is the product of highest culture. Steeped in the legacy of ancient Greece, he tends to soar off into the realm of eternal values, Platonic absolutes and to ignore the human world, the realm of relativity. As the Prinzessin remarks in the opening scene, he is driven by metaphysical longing, inhabiting the realm of "süßer Träume." Yet he also clings to the real, physical world, "das Wirkliche." Again, then, Tasso is seen to insist on living unconditionally, beyond all boundaries and divisions. His urge to experience totality is summed up by Antonio in act 3, iv:

> Dann will er alles fassen, alles halten,
> Dann soll geschehen, was er sich denken mag
> [. . .]
> Die letzten Enden aller Dinge will
> Sein Geist zusammen umfassen [. . .] (2127–36)

[Then he wants to encompass and hold everything,
Then what he thinks should be turned into action.
His spirit endeavors to bring together
The ultimate ends of all things.]

These lines, the stress on "alles," and "zusammen umfassen" strikingly echo the disposition of Faust.

Goethe defined the play's theme as the disproportion between genius and normality, the "Disproportion des Talents mit dem Leben" (503). This disproportion emerges as early as act 1, iii when Tasso is crowned. The court views the laurel wreath as a social symbol of respect; but for the poet, the laurel is a divine symbol, the attribute of Apollo, and it fills him with holy terror. Typically, he conjures up a vision of Elysium, the Paradisal fields in Greek mythology where heroes and poets are united after death:

Oh, säh ich die Heroen, die Poeten
Der alten Zeit um diesen Quell versammelt!
[. . .]
O daß ich gegenwärtig wäre, sie
Die größten Seelen nun vereint zu sehen! (545–57)

[If only I were to see the heroes, the poets
Of olden times assembled round this spring.
If only I were present to see
Them, the great souls now united.]

One notes the precariousness of these lines: they are held in the subjunctive of the wish-dream. Tasso is, then, neither at home in the everyday nor in the realm of myth. Suspended between the realm of the absolute and the relative, he is prone to misread reality. He cannot find his cognitive way; hence the motifs of "kennen" and "verkennen" form a dominant strand in the play. The danger of misreading culminates in the manifestation of paranoia. Thus in act 4, iii, he no longer trusts Leonore, and in act 5, v, he denounces the court's conspiracy against him.

So far, we have focused on Tasso's mental decline in terms of his temperament, both as a person and as a poet. Let us now turn to a socio-cultural argument which defines Tasso's agony in terms of radical social alienation. As critics have generally noted, the ethos of courtly culture is a stifling force. On this socio-critical perspective, Tasso's seeming pathology takes on a revelatory function: his tantrums, his suspicions, and his defiance of the courtly ethos show up the inauthenticity of this culture. It is a culture that rests on the imperative of "sich verstellen," of self-repression.

This inauthenticity pervades all. Take, for example, the court's tolerance toward the wayward, at times most irritating poet, which comes across as a generous form of "Sittlichkeit," but in fact it interlinks with self-interest, both personal and above all public. Tasso constitutes a precious commodity, which serves to maintain the authority of Ferrara within the rivalry of political reality. More importantly, the text increasingly highlights the human price of this self-repressive "Sittlichkeit." The motif of role-playing is the opening chord of the play. The Prinzessin and Leonore have dressed up as shepherdesses, in typical ancien régime fashion. They seem utterly at home in these roles, yet the dialogue alerts us to the sheer artifice by foregrounding the verb "scheinen": it is repeated three times within the opening lines. In addition, the two women are intensely self-conscious: each is keenly aware of the other, and each watches and comments on herself as an object:

PRINZESSIN: Du siehst mich lächelnd an, Eleonore,
             Du siehst dich selber an und lächelst wieder.
             Was hast du? Laß es eine Freundin wissen!
             Du scheinst bedenklich, doch du scheinst vergnügt.

LEONORE: Ja, meine Fürstin, mit Vergnügen seh ich
             Uns beide hier so ländlich ausgeschmückt.
             Wir scheinen recht beglückte Schäferinnen. (1–7)

[PRINZESSIN: You look upon me smilingly, Leonore,
             You see yourself and smile again.
             What is it? Let your friend into the secret!
             You seem thoughtful, yet you seem cheerful.

LEONORE: Yes, my princess, with pleasure I see
             Us both here bedecked in country dress.
             We seem to be utterly happy shepherdesses.]

These opening lines tell us that this is a culture of perfectly controlled "Schein," so much so that it displaces authenticity altogether. Precisely this central trait of "scheinen" makes the articulation of authenticity, of truth and truthfulness, dangerous, if not catastrophic — in sharpest contrast to Iphigenie. Take act 2, i: here, the Prinzessin urges Tasso to confide in Alfons and Antonio. But her advice proves disastrous: Tasso does as she tells him, and offers Antonio friendship — "Hier ist meine Hand" (1283; Here is my hand). But this gesture of communication cannot break through; on the contrary, it generates suspicion and thus reinforces the alienation between the two men. Antagonism grows and culminates when Tasso finally draws his sword.

Overall, the court can only maintain itself by an ethos of total self-repression. The four figures move in carefully gauged steps. Just as Alfons and Antonio negotiate the slippery stage of politics, so, privately, the characters tread carefully in their personal dealings. Their discourse is that of convention; in the words of the Prinzessin it is a discourse of "Sitte und Höflichkeit," of the "Gebrauch der Welt" (1692–93). This discourse may guarantee a stable order, both externally and internally, but the price is heavy: the loss of authentic, individual being.

The issue of repression openly erupts in act 2, i, the discussion between Tasso and the Prinzessin. He insists on the unrestrained life: "Erlaubt ist was gefällt" (994; what gives pleasure is permitted). These lines are a direct quotation from his pastoral play *Aminta* (1573), a play which delights in sensuousness and sensuality. Typically enough, the Prinzessin rejects his advocacy of the life of the senses: "erlaubt ist was sich ziemt" (100; what is seemly is permitted). Her stress on the decent, seemly, may come across as a superior form of "Sittlichkeit," but it is in fact a devastating tautology: her words amount to the dictum "that which is permissible is permitted." This tautology literally spells out the deadly constriction of courtly life. Given these constrictions, it is no surprise that the court is appalled by Tasso's two transgressions. On both occasions the reaction is one of total horror. In the eyes of Antonio, Tasso drawing his sword, let alone his embracing of the Prinzessin, spells the end of civilization:

> Nun sehen wir nach langem, schönem Frieden
> In das Gebiet der Sitten rohe Wut
> Im Taumel wiederkehren [. . .] (1513–15)

> [Now we see after a long and lovely time of peace
> Rough anger returning tumultuously
> To the domain of seemliness.]

The extremity of such terms as "rohe Wut," raging brutality, or, later "das Ungeheure" (3291), the monstrous, suggests a kind of hysteria — the hysteria of a culture that relies on utter repression, the rule of the taboo.

This analysis of courtly culture generates a wider argument, an argument about the mechanisms of socialization as such, about the discontent which haunts the individual self within the order of civilization. In this sense, the play prefigures Sigmund Freud's famous essay *Das Unbehagen in der Kultur* (1930), which traces the latent discontent within civilization. In this context act 3, ii is of crucial importance: here, the suppressed, the inadmissible suddenly erupts. At this point, the climax of any five act drama, Tasso is absent from the play whose very title bears his name. He is imprisoned in his room, and the Prinzessin and Leonore hold the stage. But in an extraordinary transfer, Tasso's voice shifts to the Prinzessin. In a series of monologues, she laments the condition of imprisonment, the resentment of a self entrapped in the conventions of civilization. To Leonore's horror, the Prinzessin breaks out of her role as an upholder of restraint, and takes on traits which we associate with Tasso and with Faust. Up to now she has figured as a willing member of civilization, of "Maß" and "Mäßigung": "gern" is her leitmotif. But now she pours out her discontent. Faced with the prospect that she might lose Tasso, she gives voice to unrelieved lament:

> Muß ich denn wieder diesen Schmerz als gut
> Und heilsam preisen? Das war mein Geschick
> Von Jugend auf. (1776–78)

> [Must I then again praise this pain as good
> And wholesome? That was my fate
> from youth onwards.]

The category of "gern" is here replaced by that of "müssen." Critics usually speak of her stoic acceptance, her resignation, and they link it to Goethe's later concept of "Entsagen," the moral art of learning to do without. But the key word in this scene is "entbehren," and it acquires the full force of deprivation. The phrase "soll entbehren" is repeated three times. Like Faust, who cries "entbehren sollst du, sollst entbehren" (1549), the Prinzessin rails against the condition of lack. Leonore desperately holds out the prospect of hope, of "Glück," but this only serves to intensify the Prinzessin's despair: "Glücklich? Wer ist denn glücklich?" (1782–83; Happy? Who is ever happy?), she asks, and she goes on to destroy the notion of happiness, a concept which is so much part of civilization's efforts. Her dissection reveals profound discontent and suffering within her family, a plight which is silenced, tabooed by the courtly ethos. The text here reads like short-hand, but Goethe's audience was familiar with the facts. Alfons figures no longer as the serene sovereign and instead appears as a man whose personal and political dreams have not been fulfilled. (He was in fact married three times, yet had no heir, and he strove in vain to become King of Poland. After his death, Ferrara was re-appropriated by the Pope.) Then there is Lukrezia, the sister. She hovers on the horizon of the play as a figure of radiant happiness. Now suddenly, the Prinzessin reveals her suffering: Lukrezia is childless and cannot provide her younger husband with an heir. (Her real fate was much worse: her husband treated her viciously; she finally took a lover who was promptly murdered in the presence of her brother, Duke Alfons.) Above all, the Prinzessin highlights the blighted childhood which she, Lukrezia and Alfons had to endure. Their mother turned Protestant, and the brutal logic of the Counter-Reformation dictated that she be separated from her children. There follows an account of the Prinzessin's childhood, years of illness, which were only relieved by art, by singing — a comfort which was then, on doctor's orders, also denied to her. Throughout these passages, the Prinzessin rejects "Geduld," the patience that puts up with lack. In this sense, her words point across to the most unlikely kinsman, to Faust, who curses the quality of patience: "Und Fluch vor allen der Geduld!" (1606; And a curse, above all, on patience!).

In short, act 3, ii opens up a massive gap at the very center of the play. The force of the long repressed totally displaces the court's argument that civilization offers protection, security, as Antonio suggests in act 2, iv. Rather, the outburst suggests that those "Mauern" of "Sicherheit" (1505–6) are walls of socially sanctioned silence. Typically enough, after act 3, ii, the Prinzessin never again speaks out. So internalized has she the walls of "erlaubt ist, was sich ziemt" that in act 5, iv, she recoils in horror from Tasso's embrace. Everything she tells him there, however coded, bespeaks desire; yet desire shrinks back at the last moment: "Hinweg!" (3284; Away!).

Read against the background of act 3, ii, Tasso's lack of restraint takes on a different aspect: it is no longer merely the voice of personal agony. Rather: he articulates the condition of lack, of "fehlen," and his voice, like the Prinzessin's, thus amplifies the discontent of all those whose authentic voice remains silent within the conventions of that civilization.

The play offers, then, a somber critique of civilization; but the text acquires even darker aspects when we turn to the level which addresses existential issues. Here, we find the image of a humanity marked by lack and division. On this existential level, one notes that the text is shot through with motifs of paradise lost, of an exiled humanity. The motif of banishment, "verbannen," is dominant; in the first instance, it is of course linked to the figure of Tasso: in act 2, he is banished to his room, and by act 5, he is separated from the courtly circle: "Ich bin verstoßen, bin verbannt, ich habe mich selbst verbannt" (3999–3400; I am cast out, am banished, I have banished myself). But in a much wider sense, the motif reverberates in the references to the blighted childhood of both the Prinzessin and Tasso, the exile of his father and the ban imposed on her mother. Such patterns of loss gain a particular tragic force when set against the motif of "neu," the most sustained leitmotif in this text. It recurs in countless variations, and, as in *Iphigenie*, it bespeaks hope, the longing for regeneration. But this hope of "neu" is not fulfilled: the conclusion is dominated by the motif of loss, separation, the three times sounded "Abschied."

We have come to the end of our discussion of Goethe's four major plays (apart from *Faust*, which, for obvious reasons, has a chapter to itself). *Torquato Tasso* was finished in August 1789 and is almost contemporary with the promulgation of the Rights of Man issuing from revolutionary France. Apart from *Faust*, which continues to preoccupy him until his death in 1832, Goethe seems never to have hit his stride again as a dramatist. Yet not for want of trying; and, curiously, the subject of the French

Revolution persistently triggers in him the idea for a play. But each attempt ends in failure. For Goethe, the French Revolution was anathema; everything in him rejected the violent. He was a man of evolution rather than revolution, one who believed passionately in organic development. Hence he was not good at coping with political conflict, least of all on such a cataclysmic scale.

His responses as dramatist to the French Revolution are fascinating in their polarization. On the one hand, he writes comedies, attempting, as it were, to laugh revolutionary violence out of court. On the other hand, he devotes himself to the grand manner, to high classicism and elaborately wrought artistic form, no doubt in the hope of pitting aesthetic order against the turmoil of his time. Within the comic strand, the chief dramas are *Der Großkophta* (1791), *Der Bürgergeneral* (1793), and *Die Aufgeregten* (1793). Of the three, *Die Aufgeregten* is, marginally, the most noteworthy. It is set in contemporary Germany, on the estate of a countess. The local peasants are discontented because certain of their traditional rights and tax privileges are being eroded; moreover, the charter which summarizes these privileges has disappeared. However, at the key moment, when the peasants threaten open rebellion, the charter is found. Its disappearance had nothing to do with abuse of power by the countess: it was hidden by a manipulative official. The play was Goethe's response to local student unrest inspired by the events in France. But even when judged on this totally parochial level, the play — as a comedy — is inadequate. The peasants' bid for their rights parodies the Declaration of the Rights of Man, and Goethe's suggestion that the nobility may yet become enlightened is utterly threadbare. In act 3, the members of the court engage in a seemingly instructive game of political role playing: they act out the French National Assembly, as though to gain some insight into the justification of revolutionary demands. But the scene, potentially interesting, mixes political issues with facile romance, erotic trifles, and thus lacks direction. It is no wonder that the play remained a fragment. Goethe filled in the gaps with narrative prose, but to no avail: the attempt to laugh politics out of court remains profoundly feeble.

More noteworthy are his attempts to respond with artistic grandeur. *Die natürliche Tochter* (1803) is set in France toward the end of the ancien régime. Eugenie, the illegitimate daughter of the Duke, is presented to the King. She is a beautiful and highly educated young woman, and a brilliant life seems to await her. But plots have been laid against her: she is abducted and offered the chance either to live in banishment or to marry a commoner, the "Gerichtsrat." She agrees to the latter course of action, but only on conditions that ensure that the "Gerichtsrat" keeps his distance. The play has its impressive moments, and there are some passages of magnificent verse. But ultimately it is sterile. Cherished Goethean motifs appear — of hope, salvation, death and rebirth — but they seem to collapse in on themselves and lead nowhere. The figure of Eugenie is closely related to that of Iphigenie; but in the last analysis they are poles apart. Where Iphigenie challenges cultural tradition, Eugenie clings to it; where Iphigenie challenges a world of lies and deceit, Eugenie becomes ever more entrapped. The play closes on a scene in which her marriage is about to be solemnized; but despite, or because of, the grand rhetoric, it strikes us as more counterfeit than symbol.

Some eleven years later, the famous actor Iffland commissioned Goethe to write a play to celebrate the victory of Napoleon and the return to Prussia of King Friedrich Wilhelm III. Goethe obliged with a "Festspiel" *Des Epimenides Erwachen* (1814). Orchestral music, song, chorus, painting are fused into a grand allegorical design which celebrates the return of peace, of faith, hope, charity, and, of course, national unity. It is a remarkable exercise in grandiloquence: it has a kind of willed, yet vacuous simplicity.

To feel the genuine force of Goethe's imagination as a dramatist, we have to attend to the four great plays of the pre-Revolutionary period, or to *Faust*, which occupied him throughout his creative life. To *Faust* we now wish to turn.

5: *Faust*

COMMENTATORS ON GOETHE'S dramatic work have often noted that he tends to focus on the workings of one particular sensibility and to explore whether that sensibility can be true to itself, can keep some kind of faith with the deepest promptings of his or her being. Although there may be an element of truth to this, plays such as *Götz, Egmont, Iphigenie,* and *Tasso* are dramas, not monologues. As the preceding chapter has suggested, the self has its antagonists, characters that are truly distinct, not mere extensions of the central subject. In other words: there is a world outside that self, a world of history, society, politics, institutions. Moreover, in his dramas, Goethe argues and understands through the medium of the theatre. In the discussion of *Faust,* we shall pay particular attention to this dimension.

To begin at the beginning: Goethe did not invent the Faust figure, nor did he invent the primary fable in which he appears. There was a real Faust, who was born some time around 1480. He seems to have made a living as a wandering scholar, practicing medicine, perhaps also hypnosis. He cast horoscopes and he no doubt dabbled in alchemy and magic. He was also a showman, a flamboyant and, in the eyes of many, disreputable, irreligious character. In a variety of ways, then, he was manifestly the kind of person to whom legends readily attach themselves. So, when in 1587 the prose chapbook *Historia von D. Johann Fausten* appeared in Frankfurt am Main, published by Johann Spies, it brought into narrative and psychological and theological focus a colorful cluster of stories, anecdotes, rumor, gossip that all had to do with the emergent restlessness of early modern European culture. The 1587 tale recounts how Faust, an arrogant intellectual and speculator of the elements and necromancer, sells his soul to the Devil in exchange for twenty-four years of service which give him access to all manner of erotic, social, and cosmological adventures. At the end of the allotted time he dies gruesomely, and his soul is forfeit. The story, not least because it concerned itself with a figure who was known to, and firmly anchored in, the popular imagination, caught on. It was translated into various languages, one being English, and came to the attention of Christopher Marlowe. It also provided the stuff of popular adaptations for the theatre and puppet shows. It was in these homely forms that the legend captured the youthful Goethe's interest. Subsequently he became acquainted with the 1587 narrative, although not in the original but in a somewhat later version.

The basic thrust of the 1587 *Volksbuch* (and of the version that Goethe knew) is resolutely conservative and didactic. Moralizing commentary abounds. But even so, there is a whiff of potential complexity to be sensed in the text. Like all cautionary tales, this one cannot abstain entirely from taking a certain interest in the forms and fruits of the wrongdoing it so resolutely condemns. The basic event sequence is largely episodic and trivial; but there is a certain energy to that profusion. And in the concluding section, as the moment of reckoning comes ever closer, we hear intimations of a theological-cum-philosophical issue. The *Volksbuch* is a deeply Lutheran work, and it is at least touched by the paradox that sin and abjection may be a precondition for faith and salvation. This is not to imply that the *Historia von D. Johann Fausten* is a neglected masterpiece. But it is the soil from which Marlowe derived a great play, which moves beyond the *Volksbuch's* judgmental simplicity and explores the genuine cognitive and psychological complexity of Faust as overreacher. Marlowe understands blasphemy as a desperate, last-ditch acknowledgment of the divinity that has been eradicated in the condition of secularized modernity. Goethe's *Faust* project was conceived without any direct knowledge of Marlowe's drama (he only came across it late in his life). But, clearly, he felt in his contact with the puppet plays and the 1587 story some of the seismic shocks that his great English predecessor had discerned in the *Faust* legend, shocks to do with the theological and psychological disturbances occasioned by modernity.

Before we turn to the text of Goethe's *Faust,* a word about its structure and the layers of its genesis. It may be helpful to think of the project as being three acts of a vast drama. At its center, and constituting act 2, is the tragedy of Faust's love for, and destruction of, Gretchen. Act 1 can be understood as extending from Faust's despairing opening monologue through his contract with Mephisto to the rejuvenation in the Witches Kitchen. And the immense act 3 of the drama is provided by Part II of Goethe's text, in which Faust moves through various scenes and instances of European culture, both ancient and modern. However, such a division can be no more than a rough initial guide, for we must bear in mind that Goethe worked on the *Faust* material throughout his creative life. In essence, he made four attempts: the so-called *Urfaust* of the 1770s, the fragment of 1790, Part I of 1808, and Part II of 1832. Each time he went back to the project, he changed the framework of what had already been made, and thereby he provided a new and different context for the drama. The creative process, then, was one of shifting configurations and contextualizations. Precisely that sense of an ongoing process was clearly in his mind when he published Part I in 1808: he labeled it "der Tragödie erster Teil," indicating that it was part of a larger, yet-to-be-written whole. Moreover, he prefaced that "first part of the tragedy" with three framing statements that stood apart from the experiential flow of the drama proper. What appeared in 1808, then, was a work conceived in terms of both a text and its meta-texts. Moreover, as Goethe wrote and re-wrote, he seems not to have been unduly worried about harmonizing the various versions. He did re-work the *Urfaust* material for incorporation into Part I, but even so, he did not even out all the discrepancies. Neither the *Urfaust* nor the 1790 fragment spell out the nature of the contract between Faust and Mephisto; this was the "große Lücke," the great lacuna, that Goethe was only able to fill in Part I. When he finally did so, he clarified the Faust/Mephisto relationship, but he did not then rigorously check the earlier material for loose ends. Rather, he allowed for overlapping, but sometimes diverging, frameworks of understanding. Part I up to the "Witches Kitchen" is essentially a philosophical drama which explores the battle between Faust's energy and Mephisto's cynicism. This is followed by the "Gretchentragödie," deriving from the oldest stratum of material (the *Urfaust*); it is essentially a drama of human relationships and, by that token, a psychological and moral drama. Part II is the historico-cultural drama of modernity. Now, of course, all three frameworks of significa-tion — philosophical, psychological, and historical — are not watertight entities. Rather, each informs and comments on the other and engages us in a process of complex seeing and responding in and through the thea-tre. We shall return to these issues at the end.

Let us begin with the oldest layer of the project, the Gretchen story. It constitutes a signal achievement in two ways. One is that Goethe man-ages here to resolve a central problem that plagues so many versions of the *Faust* story which precede and succeed his work — the danger of epi-sodic triviality. This is to say: once Faust has powers that accelerate ex-perience and make it readily available, there is the risk that the play may turn into a sequence of episodes which simply illustrate his indiscriminate greed for experiences. But Goethe realized from the outset of his work on the *Faust* drama that he needed to plunge his protagonist into a unique experience of intense human substance and moral weight. The second strand of Goethe's achievement in the *Urfaust* version is that he writes one of the most richly intelligent psychological dramas of modern Europe. Faust's and Gretchen's love affair is one between a young woman of hitherto modest emotional and intellectual experience and a man — a young man as a result of the witches' magic potion — who is an intellec-tual: as one might put it, he knows it all, and knows that all is still not enough. Here, Goethe's psychological insight is masterly at every turn precisely because it is so unsentimental. Gretchen knows of, and is excited by, the differences between her and her lover, differences in class and in-tellectual sophistication. She is proud of her beauty, particularly when it is set off by the jewelry:

> Wenn nur die Ohrring meine wären!
> Man sieht doch gleich ganz anders drein. (2795–96)

> [If only the earrings were mine!
> They make all the difference to the way you look.]

Or one thinks of the hint of sexually derived irritation in the "mein Herr" of her response to Faust's characteristically male suggestion that looking after a young child must be bliss:

> Da gehts, mein Herr, nicht immer mutig zu;
> Doch schmeckt dafür das Essen, schmeckt die Ruh. (3146–47)

> [It is not, sir, a life much given to pleasure.
> But it does mean that the food and rest taste good.]

Faust is passionate, ardent; he oscillates between crude desire — "Hör, du mußt mir die Dirne schaffen!" (2618; Listen, you must get that girl for me!) and intense spirituality:

> Willkommen, süßer Dämmerschein,
> Der du dies Heiligtum durchwebst! (2686–87)

> [Welcome sweet half-light of dusk
> Which weaves its way through the sanctuary.]

On occasion he can be patronizing and sentimental, as when he bluffs his way out of answering Gretchen's question whether he believes in God with a grandiloquent version of theological relativism. During that scene (Marthens Garten) it is very striking that, while she uses his name ("Versprich mir, Heinrich!"), he uses only epithets whose cumulative force tends to be demeaning: "mein Kind," "mein Liebchen," "du holdes Angesicht," "Liebs Kind," "Liebe Puppe," "Du ahnungsvoller Engel du," "Liebchen" (my child; my darling; you sweet face; dear child; dear doll; you perceptive angel you; darling). In fact, it is only right at the end of the play that he uses her name. The cogency and sharpness of Goethe's characterization is superb.

There is a further point to be made about the psychological truth of the *Urfaust* layer of Goethe's great drama, and it concerns the characterization of Gretchen. Under the emotional pressure of her love for Faust, she finds herself desperately impelled to think, to reflect, to interrogate her experience. But how can she do it? She needs a framework of self-exploration but does not know where to look for it; she has not been given much education. Girls of her class and upbringing are not meant, as it were, to soliloquize in any sustained or complex way. But she has to; and the play needs to articulate her inwardness, without becoming arch or sentimental. Goethe's answer is both simple and profound. When Gretchen soliloquizes, she is not simply sitting and thinking. She is doing something. The hands are busy: she is trying on jewelry; she is brushing her hair and undressing for bed; she is at the spinning wheel; she is putting flowers in a vase. And frequently, when she thinks, she has recourse to old, established forms of utterance. She, as it were, borrows the discourse of inwardness: from folk song ("Es war ein König in Thule" [There Once Was a King in Thule]), work song ("Meine Ruh ist hin" [My Peace Has Gone]), prayer ("Ach, neige, / Du Schmerzensreiche" [Ah Incline, You Who Are Full of Sorrows]). This achievement, at once stylistic and human, on Goethe's part, is breathtaking. One only realizes the full scope of that achievement when one considers the whole issue of Gretchen's language. Her words are constantly close to colloquial speech. One thinks of the imperfect rhyme, occasioned by Goethe's own Frankfurt dialect, in "Ach, neige, / Du Schmerzensreiche," or of that lilting little phrase when she is drawn to the casket of jewels: "Was mag wohl drinne sein?" (What might perhaps be inside?). This linguistic characterization, never falsely grandiloquent or pretentious, is all the more remarkable when we consider that German literary culture in the 1770s was still searching for a flexible language which would make immediate experience expressible.

One final point about Faust and Gretchen which will provide the link to the preceding and succeeding phases of the drama. The wonderfully observed psychological interplay between the two lovers can also be heard as the cultural interplay between two radically different worlds: between a modern awareness, Faust's, that is secular and individualist, and Gretchen's world, bounded as it is by parents, family, house, church, school, village. When Faust destroys Gretchen, we see the energies of the modern world destroying the contained, enclosing structures of pre-modern living. Hence the scene when Gretchen asks Faust if he believes in God is supremely important. Gretchen is neither foolish nor naive. She is trying to find out what Faust believes in, what he lives by and for. She frames the question the only way she knows how: "Wie hast dus mit der Religion?" (What do you make of religion?). At this point, held wonderfully in linguistic and psychological truth (note the utterly colloquial force of the phrase "wie hast dus mit"), we sense a much broader cultural issue at work, a momentous paradigm shift caused by secularization. And we can still hear some of the force of that shift if we consider a matter of German usage: Gretchen's question — the make-or-break, the decisive question — has gone into the German language as the "Gretchen Frage." What equivalent do we have in English? One answer, conceivably, is "the $64,000 question" which radically shows up the process of secularization. The tragic love affair between Faust and Gretchen is an instance of cultural and historical change. Goethe creates not just individuated characters but a whole way of life. At one level, the play grieves for the passing of the older world. But the portrayal of that world is also utterly precise and critical. One could think of Gretchen's brother Valentin, who regards her primarily as an adjunct to his social standing, or of the bitchy Lieschen at the well, who, in a brutal couplet, rejoices at the fact that one of the village girls has got herself pregnant:

> War ein Gekos und ein Geschleck:
> Da ist denn auch das Blümchen weg! (3558–59)

> [There was a fondling and kissing
> And then suddenly the little flower was gone.]

Viewed under this aspect, then, Goethe's *Faust* diagnoses modernity, perceives both its liberating and its destructive energies. It asks us to understand processes of historical change and to count the cost.

The issue of modernity is powerfully present in the first phase of Part I and in Part II. There are three principal dimensions to Faust's modernity. First: the action of the play begins with his great soliloquy of discontent. The first human image we see is of the self alone, of radical individualism. Secondly, the man in question is a scholar, someone who is emerging from forms of older, alchemical speculation into a recognizably modern quest to understand the processes of material organization that hold the world together. In these terms, Faust is, then, a scientist. Yet he aspires to a form of cognition — "Erkenntnis" — that is both the reflective exploration of experience and the need for enhanced entry into experience itself. Hence the link is forged between the story of the thwarted intellectual and the story of the lover. We remember that the verb "to know," in its modern and biblical uses, can have both intellectual and carnal meanings. Thirdly, the man we see at the opening of the drama is a fiercely secular spirit. His despair brings him to the very brink of suicide. True, the bells and the music of Easter stay his hand, but, as the text makes clear, not because Faust is a believer, but because the sounds of Easter remind him of childhood. Here, as elsewhere in the play, Faust conceives of childhood as the closest approximation to the pre-lapsarian state. Later, the "Easter Walk" will show us a Faust delighting in the only resurrection he can know and believe in: the resurrection brought by the advent of spring.

So far, we have focused on Faust as a representative of modern culture: individualist, secular, scientific. We now need to extend that argument to the wager between him and Mephisto: it is germane to the issue of modernity, and it expresses the central philosophical concerns of the play.

Faust is aware of the mismatch between the "zwei Seelen" (two souls) within him, a mismatch between matter and mind:

Die eine hält in derber Liebeslust
Sich an die Welt mit klammernden Organen;
Die andre hebt gewaltsam sich vom Dust
Zu den Gefilden hoher Ahnen. (1113–16)

[The one holds tight, in coarse desire,
On to the world with grabbing organs;
The other lifts itself violently from the confusion
To the fields of higher beings.]

One soul, then, is deeply in love with physical immediacy, with palpable experience; whereas the other is impelled by the imperative to stand back, to reflect, to conceptualize. The friction between those two imperatives produces the Faustian energy, an energy that never comes to rest, never finds contentment. Faust believes passionately in deeds, in doing, as the scene where he translates the Bible makes clear:

Mir hilft der Geist! auf einmal seh ich Rat
Und schreibe getrost: Im Anfang war die Tat! (1236–37)

[The spirit helps me! Suddenly I see how
And confidently write "In the beginning was the deed!"]

But deeds are, inevitably, finite. And Faust's mind constantly reaches beyond each finite, circumscribed articulation of the self. The intense promptings of anticipation are not quenched by the attainment of any specific goal; rather, they are re-activated as renewed desire. The narrow framework of activity is constantly overtaken by the larger framework of reflectivity.

The two great "Studierzimmer" scenes between Faust and Mephisto bring us to the heart of the philosophical theme of Goethe's drama. As we have seen, in earlier versions of the *Faust* story the contract between Faust and the Devil was a fixed term pact: Faust sells his soul for twenty-four years of service. In Goethe's conception, much has changed, to put it mildly. Mephisto's aim is to switch off the Faustian dynamo, to bring the energy to rest. Faust goes into the contract with Mephisto in a spirit of intense skepticism. What is on offer is not a pact, not a fixed term arrangement, but rather an open-ended bet, a bet on experience and above all else on Faust's *attitude* to experience. Everything depends on what he *says,* what he thinks, what he makes of the experiential high points of his life. Are they fulfilling enough to impel him to hang on to the perfect moment? Faust is skeptical:

Werd ich beruhigt je mich auf ein Faulbett legen,
So sei es gleich um mich getan!
Kannst du mich schmeichelnd je belügen,

Daß ich mir selbst gefallen mag,
Kannst du mich mit Genuß betrügen:
Das sei für mich der letzte Tag! [. . .]
Werd ich zum Augenblicke sagen:
Verweile doch! du bist so schön!
Dann magst du mich in Fesseln schlagen,
Dann will ich gern zugrunde gehn! (1692–1702)

[If ever I lie in calmness on a bed of sloth,
Then shall I be finished.
If ever you can deceive me with flattery
To the point where I am happy with myself,
If you can cheat me with pleasure:
Then that will be my last day! [. . .]
If ever I say to the moment:
Stay a while! You are so beautiful!
Then you can put me in chains
Then I will gladly meet my end.]

Faust in fact proposes the wager to Mephisto in refutation of the latter's (traditional) offer of access to pleasure; and he does so because he believes that, for him, the onlooking, reflective persona, the meta-self to the active self, will always assert itself, condemning the present moment, however lovely, to insufficiency, always reaching out for more and different possibilities.

Faust's discontent, we might say, is both his glory and his tragedy. Intertextually, we hear implications extending back to earlier versions of the *Faust* story, and beyond, much further beyond, to Genesis Chapter 3, to the banishment of Adam and Eve from Paradise for wanting to know, for eating of the fruit of the Tree of Knowledge. And this intertext serves to highlight the issue of modernity. In the individualist, secular, scientifically-minded world the old commandments no longer apply; what matters now is energy versus quiescence, activity versus sluggishness, drive versus inertia. Such values have nothing to do with right or wrong in any traditional theological or moral sense, but everything to do with the quest for existential intensity.

All this transposition to the modern mode of course poses an acute problem. What is to be done with the figure of the Devil, so indispensable to the whole temper of the *Faust* legend? What, in the modern secular universe, is the equivalent of the evil principle? As we have already suggested, Mephisto's aim is to cut the Faustian energy down to size, to quench the drive and the intensity. True to his role in the legend, then, he is the purveyor of magical availability. And one role entailed by that strategy is that of the adept salesman, offering Faust pleasure, accelerated gratification:

Doch, guter Freund, die Zeit kommt auch heran,
Wo wir was Guts in Ruhe schmausen mögen. (1690–91)

[Yet, dear friend, the time is approaching
When we should calmly savor the good things.]

or again:

Euch ist kein Maß und Ziel gesetzt.
Beliebt's Euch, überall zu naschen,
Im Fliehen etwas zu erhaschen,
Bekomm Euch wohl, was Euch ergetzt!
Nur greift mir zu und seid nicht blöde! (1760–64)

[For you no measures, no goals are set.
If you would care to take a nibble here and there,
To grab something before you leave.
I wish you joy of whatever gives you pleasure!
Just help yourself and don't be backward.]

or again, on entering Auerbachs Keller:

Ich muß dich nun von allen Dingen
In lustige Gesellschaft bringen,
Damit du sieht, wie leicht sichs leben läßt. (2158–60)

[I must now above all else
Bring you into jolly company
In order that you see how easy life can be.]

The sales pitch, as one might put it, is not subtle; yet, given Faust's disillusionment with academic life, with living in words, concepts, and ideas, its very crudity might have a certain appeal. But Mephisto's other strategy, which is dialectically related to the first, is the one that really promises results: it is that of relentless cynicism, of devaluing anything and everything. Mephisto has, as it were, seen it all before; Gretchen is "not the first" ("Sie ist die erste nicht"); the process of seduction is simply "der Lauf der Welt" (3203; the way of the world). Mephisto is the master of the doctrine of reductive interchangeability, of the throw-away line. And in this sense he knows that he can appeal seductively to the knowing, debunking agency housed in Faust's consciousness. Faust's experience has taught him that the promise is better than the actuality, that anticipation is richer than any attainment. That devaluing of each particular experience is the source of Faust's energy and restiveness. It is for this reason that it would take so little for Mephisto's cynicism to find a hold in Faust's con-

sciousness. Tellingly enough, Mephisto's first introduction of himself to
Faust is in terms of the nihilist's stance:

> Ich bin der Geist, der stets verneint!
> Und das mit Recht: denn alles, was entsteht,
> Ist wert, daß es zugrunde geht;
> Drum besser wärs, daß nichts entstünde. (1338–41)

> [I am the spirit who always denies!
> And rightly so: for anything that comes into being
> Deserves to be swallowed up and destroyed.
> So it would be better if nothing came into being in the
>   first place.]

Hence also, in the soliloquy that precedes the entry of the naive young
student at the end of the second "Studierzimmer" scene, Mephisto looks
forward to Faust's succumbing to the sheer negativity of everything that
the world has to offer:

> Den schlepp ich durch das wilde Leben,
> Durch flache Unbedeutenheit,
> Er soll mir zappeln, starren, kleben,
> Und seiner Unersättlichkeit
> Soll Speis' und Trank vor gier'gen Lippen schweben.
>
> (1860–64)

> [I will drag him through the wildness of life
> Through banality and triviality,
> He will twitch, stare, and cling
> And food and drink will hover
> Before his insatiably parched lips.]

Within this framework of argument the battle between Faust and Mephisto
is electrifying. Time and time again Mephisto is right in his diagnosis of
what drives Faust experientially — as when he calls Faust a "supra-sensual,
sensual wooer" — "du übersinnlicher, sinnlicher Freier" (3533). Yet the
conclusion he hopes for, disillusionment, despair, is not reached. Even so,
it is a close-run thing. We recall that Faust nearly commits suicide; and
when Mephisto reminds him that he did not, in fact, take the irrevocable
step, his response is a savage curse on everything that promises fulfillment
in the human sphere and thereby deflects the self from the full knowledge
of its desperate condition:

> Fluch sei dem Balsamsaft der Trauben!
> Fluch jener höchsten Liebeshuld!

Fluch sei der Hoffnung! Fluch dem Glauben,
Und Fluch vor allen der Geduld. (1603–6)

[Curse on the balsamic juice of grapes!
Curse on the highest bliss of loving!
Curse on hope! Curse on faith
And curse above all else on patience.]

Potentially Faust is perilously close to the nihilistic condition. As we have seen from the wager, everything turns on what Faust says about his experience, and on how far his attitudes sustain his energy or on how far they diminish it. The center of this debate has not so much to do with pleasure as with unfulfillment. Will unfulfillment in the last analysis energize Faust or will it disillusion him? Which will it be?

Thus far we have been attending to the philosophical implications of the wager. But there is also the historical context to be considered. Mephisto's magic serves not so much to change or transform experience as to accelerate it; and, in the modern world, the impact of science, technology, industrialization has accelerated our experiential capacities. But in the process, has the value of our experience been enhanced? Perhaps rapid availability devalues whatever it touches; it is no coincidence that Mephisto conjoins the roles of cynic and salesman. Indeed, in the context of late-capitalist consumerism and the hyped omnipresence of virtual reality, Goethe's diagnosis of the modern and the post-modern condition strikes one as very acute. The historical inflection of the wager between Faust and Mephisto takes us into Part II, in which Goethe is particularly concerned to situate the *Faust* legend at the heart of modern European culture. *Faust II* opens with Faust restored by the powers of nature which have been at work beneath and within him as he slept. He recovers from the tragedy that dominates the closing phase of Part I, not by some act of moral self-analysis but by allowing nature to do its work, to refresh mind and body. To the thematic presence of the sheer power of natural forces we shall need to return later. At this stage we simply note that the acknowledgment of nature goes hand in hand with an assertion of the drama of human self-consciousness. As Faust gazes at the waterfall, he realizes that even the act of seeing is a conceptualization of, and on that account an abstraction from, what is empirically given. The materiality of the scene is millions of droplets of rushing water with the sun shining through them. What the eye makes of this materiality is a waterfall — and, even more insubstantial this, a rainbow. Goethe, with superb economy and in verse of great splendor allows us to hear again the philosophical issue from the first phase of Part I: the drama deriving from the interplay of mind and matter in human experience. Faust at this point speaks to and for humanity at large:

Allein wie herrlich, diesem Sturm ersprießend,
Wölbt sich des bunten Bogens Wechseldauer,
Bald rein gezeichnet, bald in Luft zerfließend,
Umher verbreitend duftig-kühle Schauer!
Der spiegelt ab das menschliche Bestreben.
Ihm sinne nach, und du begreifst genauer:
Am farbigen Abglanz haben wir das Leben. (4719–25)

[Yet how magnificent, emerging from this storm,
The constantly changing permanence of this colorful arch
Bends itself, now clearly outlined, now dissolving into air,
Spreading round about fragrantly cool showers!
That mirrors human striving.
Think on and you will understand more perfectly:
We experience life as colorful reflection.]

What then follows is a remarkable theatrical extravaganza, a series of
scenes in which the play recreates and debates with images of European
culture. If the Faust/Gretchen story works with a magnificent sense of
psychological specificity and substantiality, Part II moves beyond the ter-
ritory of nineteenth-century realism into a series of not just modern, but
also post-modern *tableaux vivants* in which the intertexts of our culture,
both those that come before and those that come after Goethe's *Faust*
project, pass before us. We begin with the Holy Roman Empire on its last
legs, in dire financial straits, hard pressed to find a few last titles and offices to sell off. Into that world bursts the new jester figure, Mephisto,
who, thanks to the invention of paper money, manages to bring new forms
of innovative, speculative economic activity to bear.[1] Modernity also informs the various forms of entertainment on offer — gardeners peddle artificial flowers, Renaissance masques and pageants merge mysteriously
into something very like modern advertising, girls are advised about
make-up and figures from classical mythology — Paris and Helena — appear as entertainment and advertising icons. Act 2 takes us back to Faust's
study at the opening of the drama. The Baccalaureus figure spells out the
radical subjectivism of a Romantic (in this case, Fichtean) worldview; and
Wagner, the hopeless pedant of the early phase of the play, now manages
in his laboratory to create artificial life. (From our contemporary perspective it is difficult not to think of genetic engineering in this scene.) Yet
remarkably, even that which is made artificially, under laboratory conditions, can take on the energies of living nature. The little man in his protective container, Homunculus, hears the call of Eros and spills himself
into the sea. The erotic consummation brings the "Klassische Walpurgisnacht" to a close — a "Walpurgisnacht" which engages in dialectical debate with the northern "Walpurgisnacht" of Part I. In these parallel and

contrasting sequences Goethe explores the cultic imaginings of two phases of European history. In Part II we are transported to the South Eastern Mediterranean, the cradle of the classical world, a pagan culture, one that, for all that it knows of endless battles and strife, never wages that war that the modern world knows so well, a war that disparages nature and bodiliness and materiality as some kind of dreadful perversion. The "Klassische Walpurgisnacht" brings Faust closer to Helena. The governing images are of water, of un-phallic, erotic merging. That radiant, brightly-lit world appalls Mephisto because it has no sense of the indwelling sinfulness of the body. Homunculus spells out to Mephisto the all-important implications:

> Nordwestlich, Satan, ist dein Lustrevier,
> Südöstlich diesmal aber segeln wir. (6948–49)

> [In the northwest, Satan, is your realm of joy,
> But this time we are sailing southeastwards.]

The "Walpurgisnacht" of Part I knows fully of sinfulness and perversion. It is a tumult that takes Faust away from Gretchen, that distracts him from love and offers in its stead phallic prowess. Goethe's allegory suggests that the creative energies of Europe originally emerged in the South Eastern Mediterranean; but, as far as modern culture is concerned, they have passed to the North West — at considerable cost. The modern subject does not indwell securely in the material world, and, in its acute self-reflexivity (we remember the two souls of the philosophical theme), it manipulates natural matter in a scenario of unparalleled creativity and destructiveness. And the final act of Part II will show us Faust as representative of the modern world's readiness to intervene in nature.

Act 3, the "Helena Akt," gives us the erotic version of the modern world's intertextual love affair with the Ancient World. Helena appears, caught strangely in a sense of identity that is grounded in the perception of herself as a cultural icon. Her postmodern awareness of herself as an entity inscribed and transmitted in and through legend —

> Bewundert viel und viel gescholten, Helena,
> Vom Strande komm ich [. . .] (8485–86)

> [Admired much and much maligned, Helena,
> I come from the shore.]

— coexists with the recurrent tragedy of the beautiful woman whose effect on men is always disastrous:

> Wehe mir! welch streng Geschick
> Verfolgt mich, überall der Männer Busen

So zu betören, daß sie weder sich
Noch sonst ein Würdiges verschonten. (9244–47)

[Woe is me! What stern fate
Pursues me and makes me always so confuse men's hearts
That they care neither for themselves
Nor for any other noble purpose.]

Faust, now lord of a medieval castle on the Peloponnese, teaches Helena
to rhyme. The sexual meeting, in a scene of great linguistic self-consciousness, is also a scene of high cultural sophistication as modern and ancient
verse forms unite. Helena learns quickly: the rhymes come thick and fast:
not just end rhymes, but also internal rhymes. And her simple words in
celebration of her being with Faust ("da bin ich") are converted by her
interlocutor into a philosophical category ("Dasein"):

HELENA: Ich fühle mich so fern und doch so nah,
          Und sage nur zu gern: da bin ich! da!

FAUST: Ich atme kaum, mir zittert, stockt das Wort;
          Es ist ein Traum, verschwunden Tag und Ort.

HELENA: Ich scheine mir verlebt und doch so neu,
          In dich verwebt, dem Unbekannten treu.

FAUST: Durchgrüble nicht das einzige Geschick!
          Dasein ist Pflicht, und wärs ein Augenblick.
                                          (9408–15)

[HELENA: I feel myself so distant and so near,
          And say with great joy: Here! Here!

FAUST: I scarcely breathe. I tremble, words won't come;
          It is a dream, time and place have gone.

HELENA: I seem to be worn away and yet so new,
          Interwoven with you, true to things unknown.

FAUST: Do not reflect too much on unique destiny!
          Being is a duty — even if only for a moment.]

The product of the union of Faust and Helena is Euphorion, the spirit of
modern (i.e. Romantic, specifically Byronic) poetry. It is a poetry that flies
high, that always has immortal longings in it, but that, by that very token,
plummets to earth. A modern tragedy, of course. But the intertextual acknowledgement of the Daedalus/Icarus legend can be heard. Once again,
nothing is the first, the one and only, as Mephisto is adept at pointing
out. But, *pace* Mephisto, it is not thereby devalued, rendered worthless.
Helena disappears, back to the shadowy realm from which she has been
summoned. But Faust is left with her veil and dress. The Ancient World

has left material traces behind. And the nineteenth century was the age that supremely treasured and uncovered those traces, by means of archaeological investigation and exploration.

In the closing phase of act 3, the stage directions make clear that the Euphorion action is meant to be expressed in music throughout. Surely, Goethe's text here suggests the immense contribution of opera to nineteenth-century European culture. In a sense, one might say that, from the Romantic period onward, the possibilities of dramatic expression bifurcate into realistic (and subsequently naturalistic) drama in prose on the one hand, and into that heightened form of drama that reaches from Beethoven's *Fidelio* via Weber and Verdi to Wagner, on the other. It is particularly suggestive to reflect on the issue of opera because Goethe's *Faust*, like few other works before or since, has constantly claimed the attention of composers.

Act 4 shows us the political turmoil of revolution and restoration, and acknowledges the extraordinary power of clapped-out feudalism to prop itself up by the aesthetic mystique of offices, titles, privileges. It is a charm to which even the new men (such as Faust) are susceptible, and they are perfectly prepared to ally themselves with the obsolete world whenever aesthetic and political self-interest so dictates.

Act 5 brings the immense cultural panorama and camera obscura and theme park of Part II to a close. Modern economics, initiated by the introduction of paper money, now express themselves in piracy, trade, and war, in the forces of modern capitalism and colonialism. Faust, inspired by the project of reclaiming land for new settlement, has two old people evicted from their cottage. The impetus behind this decision is, as the text makes abundantly clear, pure self-interest. The glimpse we have of the old couple is a superb little cameo, at once touching and comic, of two old people overwhelmed by the changes that threaten them. The sea is pushed back to yield usable land, and, conversely, canals are dug through what was once *terra firma*. At every stage nature is transformed; even the elements now seem biddable. No wonder that Baucis says:

> Wohl ein Wunder ists gewesen!
> Läßt mich heute nicht in Ruh;
> Denn es ging das ganze Wesen
> Nicht mit rechten Dingen zu. (11108–11)

> [A miracle it has indeed been!
> And it still won't leave me in peace;
> For the whole thing did not come about
> In right and proper ways.]

Precisely because of the ability, by means of scientific and technological advance, to interfere in nature, the modern world develops a culture which passionately celebrates untouched nature, as in the songs of Lynkeus, the watchman. In terms of prosody, there are echoes of earlier (medieval) forms; but the sentiments are modern. There is the song of rapture at the glory of the created world:

> Ich blick in die Ferne,
> Ich seh in der Näh,
> Den Mond und die Sterne,
> Den Wald und das Reh.
> [. . .]
> Ihr glücklichen Augen,
> Was je ihr gesehn,
> Es sei, wie es wolle,
> Es war doch so schön! (11218–11300)

> [I look afar,
> I see nearby
> The moon and the stars
> The wood and the deer.
> [. . .]
> You happy eyes
> Whatever you have seen,
> Let it be whatever it was,
> It was so beautiful.]

The language could hardly be more simple or heartfelt (one is reminded of the glorious closing cadence of the late poem "Der Bräutigam"). Yet the song of rapt absorption is immediately interrupted as the watchman registers the flames, "Von der Zugluft angefacht" (11308), which are the result of Mephisto's brutal eviction of the old people. Rapture coexists with destruction, then, in the dizzying experiential flow of modern culture. Small wonder that even Faust should feel the need to cast off the acceleration of living that Mephisto's magic has brought, the need to return to simple indwelling in nature:

> Könnt ich Magie von meinem Pfad entfernen,
> Die Zaubersprüche ganz und gar verlernen,
> Stünd ich, Natur, vor dir ein Mann allein,
> Da wär's der Mühe wert, ein Mensch zu sein. (11401–4)

> [If only I could remove sorcery from my ways,
> Un-learn the magic spells utterly,
> If I were able to stand alone before you, Nature,
> It would be worth the effort to be a human creature.]

But this is mere wishful thinking. For good and for ill, Faust is the modern subject who cannot forego the pace of modern living. Until the very end of the play he ceaselessly urges Mephisto and his workers to press forward with the great project of land reclamation. Neither the wish for a (Rousseauesque) return to nature can quench that energy, nor can it be quenched by the four gray figures who seek entry into Faust's domain. Neither lack nor guilt nor need can impinge. Only "Sorge" — care or worry — can make some headway: because she is a version of that intense self-consciousness which is so central to Faust's being. Her portrait of the worried self is unforgettable:

> Soll er gehen? Soll er kommen?
> Der Entschluß ist ihm genommen;
> Auf gebahnten Weges Mitte
> Wankt er tastend halbe Schritte. (11467–70)

> [Should he go? Should he come?
> The decision is taken from him:
> In the middle of the clearly marked path
> He dithers, uncertain, groping, taking half steps.]

Yet, like Egmont before him, Faust is nothing if not headlong in his living; he rejects the power of "Sorge." In punishment she blinds him. This judgment is strangely appropriate: blindness is the precondition of Faust's energy; significantly, the blindness does not diminish his desire to complete the project on which he is embarked.

The Faust of the closing scene is both deluded and visionary. He hears the sound of the spades that are digging his own grave; yet he imagines that he is surrounded by the last phase of his great building project. As his physical forces wane, he is filled with a vision of the future that he is helping to bring about. His death speech must be one of the most remarkable in world literature. So many death speeches are either retrospective, in the sense that they bring the life to a firm and articulate closure; or they look forward to release into a better world, a beyond that promises fulfillment. Yet Faust's final speech is neither of these things. It is all forward-looking; but the future envisaged is on this earth and of this earth. As Faust spells out the shape of the community to come, we hear an interplay of sheer self-centered titanism on the one hand and of philanthropic idealism on the other (Marxist critics, for example, have been fond of interpreting the vision as a prediction of the classless society). For Faust, the new community will never be able to take its security for granted; it will have to fight the sea to justify its existence at every turn. It will be a place, then, of corporate effort, but also one of sheer existential striving, of ceaseless strenuousness. In this intimation of what one day might be, Faust rejoices in the supreme moment:

Solch ein Gewimmel möcht ich sehn,
Auf freiem Grund mit freiem Volke stehn!
Zum Augenblicke dürft ich sagen:
"Verweile doch, du bist so schön!
Es kann die Spur von meinen Erdetagen
Nicht in Äonen untergehn."
Im Vorgefühl von solchem hohen Glück
Genieß ich jetzt den höchsten Augenblick. (11576–83)

[Such a bustling I would love to see,
To stand with a free people on free land!
To the moment I would then be able to say:
"Stay a while, you are so beautiful.
The traces of my days on earth
Shall not fade in eons."
In anticipation of such high bliss
I now enjoy the highest moment.]

The final utterance is one of self-assertion, and not of philanthropy. More-over, even this supreme moment is one that is conditional rather than ac-tual, possible rather than grasped. Faust speaks the words of the wager — in the simple sense that they cross his lips. But they are in quotation marks; they are spoken but not underwritten, uttered but not fully meant. And this is something that they share with other moments in Faust's ex-perience that seem to promise fulfillment. One thinks, for example, of the moment in the "Easter Walk" in Part I where Faust celebrates the delight of the common people in the coming of spring. Yet the affirmation is spoken in quotation marks:

Zufrieden jauchzet groß und klein:
"Hier bin ich Mensch, hier darf ich's sein!" (939–40)

[Contentedly old and young rejoice:
"Here I am a human being; here I can truly be so."]

Or one could think of the moment we have just been discussing, where Faust wishes he could dispense with magic: once again the conditional mode prevails — "Da wärs der Mühe wert, ein Mensch zu sein!" (11404). In other words, it is important to register that to the very end of his life Faust derives his energy from his compulsion to think beyond present ex-perience, to be aware of the future, the conditional, and the subjunctive mode of living.

But at the moment of Faust's death, Mephisto will not have any truck with these post-modern subtleties in respect of words that are more text than substance, although at other times he relishes the slippage in human beings' use of language. At this moment, Mephisto goes for two basic facts: Faust has said the words of the wager, and Faust has died. When he first introduced himself to Faust, Mephisto spelled out his belief that, because of the mortality built into all experience, it would better if being were replaced by non-being: "Drum besser wärs, daß nichts entstünde" (1341). And now, in the extinction of Faust, Mephisto has what he takes to be the definitive confirmation of his victory: he even resists the word "vorbei" because that implies that there had been something worth noticing before death intervened:

> Was ist daran zu lesen?
> Es ist so gut, als wär es nicht gewesen,
> Und treibt sich doch im Kreis, als wenn es wäre!
> Ich liebte mir dafür das Ewigleere. (11596–99)

> [What does one make of that?
> It might as well simply not have been,
> Yet it drives itself round in circles as if it amounted to
>   something!
> As for me, I would much rather have the Eternal Void.]

But Mephisto does not have the last word. The angels interpose their song; even more important, they interpose their bodies. In the last minute Mephisto is distracted by the bottoms of the pretty angels. Goethe draws here on an old tradition that conceives of the devil as predominantly a comic figure. One might have thought, not least for such a professional cynic as Mephisto, that one bottom would be pretty much like another ("when you have seen one, you have seen them all," or "er ist der Erste nicht," so to speak). But even this consummate nihilist can be surprised by lust.

In its closing moments the play draws on various iconographies of redemption. But its primary force is untheological. The angels specifically invoke Faust's strenuousness as his redemptive quality:

> Wer immer strebend sich bemüht,
> Den können wir erlösen [. . .]. (11932–33)

> [Whoever is determined to strive
> Him we can redeem.]

Gretchen's forgiving love also plays a part in the justification of Faust. Most importantly, the final words of the drama conjoin the notion of the deed, of that which is "getan" (and, for Faust deeds are at the heart of the living principle), with the sense of an eternally continuing process ("hinan").

And the agent that is celebrated above all else is the eternal feminine —
that eternally beckoning process:

> Das Unbeschreibliche,
> Hier ist's getan;
> Das Ewigweibliche
> Zieht uns hinan. (12104–7)

> [The indescribable,
> Here it is done;
> The eternal feminine
> Draws us upward.]

In the last reckoning, the "Ewigweibliches" triumphs over the "Ewigleeres"
of Mephisto's searing nihilism. It cannot be too strongly stressed that the
redemptive close to *Faust* has been, and continues to be, the source of
immense critical debate and dissent. Goethe seems almost casual in his
readiness to (as one might put it) pick and mix from a whole range of available significations. Obviously, there is, however ironically employed, a
strong presence of Christian notions of grace and atonement. Within a
gender-specific thematic, there is the invocation of women as the agents
of love and goodness (we recall the voice from above that redeems
Gretchen at the end of Part I). Yet we are also invited to hear the "Eternal Feminine" as a kind of generalized principle, an experiential eros, the
male imagination's configuration of life's fullness. There is also the existential justification of Faust which seems to override all moral considerations in the name of "streben" as the supreme good. Perhaps the close of
Goethe's enormous drama means so many things that it never quite
means one thing. Or perhaps one could say that the all-pervasive uncertainty invites us to reflect on the forms of justification of human effort
that are available to the modern (and post-modern) imagination.

Let us now draw together the various strands of Goethe's remarkable
drama. We have sought to suggest that *Faust* works with at least three
frameworks of signification: as a philosophical drama, as a psychological
drama, and as a historico-cultural drama of modernity. These are, of course,
not separate dramas; rather, each contextualizes and is contextualized by
the other. The point can be illustrated briefly with reference to the whole
thematics of time. In philosophical terms, Faust's quest is to close the gap
between diachrony and synchrony, between the necessarily linear sequence of particular events and deeds on the one hand and, on the other,
the mind's ability to seize, in a moment's awareness, the conceptual totality of experience. One thinks of his challenge to Mephisto:

Zeig mir die Frucht, die fault, eh man sie bricht,
Und Bäume, die sich täglich neu begrünen! (1686–87)

[Show me the fruit that rots before it is picked,
And trees which every day turn green!]

The mind knows of the total cycle of the fruit's existence; but the linearity
of lived experience insists on sequentiality, on spring, summer, autumn,
winter. The philosophical dilemma is acute: there is no immediate vitality
without the linear finitude of materiality; there is no glimpse of wholeness
that is not an abstraction. Yet Faust wants, in Blake's lovely words, to kiss
the moment as it flies and to live in eternity's sunrise. Temporality is, then,
at the heart of *Faust* as a philosophical drama. It is also, as we have seen,
germane to the historical drama, given the acceleration of experience by
which modern culture lives. Does that acceleration merely compound the
human subject's sense of evanescence? Or does it promise a utopian moment when linearity can be accelerated to the point where it will modulate into a kind of felt synchrony? The intemperate swiftness of modern
culture also impinges directly on the moral and psychological drama of Faust
and Gretchen. We recall Faust's cry to Mephisto in "Wald und Höhle":

Hilf, Teufel, mir die Zeit der Angst verkürzen!
Was muß geschehn, mags gleich geschehen!
Mag ihr Geschick auf mich zusammenstürzen
Und sie mit mir zugrunde gehn! (3361–64)

[Help, Devil, to shorten the period of fear!
What has to be, let it happen at once!
May her fate fall in upon me
And may she perish with me.]

Here we feel the ghastly moral implications at work in a culture of expo-
nential acceleration. The philosophical and psychological and historical
themes constantly interact.

That interplay of various forms of drama, that process of contextualization and re-contextualization, of center becoming frame and frame becoming center is germane to both the manner and the matter of Goethe's
great project: when he transforms the contractual relationship between Faust
and Mephisto from pact to wager, and defines that wager in terms of
Faust's attitude to experience, the play by definition becomes one that is
concerned to explore forms, modes, horizons, domains of signification
rather than external arbitrations of right and wrong. This is the measure
of the subjectivization and secularization and dynamization of a story
originally grounded in a theological worldview.[2]

Precisely this issue of horizons and frameworks of signification is at work in the three prefatory statements that stand outside and comment on the actual drama. The "Prolog im Himmel" intertextually re-creates the assembly of the Heavenly Host in the Book of Job. The angels sing the praises of the self-renewing energies of the created world, within both Ptolemaic (the "Brudersphären Wettgesang" [244; The Competing Song of the Brotherly Spheres]) and Copernican cosmologies:

> Und schnell und unbegreiflich schnelle
> Dreht sich umher der Erde Pracht (251–52)

> [And swiftly, incomprehensibly swiftly,
> The earth's splendor rotates.]

Common to both world-pictures is the centrality of natural energy, the belief in that organic miracle whereby entities brought into being generations previously can still be "herrlich wie am ersten Tag" (250). The Lord, in tune with the natural energies of His creation, has abjured traditional notions of right and wrong, of obedience or disobedience, in favor of an ethos of activity and vigor, which abhors slackness and sloth:

> Des Menschen Tätigkeit kann allzu leicht erschlaffen,
> Er liebt sich bald die unbedingte Ruh [. . .]. (340–41)

> [The activity of humans can all too easily slacken
> They tend to like utter peace and quiet

The evaluative framework of our drama, then, is existential rather than moral in character. And it relates to, and asks us to acknowledge, the particular energizing force within human nature that is the capacity for self-reflexivity. Precisely this is at issue in the wager between the Lord and Mephisto, a wager on the energies of human selfhood, a wager that prefigures and contextualizes the wager between Faust and Mephisto. On both occasions Mephisto perceives human self-reflexivity as a source of endless bother: sound and fury signifying nothing:

> Er nennts Vernunft und brauchts allein,
> Nur tierischer als jedes Tier zu sein. (285–86)

> [He calls it reason and only uses it
> To be more animal than any animal.]

For the Lord, however, that mental endowment is the engine that drives the human drama.

Preceding and framing the "Prolog im Himmel," there are two further contextualizing statements which transpose the issue of self-consciousness

into the aesthetic mode. The poem "Zueignung" expresses a poet's wonderment at the fact that the human imagination is seized not only by immediate, present facts and circumstances, but also by absences, by the
memories and intimations of its own making. Once again, we note that
the framework of human signification is not given but made. Reality, in
human affairs, is less a matter of empirical constatation than a process of
human understanding:

> Was ich besitze, seh ich wie im Weiten,
> Und was verschwand, wird mir zu Wirklichkeiten. (31–32)

> [What I possess I see as hugely distant,
> And what has faded now becomes reality for me.]

A second prefatory statement follows, the "Vorspiel auf dem Theater." In
this prelude Goethe reflects on the interplay of abstraction and immediacy
in the theatre. The comic mode of this "Vorspiel" combines with the to-
pos of the world as stage in the "Prolog" to assert both aesthetic and
cognitive distance. Goethe highlights the issue of self-conscious theatre
because his *Faust* drama not only is theatre, it is about theatre. These implications are spelt out with arresting urgency in the moment when Faust
rejects the magic sign of the macrocosm because it condemns him to be
nothing more than an onlooker:

> Welch Schauspiel! Aber ach! ein Schauspiel nur! (454)

> [What a spectacle! But alas only a spectacle.]

The philosophical theme of the drama — the human subject as both
agent and onlooker, as both experiencing self and reflecting meta-self is
articulated in the notion of the subject as "acting" in both senses of the
word: performing deeds, and appearing on the stage. *Faust,* then, is embedded in self-conscious theatre and in the theatre of self-consciousness.
We can hear the implications of this argument if we reflect for a moment
on the forms of characterization in Goethe's drama. In the "Prolog im
Himmel" it is, of course, the philosophical level of the play's statement
that is at the forefront of attention: Faust is, for both the Lord and Mephisto, the test case of what the human species — "der Mensch" —
amounts to. But, as the drama of his experience unfolds, "Tätigkeit," that
principle of activity so esteemed by the Lord, becomes specified as deed,
as a "Tat" committed by one person in a recognizable moral universe of
other people: one thinks, for example, of Gretchen and her family. The
principle of headlong activity may be splendid; but the deeds it generates
can often be disastrous. In one of the supreme moments of modern
drama, Gretchen, at the end of Part I calls Faust's name: "Heinrich,

Heinrich." In so doing, she names an individual agent, the man who has destroyed her. Goethe's *Faust* drama ranges, then, from, generality, both philosophical and historical, to intense psychological specificity, overwhelmingly so in the "Gretchentragödie."

Largely because of the range of statement that sustains it, Goethe's *Faust* is a drama that works richly and complexly on the stage. And it is a drama and not a foregone conclusion. Once the text is moved from page to stage, one discovers an animating rhythmic coherence to the work. Constantly we move from scenes of spatial and mental expansiveness and overview ("Prolog im Himmel," "Vor dem Tot," Faust's opening monologue in Part II) to scenes of spatial and mental containment (room, study, prison). On stage, Goethe's drama makes us feel the rhythms of opening and closing, of diastolic and systolic, of expanding and contracting frames of meaning. The theatrical statement serves to thematize different parameters of understanding, philosophical, psychological, historical. Classical culture, medieval culture, modern culture, postmodern culture — these all constitute different domains of signification, for which Goethe finds the theatrical correlative. In consequence, his great drama asks us to enter and to respond within varying universes. His play moves us — moves us in both senses of the word: it places, displaces, replaces us; and it also hits us in the pit of the stomach. *Faust* has immense emotional force, as well as a high degree of self-consciousness. Once a particular theatrical frame is in place, it works, it is binding for the duration of that particular experiential statement. Of course, we know that the scene will change, that there are other domains to which the drama will take us. Of course, we have a kind of meta-awareness in respect of each particular scene. But once we are within the scene, its truth has to be respected, not as the only truth, but as a powerfully operative one. Sometimes critics tell us that there is no contest between Faust and Mephisto. They argue that we know that the Lord cannot lose and therefore that Faust cannot lose. Yet this is to ignore two things: first, that the wager depends on Faust's attitude to experience, not on what the Lord or anybody else thinks or believes; secondly, there are moments in the play where we forget the meta-texts and are in the presence of substantial experience. One might think of the great cascade of curses that Faust hurls at all aspects of human being in the world in the second "Studierzimmer" scene. It is a speech that demands every reserve of vocal and emotional power at the actor's disposal. If one plays that moment right, then no member of the audience will be able to feel confident that

> Ein guter Mensch, in seinem dunklen Drange,
> Ist sich des rechten Weges wohl bewußt. (328–29)

[A good person, in his dark promptings,
Is still well aware of the right way.]

Similarly, the destruction of Gretchen is harrowing; and no member of the audience will leave Part I feeling "Es irrt der Mensch, solang er strebt" (317; Humans err as long as they strive). And yet, of course, not even that scene, lacerating as it is, has the last word. Because there are not really any last words; there are only constantly repositioned frameworks of reference.

Goethe's *Faust* is the great secular drama of our pre-modernity, modernity, and postmodernity. It is both comedy and tragedy, both morality play and realistic drama and theatrical extravaganza — and all these generic possibilities are matters of frameworks and horizons of understanding. It is difficult to think of any other single drama in the Western European tradition that attempts, and achieves, so much. That achievement is, as we have seen, one that depends crucially on theatrical statement. Watching Peter Stein's remarkable production of both parts of *Faust* in their entirety, one has the sense that perhaps now, in a cultural climate which takes the idea of virtual reality very much in its stride, the totality of Goethe's great drama has become truly stageable.

6: Goethe's Discursive Writings

THE VARIETY AND EXTENT of Goethe's expository writing is prodigious. Indeed, one is hard pressed to think of any other writer of modern Europe who has left such a voluminous corpus of treatises, essays, letters, memoirs, journalism, diaries, maxims, jottings, and so on. Given the fact that Goethe was clearly at ease writing in the discursive mode, it is intriguing to register both what he wrote and what he chose not to write. One extraordinary omission stands out: as we have already noted, he did not produce anything remotely resembling a systematic philosophy of life, a circumstantial inventory of his beliefs, convictions, hopes, fears, values. Nor — and this is the second fact that strikes one — did he set out to give an overview over his understanding of art, of aesthetics, of the significance of culture generally. Yet the need to reflect on these matters was a significant part of his creative make-up; it is not as though we have no idea of what he thought under these headings. But we glean what he thought from other contexts, from other modes of statement. Let us put this issue the other way round and ask: what did he produce within the discursive mode? In terms of the principal concentrations of his output there are three fields that consistently attracted his attention: autobiography, letters, and science. We shall look at his achievement in these three forms, particularly because this material gives us a sense of some of his deepest beliefs. These beliefs emerge within a context of considerable indirection, as part of a thinking, communicating process and not as a clear-cut system. One feels, in other words, that Goethe is constantly in quest of an understanding of experience, and the dynamic of the quest is more important than the achieved goal: perhaps because the quest is the goal.

A glance at Goethe's fondness for maxims can help to illustrate the theoretical point we are after. It is interesting to note that the two great collections of maxims that spring to mind — the *Maximen und Reflexionen* and the *Sprüche in Prosa* — were both collected after his death. In other words: he himself refrained from publishing a volume of his sayings of distilled wisdom. During his life time he did bring out maxims; but he did so not only in his journal *Über Kunst und Altertum* but also, intriguingly, in the literary work. To cite the three most obvious examples: there are Goethean aphorisms in the quotations from Ottilie's diary in *Die Wahlverwandtschaften,* in the "Betrachtungen im Sinne der Wanderer" and in the "Aus Makariens Archiv" sections of the later (1829) edition of

Wilhelm Meisters Wanderjahre. When one asks oneself what the status of such aphorisms is in their particular novelistic contexts, one answer surely is that these aphorisms, published in this format, acquire both the authority and the relativity of their specified gregariousness. That is to say: we are given a sense of the context, psychological, sociological, in which these maxims came together. Hence, they strike us not as absolute statements but as particular, and on that account, contingent glimpses of modes of experiential understanding. They retain the authority of the aphoristic format — relative brevity, a particular rhetoric of apodictic crispness — but at the same time we know where they have come from. We remember the moment when Wilhelm Meister, in the process of his initiation into the "Turmgesellschaft," becomes profoundly irritated by the Society's fondness for wise sayings and memorable apothegms. Goethe was, then, aware of the charms and dangers of the aphoristic mode: it claims revelatory wisdom, but it can, on occasion, move perilously close to the platitudinous. Hence he both loved and was wary of the aphorism; his sophisticatedly dialectical attitude meant that he both offered and withheld wisdom, both engaged in and criticized the attempt to find a rhetorically memorable and brief form for the disclosure of life's meaning.[1]

Because of his distrust of foregrounded discursivity Goethe elected to express the values that meant most to him by embedding them in projects that were not obviously philosophical in their primary thrust: in autobiography, in letters, and in science. We want to begin with the autobiographical writings. One of their most engaging properties is their aim to show the individual self and the world it knows as enmeshed in a process of constant complementarity and interaction. The notion of movement, of a journey, is all-important. As is the sense of experiential avidity, of a self that is eager to engage with and understand the flux and forms of experience. There is a delight in the surface textures of the world and at the same time a wish to know how those surfaces came about. Poetic and scientific responses coexist and enrich each other. Moreover, the autobiographical works are both local in their attentiveness to the immediate experiential foreground and at the same time cosmopolitan in their interpretative import.

Dichtung und Wahrheit concerns itself with Goethe's life from birth to the point where the gradual cooling of the relationship with Lili Schöne-mann sets up the possibility of the departure to Weimar. The account is very attentive to the emergence of the self as a poetically creative entity, although the claim is also advanced that such forms of creativity do bear within them the imprint of broader patterns of historical change. Early in the autobiography we come across the following comment:

> Denn dieses scheint die Hauptaufgabe der Biographie zu sein, den
> Menschen in seinen Zeitverhältnissen darzustellen, um zu zeigen,

> inwiefern ihm das Ganze widerstrebt, inwiefern es ihn begünstigt; wie er sich eine Welt- und Menschenansicht daraus gebildet, und wie er sie, wenn er Künstler, Dichter, Schriftsteller ist, wieder nach außen abspiegelt. (HA 9, 9)

> [For this seems to be the chief task of biography, to portray the human self in its temporal context in order to show how far the whole situation thwarts him, how far it favors him. It shows how he forms out of that process a view of the world and of human experience and how he, if he is an artist, a poet, a writer, expresses it in outward terms.]

The cardinal importance of the creativity is, of course, signaled by the title, which raises the issue of the truthfulness of literary art and the artifice of truth. It is worth noting that the narrative of *Dichtung und Wahrheit* begins and ends with a reference to destiny and the role of the stars in shaping that destiny. The birth is attended by a happy constellation:

> die Sonne stand im Zeichen der Jungfrau und kulminierte für den Tag: Jupiter und Venus blickten sie freundlich an, Merkur nicht widerwärtig [. . .]. (10)

> [The sun stood in the sign of Virgo and was at its highest point for the day; Jupiter and Venus were in friendly attendance, Mercury was not unsympathetic.]

And the text ends:

> wie von unsichtbaren Geistern gepeitscht, gehen die Sonnenpferde der Zeit mit unseres Schicksals leichtem Wagen durch [. . .]. (HA 10, 187)

> [As though driven by invisible spirits, the sun horses of time rush forward pulling the fragile chariot of our destiny.]

The opening register bespeaks a sense of certainty of purpose, providentiality even, whereas the final image is one of chaotic, headlong intensity. Yet even that final image does not bespeak loss of control, because it is a quotation from *Egmont*. The poet is the maker, a kind of unseen creator who knows better than the proud hero with his *amor fati*. This is not the only occasion in *Dichtung und Wahrheit* where art has a redemptive force. It is noteworthy that towards the end of the text, and particularly in the treatment of the whole relationship with Lili Schönemann, quotations from Goethe's own work abound. And even before then one registers the coexistence of literature and experience: the Sesenheim idyll is, for example, linked with Goldsmith's *Vicar of Wakefield*. On occasion Goethe connects his own creative processes with forces of nature which bring together outward and inward promptings in a concatenation at once energetic, incalculable, yet ultimately benign:

Auf einmal erfahre ich die Nachricht von Jerusalems Tode, und, unmittelbar nach dem allgemeinen Gerüchte, sogleich die genaueste und umständlichste Beschreibung des Vorgangs, und in diesem Augenblick war der Plan zu "Werthern" gefunden, das Ganze schoß von allen Seiten zusammen und ward eine solide Masse, wie das Wasser im Gefäß, das eben auf dem Punkte des Gefrierens steht, durch die geringste Erschütterung sogleich in ein festes Eis verwandelt wird. (HA 10, 585)

[Suddenly I hear the news of Jerusalem's death and, immediately after the general rumors, a most accurate and detailed description of the events; and in this moment the plan for "Werther" was there, everything came together from all sides and became a solid mass just as water, stored in a vessel and just at freezing point, will, in response to the slightest tremor, turn instantly into firm ice.]

At the center of this passage is the notion that artistic creativity comes about with the inevitability of natural processes. In the final book of *Dichtung und Wahrheit,* we come across the famous reflections, linked to the figure of Egmont, about the force of the daemonic in human affairs. Goethe defines daemonic figures in the following terms:

Es sind nicht immer die vorzüglichsten Menschen, weder an Geist noch an Talenten, selten durch Herzensgüte sich empfehlend; aber eine ungeheure Kraft geht von ihnen [aus . . .]. Alle vereinten sittlichen Kräfte vermögen nichts gegen sie [. . .]. (HA 10, 177)

[They are not always the best of people, whether in terms of their temperament or their talents, and they do not exude kindliness. But a huge energy emanates from them. All the moral energies combined can do nothing against them.]

Here, then, is a moment of philosophical generality, in which Goethe reflects on the interplay, or lack of it, between life energy and morality in human affairs. But what follows is a return to more mundane matters as Goethe comes down from the high mountain, as it were, and returns to Lili. His account both acknowledges and transcends the anticlimax:

Von diesen hohen Betrachtungen kehre ich wieder in mein kleines Leben zurück, dem aber doch auch seltsame Ereignisse, wenigstens mit einem dämonischen Schein bekleidet, bevorstanden. Ich war von dem Gipfel des Gotthard, Italien den Rücken wendend, nach Hause gekehrt, weil ich Lili nicht entbehren konnte. (HA 10, 177–78)

[From these sublime contemplations I return to my modest life in which, however, strange experiences which also had a touch of the daemonic about them were awaiting me. I had returned home from the peak of the Gotthard, turning my back on Italy because I could not do without Lili.]

The present tense in the first clause of this quotation is nicely judged. It has historic (that is, past-tense) force, referring to the rapid oscillation in life between sublime and mundane moments; but it also has present force, invoking the account being given, now, after the event, as it mediates between reflective and narrative moments. Yet, as both Goethe and his readers at the time knew full well — after all, he began writing this account in 1809 and completed it in 1831 — there was, to use the text's own term, a touch of the daemonic even to this return to normality. The young man may have turned his back on Italy then, but later he would get there, with momentous consequences. Goethe is, as he writes *Dichtung und Wahrheit,* very much aware of the biographical patterns that sustain and give significance to his life. There are no other instances of value and meaning to be found. This is a deeply secular account, which may on occasion borrow the trappings of spiritual autobiography, acknowledging forces that work in mysterious ways their wonders to perform; but its overall import is intensely and indefatigably worldly. James Joyce's youthful hero Stephen Dedalus has to work hard to throw off the toils of Catholic Ireland; a hundred years earlier Goethe has no such difficulty with his portrait of the artist as a young man. Art has become enough gospel to live and to write by. Pietism may have touched Goethe briefly in his early years; but its impact did not go, and was not allowed to go, at all deep.

The force of that triumphantly secular sensibility can also be felt in the *Italienische Reise.* The journey to Italy occurred in the years 1786 to 1788; at the time Goethe kept a journal, a detailed and immediate account of his experience, for Frau von Stein. He also wrote letters home to Weimar, particularly to Frau von Stein and to Herder. When, from 1814 on, he came to re-work this early material for the *Italienische Reise,* he found himself caught between two imperatives: on the one hand there was the need to stay close to the sensuous particulars of the Italian experience; on the other there was the wish to take stock of that experience, to see it in the context of the subsequent years. In one sense, the interplay of these two imperatives is central to any autobiographical enterprise, of course. Yet, unlike *Dichtung und Wahrheit,* which is sustained throughout by the rhetoric of retrospection and recall, the *Italienische Reise* retains the format of the diary entry. In consequence, the predominant register is that of a temporally and experientially immediate record of happenings in their chronological sequence. But even so, changes have been made. We are, in fact, only able to determine the scale of the re-writing process in respect of Book I of the *Italienische Reise:* Goethe destroyed the source material for Books II and III. As far as Book I goes, however, we can say that he made only modest changes to the *Tagebuch,* but did significantly modify the letters. The changes are chiefly with the aim of making connections, of linking experiences together to form a significant whole.

Even so Goethe was at pains to retain a sense of urgency and immediacy. It is, for example, interesting to note that the opening paragraph makes matters sound particularly dramatic. By contrast, the account in the *Tagebuch* mentions that he has made preparations for his departure. The flight to Italy was not, then, quite as unpremeditated as the later account makes it sound. In a letter to Zelter of 27 December 1814 Goethe writes the following of his work on the Italian papers:

> Ich hüte mich, so wenig als möglich daran zu ändern, ich lösche das Unbedeutende des Tages nur weg, so wie manche Wiederholung; auch läßt sich vieles, ohne dem Ganzen die Naivität zu nehmen, besser ordnen und darstellen.

> [I am endeavoring to alter as little as possible; I am merely deleting the trivial aspects of the days — and also many of the repetitions; moreover, much can be better ordered and presented without taking the naivety from the whole work.]

This passage clearly indicates that he is sifting and tidying the original material while respecting its immediacy. In any event, the *Italienische Reise* retains great vivacity and immediacy. It has many passages that exude a wonderfully zestful sense of the eager tourist coping with a foreign culture. Here is Goethe recalling an experience familiar to all travelers — moving from one room to another:

> In unserer Herberge befanden wir uns freilich sehr übel. Die Kost, wie sie der Maultierknecht bereiten konnte, war nicht die beste. Eine Henne, in Reis gekocht, wäre dennoch nicht zu verachten gewesen, hätte sie nicht ein unmäßiger Safran so gelb als ungenießbar gemacht. Das unbequemste Nachtlager hätte uns beinahe genötigt, Hackerts Juchtensack wieder hervorzuholen, deshalb sprachen wir morgens mit dem freundlichen Wirte. Er bedauerte, daß er uns nicht besser versorgen könne: "Da drüben ist aber ein Haus, wo Fremde gut aufgehoben sind und alle Ursache haben, zufrieden zu sein." — Er zeigte uns ein großes Eckhaus, von welchem die uns zugekehrte Seite viel Gutes versprach. Wir eilten sogleich hinüber, fanden einen rührigen Mann, der sich als Lohnbedienter angab und in Abwesenheit des Wirts uns ein schönes Zimmer neben einem Saal anwies, auch zugleich versicherte, daß wir aufs billigste bedient werden sollten. Wir erkundigten uns ungesäumt hergebrachterweise, was für Quartier, Tisch, Wein, Frühstück und sonstiges Bestimmbare zu bezahlen sei. Das war alles billig, und wir schafften eilig unsere Wenigkeiten herüber, sie in die weitläufigen vergoldeten Kommoden einzuordnen. Kniep fand nun zum ersten Male Gelegenheit, seine Pappe auszubreiten; er ordnete seine Zeichnungen, ich mein Bemerktes. Sodann, vergnügt über die schönen Räume, traten wir auf den Balkon des Saals, der Aussicht zu genießen. Nachdem wir diese

genugsam betrachtet und gelobt, kehrten wir um nach unseren
Geschäften, und siehe! da droben über unserem Haupte ein großer
goldener Löwe. Wir sahen einander bedenklich an, lächelten und
lachten. Von nun an aber blickten wir umher, ob nicht eins der
Homerischen Schreckbilder hervorschauen möchte. (HA 11, 289–90)

[In our inn we were anything but happy. The food, as prepared by
the servant who looked after the mule, was not of the best. A
chicken, cooked in rice, would not have been unacceptable had it
not been made as yellow as inedible by the massive addition of saf-
fron. The most unpleasant of sleeping quarters would have almost
obliged us to get out Hackert's traveling bag — hence we spoke in
the morning with the friendly landlord. He regretted that he could
not find better quarters for us: "But over there is a house where foreigners do very well and have every reason to be content." He
showed us a large corner house of which the side that was facing us
looked very promising. We went over there right away and found a
very energetic man who introduced himself as an employee of the
hotel and who, in the absence of the owner, showed us a beautiful
room next door to a large hall, and he assured us instantly that we
would find the charges very reasonable. We immediately inquired in
the usual way what the accommodation, meals, wine, breakfast and
other items would come to. It was all cheap and we swiftly moved
our belongings across and put them into the capacious and gilded
chests. Kniep now had for the first time the chance to unfold his al-
bum and he put his drawings in order. And I did the same with my
notes. Then, delighted with the beautiful rooms, we stepped on to
the balcony to enjoy the view. Once we had looked long enough at
it and praised it, we devoted ourselves to our various concerns. And
lo and behold, above our heads there was a large golden lion. We
looked at each other thoughtfully, smiled, laughed. From this moment on we looked around us to see if any other Homeric monsters
might peer out again.]

This is a delightful passage; it is full of vitality and pace and moves with
genuine ease from urgent narration to reflective commentary and back
again. Goethe here captures splendidly the response of the tourist on
holiday in a place of high cultural significance. Everyday concerns as to
how much things cost mingle with a sense of being surrounded by (in this
case) quasi-Homeric images.

Clearly the *Italienische Reise* has centrally to do with an experience of
release and regeneration; time and time again we come across delighted
expressions of what it means to see the world afresh, to connect with a
new kind of sensuous experience. That very sensuousness goes hand in
hand with an intellectual response, one that is both scientific and philo-

sophical. Frequently the southern vegetation seems to Goethe to bring him close to a direct meeting with the "Urpflanze": this was for him the primary, symbolic, and phenomenal manifestation of plant life. In the famous passage in which he rejoices at the sheer rightness of the little sea creatures, one hears both science and ontology coming into play:

> Ich wende mit meiner Erzählung nochmals ans Meer, dort habe ich heute die Wirtschaft der Seeschnecken Patellen und Taschenkrebse gesehen und mich herzlich darüber gefreut. Was ist doch ein Lebendiges für ein köstliches, herrliches Ding! Wie angemessen zu seinem Zustande, wie wahr, wie seiend! Wieviel nützt mir nicht mein bißchen Studium der Natur, und wie freue ich mich, es fortzusetzen! Doch ich will, da es sich mitteilen läßt, die Freunde nicht mit bloßen Ausrufungen anreizen. (93)

> [I turn with my narrative to the sea again, where I today saw sea snails, shell fish, and crabs and took great delight in their world. What a lovely thing is a living creature! How attuned to its condition, how true, how full of being! How greatly do I profit from my modest study of nature and how fervently do I long to continue it. Yet, given that it can be expressed, I do not want to irritate my friends with mere exclamations.]

The final sentence, in which he checks his own tendency to effusions, is wonderfully appealing, not least because Goethe is aware of the sheer profusion of the Italian experience. It is a profusion that extends from the very small, as we have seen above, to the immense: Mount Etna, for example, serves to confirm Goethe's "neptunist" reading of the coming into being of the earth's surface. At times, Italy in general and Rome in particular offer so much that the self is in danger of being overwhelmed:

> Anderer Orten muß man das Bedeutende aufsuchen, hier werden wir davon überdrängt und überfüllt. Wie man geht und steht, zeigt sich ein landschaftliches Bild aller Art und Weise, Paläste und Ruinen, Gärten und Wildnis, Fernen und Engen, Häuschen, Ställe, Triumphbögen und Säulen, oft alles zusammen so nah, daß es auf ein Blatt gebracht werden könnte. Man müßte mit tausend Griffeln schreiben, was soll hier eine Feder! und dann ist man abends müde und erschöpft vom Schauen und Staunen. (131)

> [Elsewhere you would have to go in quest of important things to see. Here we are overwhelmed and overcome. Wherever you walk or stand, you are confronted by a landscape of various kinds — palaces and ruins, gardens and wildernesses, distant prospects and intimate foregrounds, houses, stables, triumphal arches and columns, often all of them in such proximity that it could all be captured on one sheet

of paper. One would have to use thousands of slate pencils — one pen would not do it. And then, by evening, one is tired and exhausted from all that looking and marveling.]

It is worth noticing that, in mentioning art, Goethe refers to "Paläste und Ruinen." He has little time for the Christian art of the Middle Ages and the Renaissance; indeed he often positively regrets the way in which it overlays and supplants the great works of the classical, that is, pre-Christian, past.

No commentary on Goethe's autobiographical writings would be complete without reference to the two works which show him in the role of eye witness to historical events: the *Campagne in Frankreich* (1792) and *Die Belagerung von Mainz* (begun 1793, completed 1820). The *Belagerung* retains a fragmentary, stenographic character, and is impressive for precisely this refusal to understate or to muffle the brutalizing disconnectedness of the experience of war. The *Campagne,* interestingly, has both the ability to acknowledge the sheer mess of warfare on the one hand and also the will to make grand historical generalizations on the other. As an example of the former one might quote the following pained reflection:

> So zwischen Ordnung und Unordnung, zwischen Erhalten und Verderben, zwischen Rauben und Erzählen lebte man immer hin, und dies mag es wohl sein, was den Krieg für das Gemüt eigentlich verderblich macht. Man spielt den Kühnen, Zerstörenden, dann wieder den Sanften, Belebenden; man gewöhnt sich an Phrasen, mitten in dem verzweifeltsten Zustand Hoffnung zu erregen und zu beleben; hiedurch ensteht nun eine Art von Heuchelei, die einen besonderen Charakter hat. (HA 10, 213–14)

> [So, between order and disorder, between keeping and destroying, at one moment pillaging, at another storytelling, one always got on with one's life, and this may be the reason for the way in which war gets at the emotions. One plays the role of the bold destroyer and then of the gentle protector of life. One gets used to clichés, which, in the midst of the most desperate conditions, manage to arouse and sustain hope. The upshot is a kind of hypocrisy, which takes a form all of its own.]

This is an impressive passage, primarily for its anguished recognition that the insanity of war is something that gets right inside people and destroys their ability to think straight. At the opposite end of the spectrum there are remarks such as the famous judgment passed after the defeat of the German armies at Longwy. Goethe suggests in hindsight that a decisive moment of transition in the history of European warfare has occurred: an invading army will never again believe that it can simply impose its will on an indigenous population:

Von hier und heute geht eine neue Epoche der Weltgeschichte aus, und ihr könnt sagen, ihr seid dabei gewesen. (235)

[From here and from today there begins a new age of world history. And you can say that you witnessed it.]

The rhetorical gesture is grand. The diagnosis as such has a certain force as a warning against attempts to resist the sea-change marked by the French Revolution, but it claims a greater historical overview than probably the occasion warranted. Yet what is undeniably impressive about Goethe's *Campagne in Frankreich* is the central cognitive and stylistic irresolution: on the one hand, the will to record the chaos, confusion, and pain of war, and on the other hand, the need to interpret the particular instance of armed conflict as symptomatic of larger processes within European political culture. Both pieces of wartime journalism show Goethe exploring in political terms that interplay of interpretative imperatives that is so central to his autobiographical writing in general: the wish to stay close to the experiences evoked, but also the need to stand back, to reflect, and to generalize from particular incidents.

That dialectic also informs Goethe's letters, which we now wish to consider. The sheer bulk of his correspondence — there are some 14,000 letters extant — is prodigious. It is virtually impossible to reduce this extraordinary corpus to a common denominator. But perhaps it is worth registering at the outset the remarkable range of his epistolary tone which moves effortlessly from the personal and intimate on the one hand to the public, even declamatory, on the other. In this context we must bear in mind one particular point: it was part of eighteenth-century epistolary culture in Germany that (at any rate some) letters were regarded by their recipients as public property, and were, therefore, read aloud before a circle of friends. In other words, an exchange of letters was felt to be a legitimate channel for linking one circle of like-minded friends to another. This sense of creating a possible community is nowhere more movingly apparent than in the great correspondence between Goethe and Schiller. Time and again, the center of their letters is a debate about art and culture in their socio-political ramifications and hence rests on the notion of an actual or implied circle. There are frequent glimpses of everyday chores — editing a journal, producing a play — on the one hand; and on the other there is a superbly sophisticated debate between two different minds. Schiller is the more conceptually rigorous and philosophically austere — in a sense, more Kantian — partner, whereas Goethe is more associative and intuitive in his insights. Moreover there are frequent instances of applied critical endeavor as they comment on each other's works: *Wallenstein, Maria Stuart, Wilhelm Tell,* and *Wilhelm Meister* and *Faust.* It is difficult not to feel that the Goethe/Schiller correspondence must be well-nigh unique in European letters, for their sheer intellectual variety and richness. Both men have the sense of a common enterprise, of seeking to build out of very little a genuinely sophisticated cultural climate for the reception, dissemination, and discussion of art, for reflection on questions to do with the relationship of mind and matter, of fictive and actual experience. Both men also have a sense of the particular historical juncture that contextualizes their thinking. And both men are at the height of their creative powers. All of which makes it particularly moving that there are, at frequent intervals, moments where personal tones come to the fore. There is, for example, much discussion of Schiller's poor health. And there is also the marvelous tribute which Goethe pays his friend in the letter of 6 January 1798:

> Wenn ich Ihnen zum Repräsenten mancher Objekte diente, so haben Sie mich von der allzu strengen Beobachtung des äußeren Dinge und ihrer Verhältnisse auf mich selbst zurückgeführt. Sie haben mich die Vielseitigkeit des inneren Menschen mit mehr Billigkeit anzuschauen gelehrt. Sie haben mir eine zweite Jugend verschafft und mich wieder zum Dichter gemacht, welches zu sein Ich so gut als aufgehört hatte.

> [If I served you as the advocate of many objects, you led me away from the excessively stern observation of outward things and their situation to concentrate on myself. You taught me to look at the multifariousness of the inner self with greater understanding. You gave me a second youth and made me again into a poet — which I had more or less ceased to be.]

Goethe is grateful that Schiller has enriched him as a person and writer. It was not only their personal contact (after Schiller's move to Weimar in 1799), but also their correspondence that was germane to this process.

As we know from Goethe's account in "Glückliches Ereignis" of his meeting with Schiller, what initially brought the two men together was a discussion of science, specifically of Goethe's "Urpflanze" or, as he at that time (1794) called it, the "symbolische Pflanze." Schiller comments: "Das ist keine Erfahrung, das ist eine Idee" (That is not an experience; that is an idea). To which Goethe retorts: "Das kann mir lieb sein, daß ich Ideen habe ohne es zu wissen und sie sogar mit Augen sehe" (HA 10, 540–41; That can be congenial to me, that I have ideas without knowing it — and even see them with my own eyes). The disagreement sums up perfectly the divergence of outlook, and by that token the complementarity, that obtained between them. Goethe's adherence to the belief that concepts which could help to explain the material world actually existed in that material world may strike one as quixotic, but it was at the very heart of his endeavor as a scientist, to which we now wish to turn.

Just three remarks by way of introduction. One is that Goethe was indubitably right in his sense that, for good and for ill, science was becoming the dominant paradigm of the modern world. In other words, science was to provide the source of make-or-break arbitration for modern culture. Second: for Goethe the natural world was not just an assemblage of matter; rather, it was valuable in its own right; and to that rightness his scientific endeavor bears witness. Third: it was Goethe's cardinal insight that matter was an organism rather than a machine — which meant that any adequate model of its working would have to perceive the flow of forms rather than a mechanical replicability of fixed shape. Goethe believed in fluidity rather than fixity. To recall a remark which we have already quoted: "Zustand ist ein albernes Wort; weil nichts steht und alles beweglich ist"[2] (State is a foolish word because nothing is in stasis and everything is in flux). Here we touch on some of his profoundest convictions, his philosophy of life, so to speak. Moreover, in his reverence for the various and variously interactive forms of nature one senses a kind of democratic generosity of spirit. In terms of his specific political attitudes he could be, and many commentators have resented this, utterly conservative and inflexible in outlook. But perhaps his science gives us a juster measure of the generosity of his thinking and feeling. It is, for example, fascinating to note that, in his short essay "Der Versuch als Vermittler von Objekt und Subjekt," Goethe draws on political metaphors in order to condemn that dishonest, because ideologically preconceived, relationship to matter which is in evidence when the experimenter imposes his or her will on the data of the given world:

> Man wird bemerken können, daß ein guter Kopf um desto mehr Kunst anwendet, je weniger Data vor ihm liegen; daß er, gleichsam seine Herrschaft zu zeigen, selbst aus den vorliegenden Datis nur wenige Günstlinge herauswählt, die ihm schmeicheln, daß er die übrigen so zu ordnen weiß, daß sie ihm nicht geradezu widersprechen, und daß er die feindseligen zuletzt so zu verwickeln, zu umspinnen und beiseitezubringen weiß, daß wirklich nunmehr das Ganze nicht mehr einer freiwirkenden Republik, sondern einem despotischen Hofe ähnlich wird. (HA 13, 16)

> [One will be able to note that a good mind will tend steadily to increase its creative endeavors the fewer data it has to work on. In order to show its power and authority, it will, as it were, select from all the data a few favorites that flatter it, and will order the remainder in such a way that they do not actually contradict it. And the more refractory ones will be so wrapped up, cocooned, and pushed to one side that finally the whole thing resembles less a freely functioning republic than a despotic court.]

The key terms here are "Herrschaft," "Günstlinge," "schmeicheln," "wider-
sprechen," "freiwirkende Republik," "despotischer Hof." Goethe may have
spent much of his life in the service of a duke; but he was not unmindful
of the fact that benevolent despotism was despotism nonetheless. Nor was
he unaware of the fact that a post-aristocratic world might well have its
forms of despotism, one of which was the tendency of modern science to
manipulate and destroy the world which it claims to understand.

Wherever we look in Goethe's scientific work we find a common
concern in evidence: the will to respect both the distinctness and the connectedness of the forms of the natural world, and to extend that perception to the nature and role of the human observer. The argument in
respect of the human world has a dual force: existentially the self is both
distinct from, yet also profoundly related to, the workings of natural materiality; intellectually (and this applies as much to science as to any other
kind of human inquiry), the thinking process entails both separation and
integration, both taking apart and putting together, both analysis and
synthesis. Because of his feeling for the forms of living matter, Goethe
was perhaps particularly attuned to work in what we now call the life sciences generally. His morphological cast of mind allowed him to range
over a number of areas: anatomy, biology, botany, zoology. His belief in
the "Urpflanze" entailed a respect for both the integrity of each individual plant (as expressed in, for example, the many transformations of leaf
structure) and the integrity of the vegetable kingdom as a whole. As regards anatomy, Goethe worked on the "Zwischenkieferknochen," the in-
termaxilliary bone, which orthodox wisdom had denied to be present in
the human species. For him it was proof of the interconnectedness of the
animal and human kingdoms. Some commentators have suggested that
he thereby prefigured the whole notion of Darwinian evolution. While
there may be some truth to this, it has to be said that Goethe's integrative
cast of mind would not easily have adjusted to such notions as the survival
of the fittest. Similarly, in his geological work he belonged to the neptunist rather than the vulcanist school: that is to say, he believed in notions of
primary rock form, such as crystals, realizing themselves through processes of evaporation and sedimentation, and above all through constant
and gradual interaction with water. The notion of the eruptive emergence
of rock through volcanic activity was quite incompatible with his mindset.
Insistence on the interactive principle also informs his meteorology where
he stresses the ceaseless interplay of rising and falling energies, of evaporation and precipitation. It is characteristic of him that he should begin his
"Versuch einer Witterungslehre" with the following passage which recalls
Faust's great opening monologue at the start of Part II:

> Das Wahre, mit dem Göttlichen identisch, läßt sich niemals von uns direkt erkennen, wir schauen es nur im Abglanz, im Beispiel, Symbol, in einzelnen und verwandten Erscheinungen; wir werden es gewahr als unbegreifliches Leben und können den Wunsch nicht entsagen, es dennoch zu begreifen. (HA 13, 305)

> [The true, which is identical with the divine, can never be directly apprehended by us; we see it only in its reflections, in examples, symbols, in specific and related phenomena. We register it as incomprehensible life, yet we cannot renounce the wish to get hold of it fully.]

One notes the urgency, the human engagement of the writing in the "wir" form that addresses common human experience. Moreover the opening phrase, which serenely identifies truth and divinity, suggests that so much of Goethean science issues from what one might describe as a form of secular reverence, religiosity even. In a noteworthy study of Goethe's work on color and optics, Albrecht Schöne has helped us to think in terms of a "theology of color"; and it is to this area of Goethe's endeavor that, by way of conclusion, we now turn.[3]

At the outset one should note that Goethe worked on the *Farbenlehre,* in one form or another, for many decades. It thus joins the two other great projects — *Faust* and *Wilhelm Meister* — that never relinquished their hold on his creative commitment. Moreover, he himself was disposed to rate it very high, even as his chief legacy to posterity. If we ask why this particular project was so important to him, two answers suggest themselves. One is that Goethe was an "Augenmensch," that seeing, light, and color were utterly central to his sense of human indwelling in the world. And the other is that he felt that optics provided the particular battle ground, the test case, as it were, for arguing out the dangers and opportunities of modern science because of the work (and the prestige) of Isaac Newton. The battle was engaged head-on: the *Farbenlehre* consists of three sections: one on the theory and psychology of color, one on the history of work on color, and a polemical part, which is an onslaught on Newton. That onslaught is, as we shall see, intemperate and misguided, but it is explicable in a wider perspective. Newton's doctrine that color was produced by the refractability of white light was, for Goethe, symptomatic of everything that was wrong with modern science. He thought that the experiments on which Newton's conclusions were based were wrong on two counts: wrong in that they did not acknowledge the ways in which color came about in our experience of the world; and they were morally wrong in that they entailed the tormenting and fracturing of a primal phenomenon of nature.

To begin with the issue of Newton's misrepresentation of the phenomenon of light. The experiment with refraction does work; Newton was, in other words, right. But the experiment requires quite particular conditions. Small wonder, therefore, that Goethe was not able to replicate the experiment. But he was prepared to rush to judgment, because, for him, color was an event in the world: "die Farben sind Taten des Lichts" (HA 13, 315). Color comes about from the interaction of two "Urphänomene," light and darkness, which intersect in the resistant, opaque materiality of the concrete world:

> Wir sehen auf der einen Seite das Licht, das Helle, auf der andern die Finsternis, das Dunkle; wir bringen die Trübe zwischen beide, und aus diesen Gegensätzen, mit Hülfe gedachter Vermittlung, entwickeln sich, gleichfalls in einem Gegensatz, die Farben, deuten aber alsbald, durch einen Wechselbezug, unmittelbar auf ein Gemeinsames wieder zurück. (368)

> [We see on the one side the light, brightness; and on the other darkness, obscurity. We locate solid matter between the two, and from these contradictions, by means of mediating thought, colors develop, once again in contrasts, but also directly indicating, through reciprocal connections, a common ground.]

For Goethe, then, color presupposes not the splitting and atomization of an "Urphänomen," but a myriad of occurrences in the material world.

Moreover, he also was aware that the eye of the sentient being had a key role to play in the phenomenon of color. The eye perceives, compensates for, and recreates the events before it; it therefore makes afterimages. Goethe's illustration in the following anecdote is wonderfully vivid:

> Ich befand mich gegen Abend in einer Eisenschmiede, als eben die glühende Masse unter den Hammer gebracht wurde. Ich hatte scharf darauf gesehen, wendete mich um und blickte zufällig in einem offenstehenden Kohlenschoppen. Ein ungeheures purpurfarbnes Bild schwebte nun vor meinen Augen, und als ich den Blick von der dunkeln Öffnung weg nach dem hellen Bretterverschlag wendete, so erschien mir das Phänomen halb grün, halb purpurfarben, je nachdem es einen dunklern oder hellern Grund hinter sich hatte. (339)

> [Towards evening I found myself in a metal forge at the moment when the glowing mass was about to be hammered. I had looked at it very intently and then looked away, purely by chance, into a coal store. A huge purple-covered shape hovered now before my eyes, and as I turned my gaze away from the dark opening to the bright boards of the forging area, the phenomenon seemed to me now green, now purple, depending on whether it had a darker or lighter background.]

This is a characteristically Goethean moment in which the interplay of material entities and the consciousness of the perceiving agent is vividly brought out. Eckermann reports Goethe as saying (1 February 1827) that, just as the human eye needs the world, so the world needs the human eye:

> Sie sehen, es ist nichts außer uns, was nicht zugleich in uns wäre, und wie die äußere Welt ihre Farben hat, so hat sie auch das Auge.

> [You see there is nothing outside us that is not also within us, and, just as the outer world has its colors, so too does the eye.]

The eye is, then, anything but a passive organ in receipt of stimuli from the outer world; rather, it compensates for any particular exclusive color-input, and thereby constantly produces that balancing response that conduces to harmony and totality. And, given that colors are frequently associated with moods or feelings — "Die Erfahrung lehrt uns, daß die einzelnen Farben besondre Gemütsstimmungen geben" (495; Experience teaches us that individual colors generate particular moods) — the compensatory tendency in the eye has, as we might put it, a moral mission to fulfil:

> Wurden wir vorher bei dem Beschauen einzelner Farben gewissermaßen pathologisch affiziert, indem wir, zu einzelnen Empfindungen fortgerissen, uns bald lebhaft und strebend, bald weich und sehnend, bald zum Edlen emporgehoben, bald zum Gemeinen herabgezogen fühlten, so führt uns das Bedürfnis nach Totalität, welches unserm Organ eingeboren ist, aus dieser Beschränkung heraus; es setzt sich selbst in Freiheit, indem es den Gegensatz des ihm aufgedrungenen Einzelnen und somit eine befriedigende Ganzheit hervorbringt. (502)

> [We were initially in our contemplation of individual colors pathologically fixated, in that we were carried away by certain responses, feeling now lively and energetic, now soft and yearning, now raised up to noble things, now drawn down to common things. Yet the need for totality, which is built into our organism, leads us out of this limitation. It posits its own freedoms and brings forth the countervailing response to the specific and individual, and therefore brings about a satisfying totality.]

We recall the rhetorical register with which Goethe opened the "Witterungslehre" essay, one that appealed to us (wir), to our quest for intimations of wholeness. For him, science was part of this quest. Hence his bitter hostility to Newton, a hostility that is both intellectual and moral.

To that moral issue we wish now to turn. Goethe's attack on Newton does have something of the moral fervor of a crusade. He sees himself as defender of the true faith. And what he defends is nature understood not just as another name for the material world, but as a value, a force for good. By this token, then, Newton is not only misguided but wicked. Moreover, and this is a recurrent attack, Newton is immensely powerful and influential. He has, according to Goethe, more or less been given the Royal Society as his fiefdom: it is an organization over which he presides with the authority of some kind of secular archbishop. In the process, orthodoxy is enforced at every turn; heterodoxy is labeled as heresy. Scientific inquiry has been centralized and ideologized by Newton. Goethe's onslaught is remarkable, and it is certainly not without its impressive insights, some of which we have mentioned above. But, even so, it has to be conceded that a little of the polemical section of the *Farbenlehre* goes a long way.

Because it is so problematic, that section inevitably makes us wonder what we can nowadays claim for Goethe's work on optics and color, indeed for his science generally. Under the first heading it is important to register that there still are impressive passages in the *Farbenlehre*. Much of the material on the history, the psychology and the phenomenology of color is genuinely interesting. And developments in the wave theory of light have gone some way toward suggesting that Goethe's resistance to Newtonian optics was not merely an exercise in quixotic spleen. Up to a point this dimension of modernity can be claimed for his science in general. It would be broadly true to say that there are nowadays two traditions of scientific inquiry, one of which believes that the enterprise of understanding any given phenomenon entails reducing that phenomenon to its component parts, whereas the other believes that one needs to work relationally by relating the phenomenon to its generic context. Broadly speaking, the first approach characterizes classical mechanics of the eighteenth and nineteenth centuries, and the second approach characterizes the changed paradigm of twentieth-century quantum mechanics. In this context, Goethe could be seen as anticipating the primarily relational mindset of the moderns. This is not, of course, to enthrone him as a key forerunner of modern science; but it is to suggest that there was much more than personal idiosyncrasy at work in his scientific projects.

Moreover, in cultural and philosophical terms there are many ways in which his science can speak to present-day readers. One of the defining features of the European nineteenth century is the battle between science and religion, and Goethe felt the coming tremors with extraordinary acuity. He was not, as we have noted on a number of occasions, in any conventional sense of the word a believer. But he had a powerful reverence for the created world that allowed him to understand the claims being advanced by both scientific and religious camps and, on that account, to feel the implications of the great contest that would soon be everywhere in evidence. And, to repeat a point we made earlier, much of his science acquires persuasive force when we hear it as a particular form of (for want of a better term) philosophy of life. It issues from Goethe's avidity for experience, and from the need to understand the phenomena that spoke so urgently to him. It is, for example, significant that the essay "Der Versuch als Vermittler von Objekt und Subjekt" speaks of the experiment less as an austere exercise pursued under laboratory conditions than as a process of "Entäußerung" (HA 12, 10), whereby the external world is respected in and for itself:

> Ein weit schwereres Tagewerk übernehmen diejenigen, die durch den Trieb nach Kenntnis angefeuert die Gegenstände der Natur an sich selbst und in ihren Verhältnissen untereinander zu beobachten streben [. . .]. (10)

> [A much more weighty daily task is shouldered by those who, inspired by the will to know, seek to contemplate the objects of nature in themselves and in relationship to each other.]

What Goethe implies here is the difficulty involved in the attempt to achieve that reciprocity that is at the heart of "experimental" wisdom. Such wisdom acknowledges the interdependence of experimenter and experiment; and that interdependence is at the heart of Goethe's belief in the multiple levels of overlap which link natural life and mental life. Cherished Goethean notions such as polarity, intensification, and totality come into play here. In a formulation that characteristically balances the claims of matter and mind, Goethe writes of the

> zwei großen Triebräder aller Natur: der Begriff von Polarität und Steigerung, jene der Materie, insofern wir sie materiell, und diese ihr dagegen, insofern wir sie geistig denken, angehörig. (HA 13, 48)

> [The two great engines of all nature: the notion of polarity and intensification, at one level physically operative as long as we are thinking in material terms, and at another level belonging to the mental world when we think in spiritual terms.]

The energies of separating and conjoining, of contracting and expanding, give the energy and processual dynamic to both material and mental life:

> Ist das ganze Dasein ein ewiges Trennen und Verbinden, so folgt auch, daß die Menschen im Betrachten des ungeheuren Zustandes auch bald trennen bald verbinden werden. (WA, Abt 2, Bd 11, 13)

> [If the whole of existence is a constant process of separating and conjoining, so it follows that human beings, in contemplating remarkable situations, will now separate things, now conjoin them.]

This need to establish a kinship between physical and mental life is not a determinist model. Goethe's holism resists reductive doctrines at every turn, resists the temptation to establish simplistic equations. Neither matter nor mind is accorded primacy. That resistance to cognitive primitivism is at the heart of Goethean science. And, when viewed in the context of European culture since his time, it seems to represent a not inconsiderable achievement.

7: Conclusion

THIS BOOK IS ENTITLED *Reading Goethe,* and it is our hope that, whatever it may not have achieved, it will have served to encourage the reading of Goethe's works, not as an adulatory act, but as an exercise in critical reflection. Surveying that oeuvre and our attempts to assist in the reading of it, we inevitably find ourselves looking for some summary definition of why Goethe still has urgent claims to make on us today. Three reflections suggest themselves.

One has to do with his ability to address and express what one might describe as a central philosophical concern in human living, namely the issue of self-consciousness, of the relationship between mind and body. *Faust* is a central text in this respect, of course; but throughout the oeuvre one senses Goethe reflecting on the human ability, and need, to reflect. Time and time again he conveys the ways in which, and the extent to which, consciousness both problematizes and intensifies human experience. Goethe is one of the greatest philosophical writers of modern Europe, not in the sense that he has a preordained philosophy that he wishes to put across, but rather in the multiple ways in which he anchors the process of thinking, of philosophizing, in the dynamic of living.

Our second consideration in respect of Goethe's immediacy derives from his ability to interrogate and thereby define modern culture. As we have seen, *Faust* is again a key text in this regard. And it is worth reminding ourselves that all the central projects which claimed Goethe's attention more or less throughout his creative life — *Faust, Wilhelm Meister,* and the scientific work — are germane to the understanding of the modern world with its secular, individualist, scientific mindset.

The third aspect of Goethe's art that brings him close to us is somewhat more difficult to define: it has to do with what one can perhaps best describe as his tone. On frequent occasions, and especially in respect of the poetry, we have sought to draw attention to the intimate connection between Goethe's diction and colloquial speech. And, strikingly, such moments are not just throw-away remarks, not just fleeting concessions to everyday, even banal, experience. Rather, they seem to come from the very heart of his literary and spiritual concerns. A line from the end of *Faust II* will illustrate what we mean. Mephisto rejoices over the dead body of Faust, exulting in the fact that nothing lasts on earth, that everything turns to dust. On this account, he asserts the irredeemable worthlessness of all human experience. He says:

> Ich liebte mir dafür das Ewigleere. (11600)

> [As for me, I would much rather have the eternal void.]

It is worth noting the everyday particles "mir" (which has the force of "if you ask me") and "dafür" (which expresses the reductive gesture of "I'd rather have"). We quote this line primarily in order to plead for a sense of Goethe that removes him from his Olympian perch and brings him close to our everyday modes of thinking and feeling.

Moreover, there is one final reflection to which that line gives rise. Its sentiments, and they amount to a bitter disparagement of worldly experience, are un-Goethean. They are, appropriately, given to Mephisto, but Goethe wrote them; and he gave them every ounce of expressivity that he could muster. Sometimes — to return to issues which we raised in the introduction — there has been a tendency on the part of critics and readers to stress the life-affirming aspects of Goethe's creative achievement. Or, to put the matter in slightly different terms, some commentators have been troubled, particularly in view of some of the dark times that have disfigured the twentieth century, by the fact that Goethe is too little open to the potential monstrosity of human experience. Three voices can help us to get this argument in focus. One particular criticism is advanced by Ortega y Gasset, who refers to the insulated quality of Goethe's life after the move to Weimar, the sheer security and self-possession of his sense of the world and of his place within it. Ortega writes:

> Goethe hatte sich an eine derartige Lebensform schließlich so sehr gewöhnt, daß er die Wirklichkeit nicht mehr brauchte; und wie sich dem König Midas alles in Gold verwandelte, was er berührte, verwandelt sich, verflüchtigt sich, alles zum Symbol.[1]

> [Goethe had grown so accustomed to that way of life that he did not need reality any more; just as, for King Midas, everything turned to gold, so everything that Goethe touched was transformed, indeed was dissipated, into the symbol.]

Ortega here expresses the sense of a life that is underendowed with friction and contradiction. One knows what he means of course, but even so, it is difficult to recognize the author of *Faust* in Ortega's characterization. This is also true in respect of Erich Heller's famous essay "Goethe and the Avoidance of Tragedy." He writes wonderfully and thoughtfully about Goethe's belief in Nature as the value watching over human life. He has the following to say of *Faust:*

In Faust's world there are no real loyalties to be realized and no real commitments to be broken. Both his eternal striving and his desire for peace are merely the extreme stations of his mind and heart in their neverending voyage of self-exploration. His "Tragedy" is that he is incapable of tragedy.[2]

But this is not to hear the tragedy of Gretchen's destruction, not to hear the fierce disquiet at the heart of the Faustian condition.

Finally, mention should be made of the philosopher Karl Jaspers. Particularly in the immediate aftermath of the Second World War, Jaspers became acutely aware that Goethe was both a distant and problematic figure. Distant, because Goethe did not have in his imaginative make-up a place for the scream of pain and horror that, Jaspers argued, was the only authentic image for what Europe had recently unleashed on itself and the rest of the world. Problematic, because Goethe was not strenuously self-interrogative in his relationship to his own experience, and precisely self-interrogation was what the post-war world most had need of. Jaspers writes:

> Es ist nur ein Schritt vom Ernst des sich zum vollständigen Menschen bildenden Mannes zur egozentrischen Abschließung von der Welt, — von der befreienden Übersetzung der Erfahrung in Dichtung zur ästhetischen Unverbindlichkeit, — von der Hingabe an den hohen Augenblick zur verantwortungslosen Lebendigkeit des bloßen folgenden Momentes, von der Tiefe Goethescher Weisheit zur Unentschiedenheit des Wesenlosen, — von der Alloffenheit zur Charakterlosigkeit. Es ist das Verhängnis deutscher Bildung nach Goethe, daß diese Wege gegangen wurden.[3]

> [There is but one step that separates the seriousness of the man who is trying to develop himself into a complete human being from ego-centric repudiation of the world; that separates the liberating transformation of experience into poetry from aesthetic irresponsibility; that separates devotion to high moments from the irresponsible vivacity of simply living in the moment; that separates the profundity of Goethean wisdom from the dilatoriness of the unformed self; that separates pan-openness from characterlessness. It was the nemesis of German culture after Goethe that these latter paths were taken.]

Jaspers' critique in this passage is, of course, directed not only at Goethe himself, but most particularly at the uses that had been made of him. But even so, the issue of the limitation of Goethe's sensibility will not go away.

These three voices all remind us in their different ways that it is a questionable undertaking to turn to any literary writer for the propagation of life's wisdom. Literature is more about possibilities of human being in the world than it is about the rights and wrongs of human behavior in the world, although this is not, of course, to impute moral indifference to it. Hence it tends to offer us awareness rather than judgment. With Goethe, the awareness that comes through most frequently is one that vigorously affirms the living process. This makes him an untypical voice in modern European literature. One could, for example, hazard the generalization that much creative writing in the wake of Romanticism is, in one form or another, concerned with experiences of disillusionment or disenchantment (one thinks of Byron, Heine, Baudelaire in poetry; of the tradition of social drama from Büchner to Ibsen; of the realistic novel from Stendhal to Zola). Goethe, too, knew of such experiences, of the potential entrapment of the human creature. That much is attested by Mephisto's electrifying line; and Goethe explored that condition of entrapment unforgettably in *Werther, Tasso,* and *Faust.* Yet, even so, the capacity for totalizing disparagement does not quite have the last word. Rather, the affirmation of life is made — but not as a grandiloquent or facile gesture, nor as an offer of easy comfort. Precisely that affirmation seems valuable in its ability to invite us to live thoughtfully, and by that token fully, in the world of common experience.

Notes

Chapter 1

[1] Friedrich Gundolf, *Goethe* (Berlin: Bondi, 1916), 1.

[2] Gundolf, 2.

[3] Barker Fairley, *A Study of Goethe* (Oxford: Oxford UP, 1950), 58.

[4] Fairley, 104.

[5] Fairley, 143.

[6] Nicholas Boyle, *Goethe, the Poet and the Age. Volume I, The Poetry of Desire, 1749–1790* (Oxford: Clarendon, 1991), and *Volume II, Revolution and Renunciation, 1790–1803* (Oxford: Clarendon, 2000).

[7] Boyle, I, 442–43.

[8] T. J. Reed, *Goethe: The Flight to Italy: Diary and selected Letters* (Oxford: Oxford UP, 1999), xxv.

[9] Letter to Ernst Theodor Lange, 24 November 1768.

[10] Letter to Lavater, 29 July 1782.

[11] Letter to Zelter, 9 June 1831. See David Luke, "'Vor deinem Jammerkreuz': Goethe's Attitude to Christian Belief," *PEGS*, 59 (1988–89): 35–58; and (for a somewhat different emphasis) David Bell, "Goethe's Piety," *GLL*, 53 (2000): 450–69.

[12] Letter to Frau von Stein, 7 November 1786.

[13] HA 11, 93.

[14] *Tagebuch*, 24 September 1786.

[15] HA 13, 37.

[16] HA 9, 580.

[17] MA 1, 2, 458.

[18] WA 11, 11, 131 (*MUR*, 575).

[19] WA 11, 1, xii.

[20] HA 10, 540–41.

[21] HA 10, 48.

[22] Wolfgang Leppmann, *The German Image of Goethe* (Oxford: Clarendon, 1961); Karl Robert Mandelkow, *Goethe in Deutschland: Rezeptionsgeschichte eines Klassikers,* 2 volumes (Munich: Beck, 1980–89); Hans Schwerte, *Faust und das Faustische* (Stuttgart: Klett, 1962).

[23] Hans Pyritz, *Goethe Bibliographie* (Heidelberg: Winter, 1961).

[24] Pyritz, v.

[25] Pyritz, viii.

[26] Pyritz, 183.

[27] HA 1, 454.

Chapter 2

[1] John R. Williams, *The Life of Goethe* (Oxford: Blackwell, 1998), 89.

[2] See John Margetts, "The Creative Act in Goethe's 'Mailied,'" *NGS,* 15 (1988–89): 17–21; and Gerhard Kaiser, "Goethes Naturlyrik," *Goethe Jahrbuch,* 108 (1991): 61–73.

[3] E. M. Wilkinson and L. A. Willoughby, *Goethe Poet and Thinker* (London: Arnold, 1962), 21–28. See also Wulf Segebrecht, *Johann Wolfgang Goethes Gedicht "Über allen Gipfeln" und seine Folgen* (Munich: Hanser, 1978).

[4] Regine Otto and Bernd Witte, eds, *Goethe Handbuch. Band I: Gedichte* (Stuttgart and Weimar: Metzler, 1996), 192.

[5] For a particularly helpful commentary see Theo Buck, *Goethes "Urworte. Orphisch"* (Frankfurt am Main: Lang, 1996).

[6] David Wellbery, *The Specular Moment. Goethe's Early Lyric and the Beginnings of Romanticism* (Stanford, CA: Stanford UP, 1996), 42.

[7] Goethe to Eckermann, 3 May 1827.

Chapter 3

[1] HA 6, 638.

[2] See, for example, Frank Kermode, "Poet and Dancer before Diaghilev," in Frank Kermode, *Modern Essays* (London: Fontana, 1971), 11–38.

[3] See Jeremy Adler, *"Eine fast magische Anziehungskraft": Goethes "Die Wahlverwandt-schaften" und die Chemie seiner Zeit* (Munich: Beck, 1987).

[4] Translated by John R. Russell as *Wilhelm Meister's Theatrical Calling* (Columbia, SC: Camden House, 1995).

[5] G. W. Hegel, *Ästhetik,* ed. F. Bassenge (Berlin: Aufbau, 1955), 557–58, 983.

Chapter 4

[1] See, for example, Erich Heller's essay "Goethe and the Avoidance of Tragedy" (which also, by implication, embraces the notion of Goethe's avoidance of drama) in Erich Heller, *The Disinherited Mind* (Harmondsworth: Penguin, 1961), 33–58.

[2] "O wenn ich jetzt nicht Dramen schriebe ich ging zu Grunde" (Letter to Auguste Gräfin zu Stolberg, 7–10 March 1775).

[3] Goethe to Eckermann, 6 May 1827.

[4] See especially Ilse Graham, *Goethe and Lessing: The Wellsprings of Creation* (London: Elek, 1973), 30–47; and Rainer Nägele, *"Götz von Berlichingen,"* in *Goethes Dramen: neue Interpretationen,* ed. Walter Hinderer (Stuttgart: Reclam, 1980), 65–77.

[5] Friedrich Schiller, "Über Egmont," in Friedrich Schiller, *Werke* (Nationalausgabe), ed. J. Petersen et al. (Weimar: Böhlau, 1943ff.), vol. 23, 203. See also HA 4, 583.

[6] See Wolfdietrich Rasch, *"Iphigenie auf Tauris" als Drama der Autonomie* (Munich: Beck, 1979); and T. J. Reed, *"Iphigenie auf Tauris,"* in *Goethe Handbuch, Band II: Dramen,* ed. Bernd Witte et al. (Stuttgart and Weimar: Metzler, 1996), 211–15.

[7] Goethe to Eckermann, 3 May 1827.

[8] Goethe to Eckermann, 6 May 1827.

Chapter 5

[1] On the link between those economic developments and the aesthetic statement of Goethe's drama see Hans Christoph Binswanger, *Money and Magic: A Critique of the Modern Economy in the Light of Goethe's "Faust"* (Chicago: U of Chicago P, 1994); and Heinz Schlaffer, *"Faust Zweiter Teil": die Allegorie des neunzehnten Jahrhunderts* (Stuttgart: Metzler, 1981).

[2] See Jochen Schmidt, *Goethes "Faust": Erster und Zweiter Teil: Grundlagen, Werk, Wirkung* (Munich: Beck, 1999).

Chapter 6

[1] See R. H. Stephenson, *Goethe's Wisdom Literature: A Study in Aesthetic Transmutation* (Berne: Lang, 1983).

[2] Letter of 23 November 1812.

[3] Albrecht Schöne, *Goethes Farbentheologie* (Munich: Beck, 1987).

Chapter 7

[1] Ortega y Gasset, *Um einen Goethe von innen bittend.* (Stuttgart: Deutsche Verlags-Anstalt, 1957), 40.

[2] Erich Heller, "Goethe and the Avoidance of Tragedy," in Erich Heller, *The Disinherited Mind* (Harmondsworth: Penguin, 1961), 52.

[3] Karl Jaspers, "Unsere Zukunft und Goethe," in Karl Jaspers, *Rechenschaft und Ausblick* (Munich: Piper, 1958), 51.

Works Consulted and Works for Further Reading

BECAUSE OF THE SHEER PROFUSION of secondary literature on Goethe, we have endeavored to produce a bibliography which will help both the general and the specialist reader. The latter will find, we hope, a useful and manageable survey of the main tendencies in Goethe criticism. Certain items are marked with an asterisk; these are works that have been particularly helpful to us in writing this study, and may, on that account, be of special interest to the general reader.

General Studies

Bell, Matthew. *Goethe's Naturalistic Anthropology: Man and Other Plants*. Oxford: Clarendon, 1994.

Borchmeyer, Dieter. *Weimarer Klassik: Portrait einer Epoche*. Weinheim: Beltz Athäneum, 1998.

*Boyle, Nicholas. *Goethe, the Poet and the Age: Volume I, The Poetry of Desire, 1749–1790*. Oxford: Clarendon, 1991; and *Volume II, Revolution and Renunciation, 1790–1803*. Oxford: Clarendon, 2000.

Conrady, Karl Otto. *Goethe, Leben und Werk*. 2 vols. Königstein Ts.: Athäneum, 1982–85.

*Fairley, Barker. *A Study of Goethe*. Oxford: Oxford UP, 1950.

Graham, Ilse. *Goethe: Portrait of the Artist*. Berlin and New York: De Gruyter, 1977.

*Gundolf, Friedrich. *Goethe*. Berlin: Bondi, 1916.

Hölscher-Lohmeyer, Dorothea. *Johann Wolfgang Goethe*. Munich: Beck, 1991.

Leppmann, Wolfgang. *The German Image of Goethe*. Oxford: Clarendon, 1961.

Lewes, George Henry. *The Life and Works of Goethe*. London: Everyman Dent, 1949.

Lukács, Georg. *Goethe und seine Zeit*. Bern: Franke, 1947.

*Mandelkow, Karl Robert. *Goethe in Deutschland: Rezeptionsgeschichte eines Klassikers*. 2 vols. Munich: Beck, 1980–89.

Mayer, Hans. *Goethe. Ein Versuch über den Erfolg.* Frankfurt am Main: Suhrkamp, 1973.

*Reed, T. J. *Goethe.* Oxford: Oxford UP, 1998.

———. *The Classical Centre. Goethe's Weimar, 1775–1832.* Oxford: Oxford UP, 1986.

*Staiger, Emil. *Goethe.* 3 vols. Zürich: Artemis, 1952–59.

*Wilkinson, E. M., and L. A. Willoughby. *Goethe Poet and Thinker.* London: Arnold, 1962.

*Williams, John R. *The Life of Goethe.* Oxford: Blackwell, 1998.

*Witte, Bernd, Theo Buck, Hans-Dietrich Dahnke, Regine Otto, and Peter Schmidt, eds. *Goethe Handbuch.* 4 vols. Stuttgart and Weimar: Metzler, 1996–99.

Poetry — General Studies

Fairley, Barker. *Goethe as Revealed in His Poetry.* London: Dent, 1932.

Kaiser, Gerhard. "Goethes Naturlyrik." *Goethe Jahrbuch* 108 (1991): 61–73.

———. *Geschichte der deutschen Lyrik von Goethe bis Heine. Ein Grundriß in Interpretationen.* 3 vols. Frankfurt am Main: Suhrkamp, 1988.

*Kommerell, Max. *Gedanken über Gedichte.* Frankfurt am Main: Klostermann, 1956.

Lee, Meredith. *Studies in Goethe's Lyric Cycles.* Chapel Hill: U of North Carolina P, 1978.

Paulin, Roger, ed. "Special Goethe Number." (Lectures on the Poetry by Members of the Cambridge Department of German.) *GLL* 36 (1982–83).

*Reed, T. J., ed. *Goethe: Selected Poems.* Bristol: Bristol Classical Press, 1999.

Reich-Ranicki, Marcel, ed. *Alle Freuden, die unendlichen.* Frankfurt am Main: Insel, 1987.

———, ed. *Verweile doch. 111 Gedichte mit Interpretationen.* Frankfurt am Main and Leipzig: Insel, 1992.

Sauder, Gerhard, ed. *Goethe Gedichte: Zweiunddreißig Interpretationen.* Munich: Hanser, 1996.

Weimar, Klaus. *Goethes Gedichte 1769–1775. Interpretationen zu einem Anfang.* Paderborn: Schöning, 1982.

*Wellbery, David. *The Specular Moment: Goethe's Early Lyric and the Beginnings of Romanticism.* Stanford, CA: Stanford UP, 1996.

Wünsch, Marianne. *Der Strukturwandel in der Lyrik Goethes.* Stuttgart: Kohlhammer, 1975.

Poetry — Individual Studies

Beug, Joachim. "Warum gabst du uns die tiefen Blicke." In *Versuche über Goethe*. Ed. V. Dürr et al. Heidelberg: Stiehm, 1976. 57–75.

Burckhardt, Sigurd. "The Metaphorical Structure of Goethe's 'Auf dem See.'" *GR* 31 (1956): 35–48.

Conrady, Karl Otto. "Zwei Gedichte Goethes kritisch gelesen." In *Literatur und Germanistik als Herausforderung*. Ed. Karl Otto Conrady. Frankfurt am Main: Suhrkamp, 1974. 175–85.

Dyck, Joachim. "Die Physiognomie der Selbsterkenntnis: Goethes Gedicht 'Auf dem See.'" *Euphorion* 67 (1973): 74–84.

Hoffmann, Frank. *Goethes "Römische Elegien." Erotische Dichtung als gesellschaftliche Erkenntnisform*. Stuttgart: Metzler, 1993.

Margetts, John. "The Creative Act in Goethe's 'Mailied.'" *New German Studies* 15 (1988–89): 17–21.

Rasch, Wolfdietrich. "'Ganymed': über das mythische Symbol in der Dichtung der Goethezeit." *WW* 2 (Sonderheft; 1954): 34–44.

*Segebrecht, Wulf. *J. W. Goethes Gedicht "Über allen Gipfeln" und seine Folgen*. Munich: Hanser, 1978.

Simpson, James. "Freud and the Erl King." *OGS* 27 (1998): 30–63.

Wünsch, Marianne. "Zeichen — Bedeutung — Sinn: zu den Problemen der späten Lyrik Goethes am Beispiel der 'Trilogie der Leidenschaft.'" *Goethe Jahrbuch* 108 (1991): 179–90.

Narrative Fiction — General Studies

*Blackall, Eric. *Goethe and the Novel*. Ithaca and New York: Cornell UP, 1976.

Blessin, Stefan. *Die Romane Goethes*, Königstein Ts.: Taunus Athäneum, 1979.

Lillyman, W. J., ed. *Goethe's Narrative Fiction: the Irvine Symposium*. Berlin and New York: De Gruyter, 1983.

*Lützeler, P. M., and James McLeod, eds. *Goethes Erzählwerk: Interpretationen*. Stuttgart: Reclam, 1985.

Muenzer, Clark. *Figures of Identity: Goethe's Novels and the Enigmatic Self*. University Park and London: Pennsylvania UP, 1984.

Reiss, Hans. *Goethe's Novels*. London: Macmillan, 1969.

Narrative Fiction — Individual Studies

Werther

Buch, Hans Christoph, ed. *"Die Leiden des jungen Werther": Ein unklassischer Klassiker.* Berlin: Wagenbach, 1982.

Herrmann, Hans Peter, ed. *Goethes "Werther": Kritik und Forschung.* Darmstadt: Wiss Buch, 1994.

Jäger, Georg. *Die Leiden des alten und neuen Werther.* Munich: Hanser, 1984.

Müller, Peter. *Zeitkritik und Utopie in Goethes "Werther."* Berlin: Rütten und Loening, 1969.

Scherpe, Klaus. *Werther und Wertherwirkung.* Bad Homburg: Gehlen, 1970.

Hermann und Dorothea

Elsaghe, Yahya. *Untersuchungen zu "Hermann und Dorothea."* Bern: Lang, 1990.

Morgan, Peter. *The Critical Idyll: Traditional Values and the French Revolution in Goethe's "Hermann und Dorothea."* Columbia, SC: Camden House, 1990.

Wilhelm Meister

Bahr, Ehrhard. *Johann Wolfgang Goethe, "Wilhelm Meisters Lehrjahre."* (Erläuterungen und Dokumente.) Stuttgart: Reclam, 1982.

———. *The Novel as Archive: The Genesis, Reception, and Criticism of Goethe's "Wilhelm Meisters Wanderjahre."* Columbia, SC: Camden House, 1998.

Berger, Albert. *Ästhetik und Bildungsroman: Goethes "Wilhelm Meister."* Vienna: Braumüller, 1977.

Blair, John. *Tracing Subversive Currents in Goethe's "Wilhelm Meister's Apprenticeship."* Columbia, SC: Camden House, 1997.

Brown, Jane K. *Goethe's Cyclical Narratives: "Die Unterhaltungen deutscher Ausgewanderten" and "Wilhelm Meisters Wanderjahre."* Chapel Hill, NC: U of North Carolina P, 1975.

*Gille, Klaus F. *Wilhelm Meister im Urteil seiner Zeitgenossen.* Königstein Ts.: Taunus Athenäum, 1971.

Mayer, Mathias. *Selbstbewußte Illusion: Selbstreflexion und Legitimation der Dichtung in "Wilhelm Meister."* Heidelberg: Winter, 1989.

Neumann, Michael. *Roman und Ritus: "Wilhelm Meisters Lehrjahre."* Frankfurt am Main: Suhrkamp, 1992.

Schlechta, Karl. *Goethes "Wilhelm Meister."* Frankfurt am Main: Suhrkamp, 1985.

Steer, A. G. *Goethe's Science and the Structure of the "Wanderjahre."* Athens Georgia: U of Georgia P, 1979.

Steiner, Jacob. *Goethes "Wilhelm Meister": Sprache und Stilwandel.* Stuttgart: Kohlhammer, 1966.

Die Wahlverwandtschaften

*Adler, Jeremy. *"Eine fast magische Anziehungskraft": Goethes "Wahlverwandtschaften" und die Chemie seiner Zeit.* Munich: Beck, 1987.

Barnes, H. G. *Goethe's "Die Wahlverwandtschaften": A Literary Interpretation.* Oxford: Clarendon, 1976.

Blessin, Stefan. *Erzählstruktur und Leserhandlung: Zur Theorie der literarischen Kommunikation am Beispiel von Goethes "Wahlverwandtschaften."* Heidelberg: Winter, 1974.

Bolz, Norbert W. *Goethes "Die Wahlverwandtschaften."* Hildesheim: Gerstenberg, 1981.

Nemec, Friedrich. *Die Ökonomie der "Wahlverwandtschaften."* Munich: Fink, 1973.

Rösch, Ewald, ed. *Goethes Roman "Die Wahlverwandtschaften."* Darmstadt: Wiss Buch, 1975.

Schwan, Werner. *Goethes "Die Wahlverwandtschaften": Das nicht erreichte Soziale.* Munich: Fink, 1983.

Winkelman, John. *Goethe's "Elective Affinities": An Interpretation.* New York: Lang, 1987.

Novelle

Meyer, Herman. *Natürlicher Enthusiasmus: Das Morgenländische in Goethes "Novelle."* Heidelberg: Stiehm, 1973.

Wäsche, Erwin. *Honorio und der Löwe: Studie über Goethes "Novelle."* Säckingen: Stratz, 1947.

Drama — General Works

Brandmeyer, Rudolf. *Heroik und Gegenwart: Goethes klassische Dramen.* Frankfurt am Main: Lang, 1987.

Flemming, Willi. *Goethe und das Theater seiner Zeit.* Stuttgart: Metzler, 1968.

Hinck, Walter. *Goethe, Mann des Theaters.* Göttingen: Van den Hoeck und Ruprecht, 1982.

*Hinderer, Walter, ed. *Goethes Dramen: Neue Interpretationen.* Stuttgart: Reclam, 1992.

Keller, Werner. "Das Drama Goethes." In *Handbuch des deutschen Dramas.* Ed. Walter Hinck. Düsseldorf: Bagel, 1980. 133–56.

Melchinger, Siegfried. "Das Theater Goethes: Am Beispiel der *Iphigenie.*" *Jahrbuch der deutschen Schillergesellschaft* 11 (1967): 297–319.

*Peacock, Ronald. *Goethe's Major Plays.* Manchester: Manchester UP, 1959.

Schanze, Helmut. *Goethes Dramatik. Theater der Erinnerung.* Tübingen: Niemeyer, 1989.

*Wagner, Irmgard. *Critical Approaches to Goethe's Classical Dramas.* Columbia, SC: Camden House, 1995.

Drama — Individual Studies

Götz von Berlichingen

Graham, Ilse. "Götz von Berlichingen's dead Hand." In *Goethe and Lessing. The Wellsprings of Creation.* Ed. Ilse Graham. London: Elek, 1973. 30–47.

Lindenberger, Herbert. *Historical Drama.* Chicago: Chicago UP, 1975.

Michelsen, Peter. "Goethes *Götz:* Geschichte dramatisiert." *Goethe Jahrbuch* 110 (1993): 41–60.

Neuhaus, Volker. *Johann Wolfgang Goethe, "Götz von Berlichingen."* (Erläuterungen und Dokumente.) Stuttgart: Reclam, 1973.

Egmont

Brück, Max von. *Johann Wolfgang Goethe, "Egmont": Deutung und Dokumentation.* Frankfurt am Main: Ullstein, 1969.

Ellis, J. M. "The Vexed Question of Egmont's Political Judgment." In *Tradition and Creation.* Ed. C. P. Magill et al. Leeds: Maney, 1978. 116–30.

Haile, Harry G. "Goethe's Political Thinking and *Egmont.*" *GR* 42 (1967): 96–107.

Hobson, Irmgard. "Oranien and Alba: The Two Political Dialogues in *Egmont.*" *GR* 50 (1975): 260–74.

Keferstein, Georg. "Die Tragödie des Unpolitischen. Zum politischen Sinn des *Egmont.*" *DVjS* 15 (1937): 331–61.

Michelsen, Peter. "Egmonts Freiheit." *Euphorion* 65 (1971): 274–97.

Schröder, Jürgen. "Poetische Erlösung der Geschichte: Goethes *Egmont.*" In *Geschichte als Schauspiel. Deutsche Geschichtsdramen.* Ed. Walter Hinck. Frankfurt am Main: Suhrkamp, 1981. 101–15.

Sharpe, Lesley. "Schiller and Goethe's *Egmont.*" *MLR* 77 (1982): 629–45.

Wagener, Hans. *Johann Wolfgang Goethe, "Egmont."* (Erläuterungen und Dokumente.) Stuttgart: Reclam, 1974.

Iphigenie auf Tauris

Adorno, Theodor W. "Zum Klassizismus von Goethes *Iphigenie.*" In Theodor W. Adorno. *Noten zur Literatur.* Frankfurt am Main: Suhrkamp, 1981. 495–514.

Angst, Joachim. *Johann Wolfgang Goethe, "Iphigenie auf Tauris."* (Erläuterungen und Dokumente.) Stuttgart: Reclam, 1969.

Brown, Kathryn, and Anthony Stephens. "'Hinübergehn und unser Haus entsühnen.' Die Ökonomie des Mythischen in Goethes *Iphigenie.*" *Jahrbuch der deutschen Schillergesellschaft* 32 (1988): 94–115.

Burckhardt, Sigurd, "'The Voice of Truth and Humanity': Goethe's *Iphigenie.*" In Sigurd Burckhardt. *The Drama of Language: Essays on Goethe and Kleist.* Baltimore and London: Johns Hopkins UP, 1970. 33–56.

Fischer-Lichte, Erika. "Probleme der Rezeption klassischer Werke am Beispiel von Goethes *Iphigenie.*" In *Deutsche Literatur zur Zeit der Klassik.* Ed. Karl Otto Conrady. Stuttgart: Reclam, 1977. 114–40.

Gallas, Helga. "Antikenrezeption bei Goethe und Kleist — *Penthesilea* eine Anti-*Iphigenie*?" In *Momentum Dramaticum.* Ed. Linda Dietrick et al. Waterloo: Waterloo UP, 1990. 209–20.

*Heller, Erich. "Goethe and the Avoidance of Tragedy." In Erich Heller. *The Disinherited Mind.* Harmondsworth: Penguin, 1961. 33–58.

Henkel, Arthur. "*Iphigenie auf Tauris* und die 'verteufelt humane' Iphigenie." In Arthur Henkel. *Goethe-Erfahrungen: Studien und Vorträge.* Stuttgart: Metzler, 1982. 61–83, 85–101.

Hobson, Irmgard. "Goethe's *Iphigenie:* A Lacanian Reading." *Goethe Yearbook* 2 (1984): 51–67.

Jenkins, Sylvia P. "The Image of the Goddess in *Iphigenie auf Tauris.*" *PEGS* 21 (1952): 69–106.

Rasch, Wolfdietrich. *"Iphigenie auf Tauris" als Drama der Autonomie.* Munich: Beck, 1979.

*Reed, T. J. "Iphigenies Unmündigkeit: Zur weiblichen Aufklärung." In *Germanistik: Forschungsstand und Perspektiven.* Ed. Georg Stötzel. Vol. 2. Berlin and New York: De Gruyter, 1985. 505–24.

Wagner, Irmgard. "Vom Mythos zum Fetisch: Die Frau als Erlöserin in Goethes klassischen Dramen." *Goethe Yearbook* 5 (1990): 121–43.

Weimar, Klaus. "'Ihr Götter.'" In *Unser Commercium: Goethes und Schillers Literaturpolitik.* Ed. W. Barner. Stuttgart: Cotta, 1984. 303–27.

Torquato Tasso

Ammerlahn, Hellmut. *Aufbau und Krise der Sinn-Gestalt: Tasso und die Prinzessin im Kontext der Goetheschen Werke.* Bern: Lang, 1990.

Bürger, Christa. "Der bürgerliche Schriftsteller im höfischen Mäzenat: literatursoziologische Bemerkungen zu Goethes *Tasso.*" In *Deutsche Literatur zur Zeit der Klassik.* Ed. Karl Otto Conrady. Stuttgart: Reclam, 1977. 141–53.

Girschner, Gabriele. *Goethes "Tasso." Klassizismus als ästhetische Regression.* Königstein Ts: Athenäum, 1981.

Grawe, Christian. *Johann Wolfgang Goethe, "Torquato Tasso."* (Erläuterungen und Dokumente.) Stuttgart: Reclam, 1981.

Merkl, Helmut. "Spiel zum Abschied. Betrachtungen zur Kunst des Leidens in Goethes *Torquato Tasso.*" *Euphorion* 82 (1988): 1–24.

Neumann, Gerhard. *Konfiguration: Studien zu Goethes "Torquato Tasso."* Munich: Fink, 1965.

Rasch, Wolfdietrich. *Goethes "Torquato Tasso": die Tragödie des Künstlers.* Munich: Beck, 1979.

Reed, T. J. "Tasso und die Besserwisser." In *Texte, Motive und Gestalten der Goethezeit.* Ed. John Hibberd et al. Tübingen: Niemeyer, 1983. 95–112.

Ryan, Lawrence. "Die Tragödie des Dichters in Goethes *Torquato Tasso.*" *Jahrbuch der deutschen Schillergesellschaft* 9 (1965): 283–322.

Wilkinson, E. M. "Goethe's *Tasso:* The Tragedy of a Creative Artist." In *Goethe Poet and Thinker.* Ed. E. M. Wilkinson and L. A. Willoughby. London: Arnold, 1962. 75–94.

Williams, John R. "Reflections in Tasso's Final Speech." *PEGS* 47 (1977): 47–67.

Faust

Arens, Hans. *Kommentar zu Goethes "Faust I."* Heidelberg: Winter, 1982.

———. *Kommentar zu Goethes "Faust II."* Heidelberg: Winter, 1989.

Atkins, Stuart. *Goethe's "Faust": A Literary Analysis.* Cambridge and London: Harvard UP, 1958.

Beddow, Michael. *Goethe: "Faust I."* London: Grant and Cutler, 1986.

Bennett, Benjamin. *Goethe's Theory of Poetry: "Faust" and the Regeneration of Language.* Ithaca and London: Cornell UP, 1986.

*Binswanger, Hans Christoph. *Money and Magic. A Critique of the Modern Economy in the Light of Goethe's "Faust."* Chicago: Chicago UP, 1994.

Brown, Jane K. *Goethe's "Faust": The German Tragedy.* Ithaca and London: Cornell UP, 1986.

Emrich, Wilhelm. *Die Symbolik von "Faust II."* Königstein Ts: Athenäum, 1964.

Friedrich, T., and L. J. Scheithauer. *Kommentar zu Goethes "Faust."* Stuttgart: Reclam, 1973.

Gaier, Ulrich. Goethes *"Faust"-Dichtungen: Ein Kommentar. I "Urfaust."* Stuttgart: Reclam, 1989.

Gearey, John. *Goethe's "Faust": The Making of Part One.* New Haven: Yale UP, 1981.

———. *Goethe's Other "Faust": The Drama, Part II.* Toronto: Toronto UP, 1992.

Hamm, Heinz. *Goethes "Faust": Werkgeschichte und Textanalyse.* Berlin: Volk und Wissen, 1978.

Hesse-Belasi, Gabriele. *Signifikationsprozesse in Goethes "Faust Zweiter Teil."* Frankfurt am Main: Lang, 1992.

Jantz, Harold. *The Form of "Faust": The Work of Art and Its Intrinsic Structures.* Baltimore: Johns Hopkins UP, 1978.

Kaufmann, Hans. *Goethes "Faust" oder Stirb und Werde.* Berlin and Weimar: Aufbau, 1991.

Keller, Werner, ed. *Aufsätze zu Goethes "Faust I."* Darmstadt: Wiss Buch, 1974.

———. *Aufsätze zu "Faust II."* Darmstadt: Wiss Buch, 1991.

Lohmeyer, Dorothea. *Faust und die Welt. Der zweite Teil der Dichtung.* Munich: Beck, 1975.

Mason, Eudo. *Goethe's "Faust": Its Genesis and Purport.* Berkeley: California UP, 1967.

Matussek, Peter. *Naturbild und Diskursgeschichte: "Faust"-Studie zur Rekonstruktion ästhetischer Theorie.* Stuttgart: Metzler, 1992.

Meyer, Herman. *Diese sehr ernsten Scherze. Eine Studie zu "Faust II."* Heidelberg: Stiehm, 1970.

Requadt, Paul. *Goethes "Faust I." Leitmotivik und Architektur.* Munich: Fink, 1972.

*Schlaffer, Heinz. *"Faust Zweiter Teil." Die Allegorie des neunzehnten Jahrhunderts.* Stuttgart: Metzler, 1981.

*Schmidt, Jochen. *Goethes "Faust Erster und Zweiter Teil."* Munich: Beck, 1999.

Scholz, Rüdiger. *Die beschädigte Seele des großen Mannes: Goethes "Faust" und die bürgerliche Gesellschaft.* Rheinfelden: Schäuble, 1982.

————. *Goethes "Faust": Ein einführender Forschungsbericht*. Rheinfelden: Schäuble, 1984.

Schwerte, Hans. *Faust und das Faustische. Ein Kapitel deutscher Ideologie*. Stuttgart: Klett, 1962.

Smeed, John W. *Faust in Literature*. London: Oxford UP, 1975.

Wieland, Renate. *Schein, Kritik, Utopie: Zu Goethe und Hegel*. Munich: Text und Kritik, 1992.

Wilkinson, Elizabeth M. "Goethe's *Faust:* Tragedy in the Diachronic Mode." *PEGS* 42 (1971–72): 116–74.

Williams, John R. *Goethe's "Faust."* London: Allen und Unwin, 1987.

Zabka, Thomas. *"Faust II" — Das Klassische und das Romantische. Goethes Eingriff in die neueste Literatur*. Tübingen: Niemeyer, 1993.

Discursive Writings

Koranyi, Stephan. *Autobiographik und Wissenschaft im Denken Goethes*. Bonn: Bouvier, 1984.

Stephenson, R. H. *Goethe's Wisdom Literature: A Study in Aesthetic Transmutation*. Bern: Lang, 1983.

Autobiography

Aichinger, Ingrid. *Künstlerische Selbstdarstellung. Goethes "Dichtung und Wahrheit" und die Autobiographie der Folgezeit*. Bern: Lang, 1977.

Barner, Wilfried. "Altertum, Überlieferung, Natur. Über Klassizität und auto-biographische Konstruktion in Goethes *Italienischer Reise*." *Goethe Jahrbuch* 105 (1988): 64–92.

Kiefer, Klaus. *Wiedergeburt und neues Leben. Aspekte des Strukturwandels in Goethes "Italienischer Reise."* Bonn: Bouvier, 1978.

Müller, Klaus-Detlef. *Autobiographie und Roman. Studien zur literarischen Autobiographie der Goethezeit*. Tübingen: Niemeyer, 1976.

Reed, T. J. *Goethe: The Flight to Italy: Diary and Selected Letters*. Oxford: Oxford UP, 1999.

Scientific Writings

Amrine, Frederick et al., eds. *Goethe and the Sciences: A Re-appraisal*. Dordrecht and Boston: Reidel, 1987.

Becker, Hans-Joachim. *Goethe — seine Biologie und seine räumliche Wahrnehmung*. Munich: Bayerische Akademie der Wissenschaften, 1994.

Burwick, Frederick. *The Damnation of Newton: Goethe's Color Theory and Romantic Perception*. Berlin and New York: De Gruyter, 1986.

Fink, Karl J. *Goethe's History of Science*. Cambridge: Cambridge UP, 1991.

Krätz, Otto. *Goethe und die Naturwissenschaften*. Munich: Callwey, 1992.

Nisbet, H. B. *Goethe and the Scientific Tradition*. London: Institute of Germanic Studies, 1972.

*Schöne, Albrecht. *Goethes Farbentheologie*. Munich: Beck, 1987.

Schönherr, Hartmut. *Einheit und Werden. Goethes Newton-Polemik als systematische Konsequenz seiner Naturkonzeption*. Würzburg: Königshausen und Neumann, 1993.

Sepper, Dennis L. *Goethe contra Newton: Polemics and the New Project for a Science of Colour*. Cambridge: Cambridge UP, 1988.

Stephenson, R. H. *Goethe's Conception and Knowledge of Science*. Edinburgh: Edinburgh UP, 1995.

Index

9239023

CPSIA information can be obtained at www.ICGtesting.com
Printed in the USA
LVOW10s0310180913

352871LV00001B/86/P